MADE IN HEAVEN

MADE IN HEAVEN

A Jewish Wedding Guide

by

Rabbi Aryeh Kaplan

MOZNAIM PUBLISHING CORPORATION
NEW YORK / JERUSALEM

For information write:
Moznaim Publishing Corporation
4304 12th Avenue
Brooklyn, New York 11219
Tel. (718) 438-7680, 853-0525

Printed and bound in Jerusalem, Israel
by Vagshal Ltd.
Printed in Israel

This book is dedicated to my children, Yosef Menachem, Yisrael Meir, Avigail Faiga, Devorah Rivka, Micha, Rochel, Reuven Yehudah, Shimeon Yitzhak, and Haim Simhah;
and to my publisher, Menachem Wagshall.

CONTENTS:

Author's Introduction IX
Introduction XI

Chapter

1. Made in Heaven 1
2. Love 8
3. Before It's Too Late 16
4. Engagement 22
5. Setting the Date 31
6. The Ring 44
7. The Tallith 54
8. The Wedding Gown 59
9. The Wedding Party 62
10. The Week Before 67
11. Spiritual Purification 74
12. The wedding Day 80
13. Outline of the Wedding 89
14. The Prenuptial Reception 91
15. The Kethubah 95
16. Understanding the Kethubah 104
17. Preparing for the Ceremony 123
18. The Marriage Canopy 133
19. The Processional 149
20. The Prenuptial Blessing 166
21. The Kiddushin 173
22. The Seven Blessings 186
23. Seclusion 206
24. The Meal 209
25. The Grace 213
26. The Bridal Week 230
27. Making Marriage Work 234

Marriage Record 235

INTRODUCTION

Whenever I write a book, people ask me, "For whom are you writing it?" Usually, my answer is, "For everyone." I always try to make my books as universal as possible.

In that respect, this is a very difficult book. If I were to write for well learned Jews, many important points would be redundant. If I were to write for the Jew of limited background, I would have to explain many points that are obvious to those who are better educated. Also, a book such as this one should contain enough information to be useful even to learned rabbis.

I therefore try to fulfill both goals in this book. On the one hand, it is directed toward the learned Jew, providing him with deeper insight into all aspects of the Jewish wedding. At the same time, it is meant to be a guide even for people with no background whatsoever. The learned person may therefore find many things in this book painfully obvious, such as the fact that a wedding dinner should be kosher. He must, however, keep in mind that for many readers, this is a point that is not obvious at all.

A huge number of original sources have been consulted in writing this book. Among the most useful references are *Shulchan HaEzer* by Rabbi Yitzhak Tzvi Leibowitz (Des, 1929; Beregszasz, 1932), and *Eduth LeYisrael* by Rabbi Yaakov Werdiger (Tel Aviv, 1968), which are among the most comprehensive works in the field. However, we have gone far beyond the scope of these works, and have included many original sources not previously quoted elsewhere.

The family has always been the strength of Judaism. Judaism may be able to survive without the synagogue, but it cannot survive without the family. The foundation of the Jewish family is the Jewish wedding, which sets the tone for the couple's future life. It is therefore my prayer that this book give all couples new insight into the depth and spiritual power of the Jewish wedding ceremony, and of Judaism as a whole.

May it help make the ceremony an event that will infuse their lives with love for each other, love for all Israel, and love for God.

Aryeh Kaplan
11 Kislev, 5742

Introduction

by Rabbi Pinchas Stolper

Made In Heaven is a unique and highly significant book. It examines the most ancient human ceremony, marriage, which is the foundation for the oldest and most important human institution — the family.

Made In Heaven explodes many myths and superstitions. It provides insights into practices and observances which hark back to the very beginnings of mankind. It not only guides the reader who wishes to create an authentic Jewish wedding, it also explains the whys and wherefores of each of the many customs and traditions in the Jewish wedding ceremony. In this sense it combines a practical guide, offering "how to" advice, with teaching the reader about ideas and concepts that appear for the first time in the English language.

A Jewish marriage is not a partnership; it is more properly viewed as a merger. While each member of the family has his and her own privileges and responsibilities, and while each retains his/her individuality, both husband and wife are expected to submerge personal and selfish goals when they run counter to the interests and aims of the unit — thus promoting and creating a new entity, or a new "personality," which is called the family. In this new entity husband and wife are able to develop their own potential as well as raise children who will learn to become human in the fullest meaning of the word.

Seen in this light, marriage offers life's greatest challenge, and at the same time presents life's greatest paradox. Can two strangers, coming from totally different backgrounds, suddenly establish a home in which they live together in peace and harmony, building and creating together so that they and their children will achieve happiness and fulfillment? Can they sublimate their own selfish motives and desires to create a home which, in Jewish tradition, is looked upon as a sanctuary, a place where the highest ideals of life are brought to fruition?

What is Jewish Marriage?

Until very recently, most people took the institution of marriage for granted, hardly ever wondering at its almost universal acceptance. But in today's society, where no aspect of life escapes close, rational, and scientific scrutiny, we must not hold back from investigating the institution of marriage as objectively as possible, in order better to understand and appreciate its significance for modern society.

Why are marriage and the family so basic to human society? Why should a "single," "happy" man willingly surrender his freedom and independence to share his life with a complete "stranger"?

Why should he want to feed this "stranger," house her, clothe her, support and educate "her" children? Why does a man assume these burdens and responsibilities — voluntarily? Yet, even in an era when marriage and the family are under attack, when young people are exposed daily to propaganda promoting so-called "alternative life styles," actual statistics indicate that as many young people are marrying as ever before. The impulse to create a permanent family relationship seems to be part of our very nature. Perhaps this is because we seek to love and to be loved, perhaps we need structure and self-respect, a home in which to grow and build, a family to mold and children to raise.

For these reasons, Jewish law strongly urges that people marry, and the earlier they marry, the better. In fact, in many observant families, it is common for a young person's education to be completed *after* marriage, so that the young couple can strive to achieve life's goals together, rather than waiting out a long period of tension and frustration before marriage.

Marriage is a mysterious force that calls upon man and woman to unite in a partnership, to build a home in which God will feel welcome and dwell, a platform on which to inscribe the major points of life's program.

The Talmud (*Yevamoth* 62b) clearly states that, "He who spends his days without a wife, has no joy, no blessing, no good." Torah law also contains a built-in bill of rights which gives the Jewish woman a unique status and position in the home, based on the Torah command that no matter how poor or troubled a man may be, with regard to his wife, "He may not diminish her support, her clothes, or her conjugal rights."

In the family structure we find the one human, social institution that is most indispensable for creating and forming the individual. Without the family, it is impossible to create a healthy individual, not only biologically, but in any sense.

Two people must act in unison in order to create a third. The highest act of human creativity calls for two to act as *one* in order to bring forth a new individual. If two can act as *one* they can draw a new soul down to earth and create a new human being, making God the third partner in a new miracle of Creation. God has given man the ability to duplicate His own greatest feat of Creation by creating a child. When we create a child we literally "play God." But if the child is the product of lust or physical passion alone, if the child is created through the rejection of God's laws — what kind of child have we created.?

The drama of man's partnership with God in creation does not end with the birth of a child. After birth, too, that father and mother must live together within the family unit. Thus, children can be reared and educated in such a way that they will develop into men or women who are capable of fulfilling their human and spiritual destinies. Each person is, to a large extent, what his parents and family make him; if they are successful parents the children may even be better than they are. Jewish parents have always hoped to rear children even more successful than themselves, each more capable of fulfilling his own individual human and spiritual destiny.

In the historic Jewish view, the family, and not the synagogue, is considered the basic institution of Jewish life and society. In fact, most of the crucial acts and experiences of Jewish living call for a family setting. The synagogue, at best, plays a secondary role.

The Jewish family has long been a model of harmony, love, and stability, the envy of the entire civilized world. The very social evils that tend to disrupt and destroy modern society, such as divorce, prostitution, adultery, wife-beating, or juvenile delinquency, were, until recent times, almost unknown among traditional, unassimilated Jews. While observant Jews in America have also been affected by this generation's tendency to solve marital problems through divorce, the difference in percentages still points to a qualitative difference of considerable weight.

Marriage, for a Jewish man, is not optional, but obligatory. The Talmud (Shabbath 31a) explains that in the World to Come, the first three questions asked of a person are: "Did you buy and sell in good faith? Did you have a set time for Torah study? Did you raise a family?" The single life is regarded as a misfortune, and a good wife is the chief delight of a man's existence. It was and is easy to obtain a Jewish divorce, but relatively few ever did so. Jews who observed tradition and law took family life very seriously and created stable, strong, and supportive family environments. They worked hard at their marriages and resorted to divorce only after many extensive attempts to keep a marriage together had definitely failed.

The family bond and its relationships are sanctified. Marriage and the family are integral parts of the divine plan. The love which attracts man and woman to each other is sacred in the eyes of God. Jews see the family as the essential force in the development of a God-fearing individual, and the creation of a home in which God dwells. If this home is dedicated to God, and His word reigns supreme there, it becomes the fulcrum for the entire structure of Jewish life.

Marriage implies the uniting of two people, two personalities, two minds, two wills, two talents — not just for now, but for always. Marriage means much more than two people who share a bedroom. It means two people who share their lives and enjoy a relationship so successful, that in thinking and acting as one, they are prepared to unite to bring children into the world. Marriage is so significant that it is the point of origin of all mankind. It is the one human institution which can bring to fruition man's greatest hopes and dreams.

May we hope that, in developing a deeper understanding of the Jewish wedding, the reader will approach the day of a person's greatest joy with a deeper sense of responsibility, and with greater sensitivity so that each family might aspire toward the ideals described in this book.

Chapter I

MADE IN HEAVEN

He knows that she is special. And she knows that he is unique. Of all the people in the world, they realize that they are meant for each other. It is as if it has been set up since the time of creation. And in a sense it was.[1]

Behind every couple that meets, there is a chain of events that stretches back through the eons. If we trace the chain to its very beginning, we find that it actually does go back to creation.

Take the following case:

He is introduced to her by a friend. But how did he meet the friend? All the events that brought him together with his friend must also be taken into account. Let us say that he met the friend in school. Why did he go to that particular school? Why was he attracted to that particular friend? How did *she* make contact with that friend? The answer can take one back years, and even generations.

Or take another case:

She and he lived next door to each other all their lives. Then, one day, she realized that of all the men in the world, there was something very special about him. But why did they live next door to each other in the first place? Because both their parents decided to buy houses there. But what went into their parents' decisions? Perhaps ideas that they got from *their* parents. And these ideas may have come from their parents' parents. Again, the chain of events goes back from one generation to the next.

Or still another case:

1. It is taught that Bathsheva was destined to marry David from the time of creation (*Sanhedrin* 67a). In a sense, a husband and his wife existed together in the undifferentiated Divine Essence that existed before creation (see *Noam Elimelekh, VaYechi*, 27a, quoted in *The Light Beyond*, p. 60).

She came from California to Israel to study. He was on a tour from Australia. A chance meeting and something clicked. They may have come from opposite ends of the world, but somehow they are now together.[2]

Whenever a person meets the special "one," it is something of a miracle.[3] Somehow, through a particular set of coincidences and chains of events, God has brought them together. It is a miracle that will bring happiness to the couple, and in a sense, begin the creation of a new world.[4]

In addition to the factors that brought the couple together, there are also the factors that brought them into existence. These factors also trace their beginnings all the way back to creation. Pondering this, we see every marriage as being initiated at the very beginning of time. Thus, every marriage is like a crossroads in eternity.

Consider for a moment the ancestry of the boy and girl. Each one obviously has two parents. Go back another generation, and there are four grandparents. One more generation, and there are eight great - grandparents. Continue in this fashion, and you find sixteen great - great - grandparents, and 32 great - great - great - grandparents.

The calculations then become a bit more difficult, especially if one is not mathematically minded. But the results are fascinating. A few minutes with a pocket calculator, and it becomes obvious that going back ten generations, a person has 1024 ancestors. Back twenty generations, he has 1,048,576 — over a million!

2. It is taught that God can bring a man and a woman together from the opposite ends of the world; *Yerushalmi, Kiddushin* 3:12 (Vilna, 1922) 40a; *Bereshith Rabbah* 65:2, from Psalms 68:7; *Bereshith Rabbah* 68:3, *BeMidbar Rabba* 3:4; *Tanchuma, Ki Thisa* 5.

3. The Talmud teaches that bringing a couple togther is as great a miracle as splitting the Red Sea; *Sotah* 2a; *Sanhedrin* 22a; *Bereshith Rabbah* 68:4; *Va Yikra Rabbah* 8:1; *Midrash Tehillim* 59:2; *Zohar* 1:21b, 1:207b, 2:170b, 3:283b; Maharl, *Beer HaGolah* 4 (Zolkiev, 1848), p. 40b.

4. Every match is like the creation of a new world; *Zohar* 1:89a.

After this, the numbers become almost absurd. After thirty generations the number of one's ancestors would be 1,073,741,824 — over a billion. After forty generations, it would be 1,099,511,627,776 — over a trillion!

This last number is obviously absurd. It is greater than the total number of people who have ever lived. No one can have more ancestors than there are people. This number simply means that the ancestral lines cross, and a person is descended from the same individual in more than one way. Going back something like forty generations, one will find the same ancestors coming up again and again in different places on the family tree.

In any case, it takes fewer than forty generations for a person to find a number of ancestors that is greater than the total population of the world. But forty generations is not an impossibly long time. If we consider the average generation to be around 25 years, forty generations is only one thousand years.

This is a fascinating point. If we trace a single person's ancestry back for a thousand years (actually, much less), we find that he can possibly be descended from every human being alive at the time. To put it another way, it took the entire world population of one thousand years ago to provide the unique ingredients of heredity and environment that produced the unique individual as he is today.

(Of course, if the person in question is Jewish, this will be restricted to the Jewish world. Since there are around fourteen million Jews in the world, this entire process would take only around 24 generations, or approximately 600 years. However, since conversions to Judaism have always taken place, the non-Jewish world is also a contributing factor after several generations.)

In any case, if one could look at the world of a thousand years ago, every person one saw would most probably be an ancestor of the young man or woman standing here today. Every marriage that took place one thousand years ago would have led to this unique person as he is today. If one man in the past had married one woman instead of another, his children would have been different. This, in turn, would have affected all subsequent generations — to this very day.

This has awesome implications. A single marriage one thousand years ago could have changed every single person alive today. A marriage is therefore an event of tremendous consequence. It is a miraculous event in more ways than one.

Now let us assume that our boy and girl marry. Assume that they have a "small" family of only two children. And assume that each of their descendants also has a similar family, averaging two children.

We again see that the number of descendants doubles in each generation. (In mathematics, this is known as a geometric progression.) The couple has two children, four grandchildren, eight great-grandchildren, sixteen great-great-grandchildren. With each generation, the number doubles.

Again, after ten generations, this couple has 1024 descendants. After twenty generations, there will be 1,048,576 descendants. And after only 24 generations — a mere 600 years - there will be 16,777,216 descendants. This is very close to the current world Jewish population.

Thus, when a couple decides to marry, it is much more than a personal decision. It is a decision that will ultimately affect the entire Jewish people. This explains why boy meeting girl is such a great miracle, and is so carefully planned by God.

If a couple meets and decides to marry, then, in the course of time, every Jew in the world will have in his heredity the unique characteristics that result from this union. If they decide not to marry, then every Jew in the world will ultimately be just a little bit different. The same is true of the human race as a whole.

In a way, the Talmud alludes to this. It says, "Why was Adam created alone? To teach that whoever destroys a single Jewish life is counted as if he has destroyed an entire world.

And whoever saves a single Jewish life is counted as if he has saved an entire world."[5]

The Torah tells us that Adam was a single individual. Yet, all the billions of people alive today are descendants of Adam and Eve. Every couple who marries is just like Adam and Eve. In the course of time, their descendants will number in the millions, forming a huge population.

It is obvious that if God is concerned with the destiny of even the most insignificant individual, then He is all the more concerned with the population of the entire world. But every marriage can, in time, produce an entire world population. Creating a marriage is therefore just like creating an entire world.[6]

On the day that a person is conceived,[7] all the forces of Providence set into motion chains of events that will lead to his or her eventual marriage. The Talmud teaches that at this time, it is announced on high, "The daughter of this man shall be for that man."[8]

Of course, each person has free will. Therefore, even when something is destined (*"beshert"*), free will comes into play. But God's interaction with a person's free will allows Him to arrange things the way He desires.

Imagine that you were playing chess with a world class grandmaster. Although you have free will, and can make any move you desire, he can manipulate you all over the board at

5. *Mishneh, Sanhedrin* 5:5, 37a.

6. *See* note 4.

7. The Talmud speaks of this euphemistically as "forty days before the formation of the embryo;" *see* next note. It takes an embryo forty days to form from the time of conception; *Kerithoth* 10a; *Niddah* 30a.

8. *Sotah* 2a; Maharsha, Maharitz Chajath *ad loc; Sanhedrin* 22a; *Midrash Tehilim* 125:2; *Zohar* 1:91a, 1:229a; *Tikkuney Zohar* 14, 30a; *Teshuvoth HaRambam* (Leipzig, 1859) 119; *Sheviley Emunah* 3 (Warsaw, 1887) 26c; *Akedath Yitzchak* 8 (Pressburg, 1849) 1:60a, 22, 1:149a, *Teshuvoth* 2:1. Cf. *Bava Bathra* 110a; *Sefer Chassidim* 1092, 1099, 1100.

will. No matter how you move, he knows how to move to make the game come out as he wants it. He can determine the outcome of the game, virtually at will.

Of course, God is much more than a grandmaster. But He too anticipates our moves in the game of life, and He reacts to them. No matter how we move, He countermoves and maneuvers us where He wants us to be. Thus, no matter what a person does, God can arrange things so that he or she will meet his or her destined one.

It is taught that there are times when, although a person may be destined to marry one individual, his own acts lead him to marry someone else. In such cases, he does not marry his "destined one," but another person.[9] His choice of a wife has been changed by his own acts, and his own moral value system, which involves an area where God allows each person absolute free choice.[10] In such a case, it is said that the person was not worthy of finding his destined mate. This is often true in cases where a marriage ends in divorce.

There are also factors that may change a person's destiny for the better. Thus, a person may have some merit that helps him get a better mate and have a happier marriage than originally destined for him.[11] As in all aspects of a person's destiny, prayer can have a powerful effect.[12] But after all is said and done, no matter what a person does, the making of a marriage is in God's hands. For a marriage to be successful, it must be made in heaven.[13]

9. See *Sotah* 2a.

10. *Niddah* 16.

11. *Akedath Yitzchak* 22, 1:159a.

12. *Moed Katan* 18b; *Yerushalmi, Betza* 5:2, 20b; *Yerushalmi, Taanith* 1:8, 7b, 4:6, 25b; *Yerushalmi, Kethuboth* 1:1, 2a; Targum on Psalms 68:7; *Bereshith Rabbah* 68:3; *Zohar* 1:85a, 1:90b, 2:109a; *Orach Chaim* 551:2. Also see *Tosafoth, Sanhedrin* 22a, s.v. *Arbayim; Zohar* 1:91a, 2:101a; *Sefer Chassidim* 283.

13. See *Yerushalmi, Kiddushin* 3:12, 40a; *Sefer Chassidim* 1092, 1099, 1100.

The Midrash relates that a Roman matron once asked Rabbi Yosi ben Chalafta, "Now that God has finished creating the universe, what does He do?" The rabbi replied that God now makes matches, bringing couples together so that they can marry each other.[14]

Rabbi Yosi's reply provides us with a unique insight into marriage. Every marriage has consequences for all mankind. Therefore, every time a couple comes together, it is as if an entire world has been created.

14. *Bereshith Rabbah* 68:4; *VaYikra Rabbah* 8:1; *BeMidbar Rabbah* 3:4; *Tanchuma, Ki Thisa* 5; *Zohar* 1:89a; Maharal, *Beer HaGolah* 4, p. 40b.

Chapter 2

LOVE

Sometimes it strikes like a thunderbolt. Sometimes it develops only after years of courtship and marriage. But when it exists, the love between man and woman is one of the strongest forces in the world.

Love usually grows in stages. To say, "I love you," is a tremendous commitment, leaving a person very vulnerable. If the declaration of love is not reciprocated, the one making it can feel very hurt and foolish.

The process of falling in love therefore usually proceeds step by step. Even when the inside feeling of love is very strong, its communication must follow a slower course. First there are tentative statements. If the answers are right, the statements become stronger. "You are very nice," leads to "I like you," and finally to, "I love you." If the words are sincere, the sentiments will also be real.

Love and lust should not be confused. While love wants to give, lust only wants to take. Love is a reciprocal sentiment, where one identifies with the wants and needs of the beloved.[1]

When the Torah provides a paradigm of love, it says, "You shall love your neighbor like yourself" (Leviticus 19:18). Love means feeling about another person exactly the same as one feels about oneself. When you love a person, the person's happiness is as important to you as your own happiness. His sadness is as painful as if you yourself were experiencing it.

It is noted that the Hebrew word for love, *ahavah* (אַהֲבָה) has the numerical value (gematria) of thirteen. This is the same as the numerical value of the Hebrew word *echad* (אֶחָד) meaning "one." In its deepest sense, love takes two people and makes them into one.[2]

1. Rabbi Yehudah (ben Yitzchak) Abarbanel, *Vikuach al Ahavah* (Lyck, 1871), pp. 6a, 13a.

2. It is thus taught that husband and wife come from the same element of the Divine Essence; *VaYikra Rabbah* 29.

But what is love? This is a question that has tantalized poets and philosophers over the ages. Psychologists have tried to analyze it, and biologists have tried to dissect it,[3] but it still remains a mystery.

Indeed, it is impossible even to describe love. When two people are in love, the whole world seems different. Colors are brighter, sounds are clearer, tastes are more refined. Life seems to flow on a higher, more lofty, more spiritual plane. Something is happening, but it cannot be described. To know what love is, one must experience it.

The Song of Songs is one of the most beautiful books of the Bible. On its surface, it appears to be a love song between a man and a woman. Not only is it a love song, but it is a beautiful ode to love. It speaks of the joys of closeness and the pangs of separation. "Kiss me with the kisses of your mouth, for your love is better than wine" (Song of Songs 1:2). "My beloved is mine, and I am his" (*Ibid.* 2:16). "At night, on my bed, I sought the one my soul loved" (*Ibid.* 3:1). "Love is as strong as death... many waters cannot quench love, neither can the floods drown it" (*Ibid.* 8:6,7). Throughout the song, the pulse of love can be felt beating in every word.

Yet, our sages teach that the Song of Songs is actually an allegory of the love between God and humanity, or between God and Israel. This is a divine love, that in its highest forms can transcend everything else in the world, even life itself.[4]

The Song of Songs speaks of this divine love in its most potent manifestation. It speaks of the highest spiritual levels to which a mortal can aspire. It is taught that if all the books of the Bible are holy, then the Song of Songs is "holy of holies."[5]

The wise King Solomon chose to use the love between man and woman as his allegory. This shows how powerful — and

3. We thus find monogamy in the dove; see *Eruvin* 100b; *Zohar* 3:61a, 3:240b; *Zohar Chadash* 31c.

4. Rabbi Akiva thus said, "All my life I wanted to experience martyrdom, to be able to fulfill the commandment to "love God with all your soul" (*Berakhoth* 61b).

5. *Yadayim* 3:5.

how holy — such love can be. In many ways, the closest mundane emotion that resembles the love between God and man is the love between man and woman.[6]

When a person is in love, his beloved is the focus of his being.[7] His entire consciousness is focused on his beloved to the exclusion of all else. Love enters the innermost recesses of the soul, and the deepest chambers of the heart.[8] His mind is on his beloved day and night, in every waking moment, and in every dream. He only lives for the times that they can be together.

Now, imagine a person having the same relationship toward God. Imagine him having the same passion toward God as the greatest passion that exists between man and woman. Such a person would be a saint — a *tzaddik*. Few people are able to reach such a level of love and closeness to God. But the paradigm that the scripture gives for it is the love between man and woman.

Love is a pure emotion that cannot be understood in terms of other feelings. It is a gift that God gave to the world, to bring man and woman together, and to allow them to give pleasure to each other. It is the foundation of the family, and hence, the foundation of the world.

Love is impossible to define, precisely because it is such a unique gift from God. It is a very special feeling, unrelated to other human emotions. One does not love a person because of anything that person has or does — but simply because he exists.

The Talmud expresses this in a very insightful teaching: "When love depends on another factor, then when the factor ceases to exist, so does the love. But when love does not depend on anything else, it never ceases to exist."[9]

Pure love, then, does not depend on anything else. One does not love another person because of any quality that the person

6. See Rabbi Mordechai Gifter, Introduction to Artscroll *Shir HaShirim* 6, p. xix.

7. *Vikuach al Ahavah*, p. 40a.

8. *Ibid.* p. 39b.

9. *Avoth* 5:16.

has. True love does not expect anything in return, nor does it merely anticipate pleasure. Pure love is a wholly altruistic feeling, where the pleasure is more in giving than in taking.

The most perfect love in the world is that between parent and child. When a mother holds an infant in her arms, her heart overflows with a most unique love. She has this love not because she expects anything from the child, but merely because the child exists. The very fact that this is *her* child makes her love him with the deepest emotion possible.[10]

Love between parent and child exists because parent and child feel like one. They are part of the same family, and feel a bond of unity. The bond between man and woman is a reflection of this.[11]

It is significant that the first mention of love in the Bible deals with the love between parent and child; that is, the love between Abraham and Isaac (Genesis 22:2). The second mention of love in the Bible is the love between man and woman, the love between Isaac and Rebecca (Genesis 24:67).

The Torah teaches that man and woman were originally created as a single, androgynous unit. God then separated the two, making man and woman into independent persons.[12] Thus, man and woman began as a single entity, and togetherness is their natural state. The love between man and woman is a result of their natural tendency to be one.

Adam recognized this as soon as Eve was separated from him. He said, "Now this is the bone from my bones, and flesh from my flesh![13]... Therefore, [every] man shall leave his father and mother, and join his wife, and they shall become one flesh" (Genesis 2:23,24).[14]

10. It is thus taught, "Although an infant is born dirty and soiled, everyone hugs and kisses it; *VaYikra Rabbah* 27:7.

11. *Moreh Nevukhim* 3:49.

12. *Berakhoth* 61a; *Eruvin* 18a; *Ketuboth* 8a; Rashi on Genesis 2:21, 1:27. The same concept is found in Plato, *Symposium* 189, in the name of Aristophanes. It is seen as having been learned from Jewish sources; *Vikuach al Ahavah*, p. 85b.

13. This is an idiomatic expression, having the same connotation as "my own flesh and blood;" see Genesis 29;14, 2 Samuel 5:1, 19:13.

14. In "one flesh", the word *echad* also denotes *ahavah*, as above.

Adam was saying that when a man marries, he takes the natural love that he has for his parents, and directs it toward his wife. Thus, until a person marries, his strongest love is naturally directed toward his parents. After marriage, it is directed toward his mate.[15]

It is significant to note that, alone of all species, man and woman began as a single entity. All the other animals were originally created male and female. But for an animal, there is no true bond of love. An animal does not feel like one with its mate. It cannot, since the male and female were created separately. But in the case of man, the two were created as a single entity.[16]

The Talmud therefore teaches, "One's wife is like one's own body."[17] It also teaches that in a perfect marriage, a man loves his wife like his own body.[18] When love is perfect, man and wife are like a single person. All barriers, no matter how insurmountable, can be overcome by this love.[19] The Talmud thus relates that one man said of his wife, "When the love between us was intense, we could have lain together on the edge of a sword."[20]

The love between man and woman can also be understood on a deeper level. When man was first created, the Torah says, "God created the human in His image, in the image of God He created them, male and female He created them" (Genesis 1:27). Neither male nor female alone is in "the image of God"; only both of them together. When the man and woman are together in perfect harmony, they form the "image of God."[21]

15. *Moreh Nevukhim* 2:30; Rabbenu Meyuchas (ben Eliahu) on Genesis 2:24 (London, 1909); Rabbi Shimshon Raphael Hirsch, *Der Pentateuch ubersetzt und erlautert*, on Genesis 24:67.

16. See Malbim on Genesis 2:18. However, see above, note 3.

17. *Berakhoth* 24a; *Kethuboth* 66a; *Menachoth* 93b; *Bekhoroth* 38a; *Zohar* 2:117a.

18. *Yevamoth* 62b.

19. "Love compresses the flesh"; *Bava Metzia* 84a.

20. *Sanhedrin* 7a.

21. See *Sotah* 17a.

God is the Creator of all things. Moreover, God's creation of the world is seen as an act of love and altruism.[22] The only time a human being can emulate God as creator is when he comes together with a member of the opposite sex. Then, just as God created life, they also can create new life. Indeed, at such a time, they are, as the Talmud teaches, partners with God.[23]

This is why both man and woman have this desire to unite. When they do so, they manifest this "image of God." This is why love in its purest form is such a spiritual emotion. This is also another reason why the love between man and woman is used as the allegory for the love between God and His creation in the Song of Songs.

The Torah stresses that pure love between man and woman can exist even in the absence of sexual desire. Although love may be the most powerful aphrodisiac, love and sexual desire are two very different feelings. The Torah states that after Adam and Eve were created, "The two of them, the man and his wife, were naked, but they were not ashamed" (Genesis 2:25). The commentaries note that they were not ashamed because there was no sexual lust between them. Before the first sin, in the absence of such lust, looking at the nakedness of the opposite sex was no different than looking at the hands or face. But, although sexual desire did not exist, the bond of love between man and woman was very strong, simply because they were "one flesh" forming the "image of God."[24]

In a sense, the entire Jewish nation is built on love. It all began, as the Torah says, when "Jacob loved Rachel" (Genesis 29:18). He loved her so deeply that he was willing to work seven years to gain her as his bride. The Torah stresses the intensity of this love, saying, "Jacob worked seven years for Rachel, but it seemed like just a few days, so much did he love her" (Genesis 29:20).[25] The Midrash states that he loved her with a "love as strong as death."[26]

22. See *The Handbook of Jewish Thought* 3:4 ff.

23. Thus, the partners in producing a child are its father, its mother, and God; *Niddah* 31a.

24. Rashi, Abravanel, Sforno, *ad loc.* Also see Ramban on Genesis 2:9.

25. See Radak *ad loc; Or HaChaim* on Genesis 29:18.

26. Song of Songs 8:7; *Yalkut Shimoni ad loc; Tanchuma B VaYeshev* 19, p.

Just as the Bible speaks of a man's love for a woman, it speaks of the woman's love for the man. We thus find that King Saul's daughter, Michal, loved David, and that this was considered a reasonable basis for marriage (1 Samuel 18:20). Love is thus seen as a reciprocal relationship.

A love relationship between man and wife is basic to the good happy life as a whole. It is thus taught, "He who finds a wife, finds good" (Proverbs 18:22). King Solomon also said, "Enjoy life with the wife you love" (Ecclesiastes 9:9).

Of course, just because love is powerful, it does not mean that it is supposed to be blind. Marriage is the most important decision that a person will make in his or her life, and it is a decision that must be made with open eyes. One must know whom one is marrying, and be certain that there are no faults that will doom the marriage to failure. Advice must be sought and heeded. But then, once the open-eyed commitment for marriage has been made, love gives it a powerful foundation. A couple who are in love when they marry are building their marriage on the same foundation on which the entire Jewish nation was built.

But sometimes a marriage feels "right" even when there is no strong love. A couple may still feel that they should get married. In such a case, love can also grow after marriage. Even when the couple is in love before marriage, the love that develops after marriage is much deeper. It becomes a love where two people are totally sensitive to each other, and where neither can imagine life without the other. It is a love that comes from building a family — and a life — together.

This paradigm also appears in the Torah. The first mention of love between man and woman in the Torah concerns the love between Isaac and Rebecca. The Torah says, "[Isaac] married Rebecca; she became his wife and he loved her" (Genesis 24:67).

Here we see that the longer Isaac and Rebecca were married, the more they grew to love each other. This was a marriage contracted at Abraham's command, through his trusted servant. It had been contracted, not by passion, but by reason and judgment. This is true of many Jewish marriages, where

94b. In *Shir HaShirim Rabbah* on 8:7 #4, this is applied to the normal relationship between husband and wife.

parents, relatives, or friends consider which young people are suited for each other, and bring them together. If the marriage is inherently good, then the longer the couple is married, the more they will grow to love each other.[27]

I recall a conversation that I had many years ago with a man who had recently celebrated his fiftieth wedding anniversary. He said, "Young couples think that they are in love. But they don't know what true love really is. After fifty years of marriage — then you know what it means really to be in love!"

The Torah clearly recognizes that the first months of marriage are crucial to forming the love bond. It is thus written, "When a man takes a new wife, he shall not go out to the army, nor shall he be given any responsibility; he shall remain free for his house for one year, and he shall gladden the woman he married" (Deuteronomy 24:5).

Even when the Israelites maintained armies to defend their borders, a man could not be drafted during his first year of marriage. From this is derived a rule that during the first year of marriage, a man should not engage in any business that will keep him away from home.[28] During the first year of marriage, a couple must be free to build on the intimacy that will provide the foundation for the rest of their lives.

We thus see that marriage sets up chains of events that affect all future generations. God created the emotion of love to form a foundation for marriage, thus making the bond between man and woman extremely strong. God's gift of love between man and woman is one of His greatest gifts to mankind. At the same time, it is a primary ingredient of society and the future.

27. Hirsch on Genesis 24:67.

28. *Yad, Melakhim* 7:10,11; *Sefer HaMitzvoth*, Positive Commandment 214, Negative Commandment 311; *Sefer Mitzvoth Gadol*, Positive Commandment 121, Negative Commandment 230; *Chinukh* 581, 582. This "rejoicing" includes physical intimacy; *Sefer Mitzvoth Katan* 285; *Charedim*, Positive Commandments 7:7.
See *Binath Adam, Shaar Beth HaNashim* 19:37.

Chapter 3

BEFORE IT'S TOO LATE

Besides its ramifications for the bride and groom, every marriage also affects the entire community. Therefore, there are certain rules regarding who may marry and who may not. Sometimes, there are other important questions that must be clarified before a marriage occurs. In many cases, a problem that can be cleared up easily before marriage can have grave consequences afterward.

If the couple comes from Torah-oriented families, there is usually little problem. The family itself is well enough versed in Torah law to be aware of any restrictions. But where the couple's background is not Torah-oriented, it is extremely important that they meet with a rabbi who is well-versed in Torah law before marriage.

There is a very important reason for this. There are problems that may arise that can have dire effects on any children born to a particular marriage. In some cases, these problems can result in a stigma that will follow the child all his life, and even be passed down to his children and grandchildren. If a marriage is not recognized in *all* Jewish circles, then the child may be considered less than a full-fledged Jew to important segments of the Jewish community.

More and more of such problems are beginning to be seen. There are children born of Jewish parents who, according to Jewish law, cannot marry other Jews. There are young men and women who are trying to rediscover their Jewish roots, only to discover that, because of a mistake made by their parents, they are not full-fledged Jews. If the Jews are to be a united people, there must be a uniform standard in marriage law.

This is especially important today, since not all marriages are recognized by the Israeli rabbinate. Here again, if a marriage is improper, it can result in children, and even grandchildren, having second class Jewish status if they ever move to Israel. No one knows what the future will bring, and as long as Israel is an important Jewish option, it should be an important consideration.

There is a standard of Jewish law that is found in the Torah. This standard was incorporated in the Talmud, which was codified around 188 c.e. as the Mishna, and around 500 c.e. as the Gemara. Halakhic Judaism, or Judaism based on Talmudic law, is thus demonstrably over 1700 years old. It is older than Islam, even though Islam is considered an ancient religion. With regard to questions of marriage, which affect future generations of the entire Jewish community, there must be a single standard. This standard is Talmudic law, which is the standard that all Jews have accepted for many centuries.

To avoid problems, every couple contemplating marriage should have a discussion with a rabbi who is expert in Talmudic law. Where more complex questions arise, they may be referred to a rabbinical count, most often in New York City, or in Israel.

It is well known that the Torah forbids marriages between many relatives by blood or by marriage. A list is found in Leviticus 18, and most are quite obvious. No one would expect marriage between parent and child, or brother and sister, to be permissible.

Significantly, there are some blood relatives who are permitted to marry one another. Thus, under Jewish law, first cousins may wed.[1] It is also permissible for an uncle to marry his niece.[2] However, an aunt is *not* allowed to marry her nephew.[3]

Therefore, if a man and woman contemplating marriage are

1. Rabbi Yosef Chaim ben Eliahu of Baghdad, *Ben Ish Chai, Shoftim* 20 (Jerusalem, 1899).

2. It is considered an act of virtue for a man to marry his niece; *Yevamoth* 62b; *Sanhedrin* 76b; *Yad, Issurey Biyah* 2:14; *Evven HaEzer* 2:6 in *Hagah*. See Bachya on Genesis 24:3; *Ben Ish Chai, Shoftim* 21.

3. Leviticus 18:12-14. For a discussion of why a niece is permitted while an aunt is forbidden, see Rabbi Kalonymus Kalman (ben Aaron) Epstein, *Meor VaShemesh* (Breslau, 1842) on Exodus 6:20; Rabbi Yisrael Chaim Friedman, *Likutey Maharich* (Sighet-Satmar, 1911) 3:128b.

in any way related, whether by blood or by marriage, they should discuss the circumstances with a rabbi who is expert in Talmudic law.

Problems can sometimes occur if the mother of either party had been divorced before they were born. In such a case, it is important to determine whether or not the mother had a proper Jewish divorce (known as a *get*). When going to a rabbi with questions of this nature, as many details as possible of both marriages of the mother, as well as the divorce, should be available.

A rabbi should also be consulted if either of the parents of either party was a convert to Judaism. Not all conversions are universally recognized. Moreover, some conversions are not recognized in the State of Israel. If one's mother was not converted properly, one's status as a Jew may be called into question.[4] In such cases, if there is a problem, it is usually readily rectifiable.

In the case of a second marriage, an Orthodox rabbi must be consulted to make sure that a proper Jewish divorce has been obtained. This is especially important for the woman, since if a woman remarries without a proper Jewish divorce (*get*), her children may have the status of *mamzer* (bastard), who may not intermarry with other Jews. Such a child is banned from the community by the commandment, "A bastard (*mamzer*) must not enter God's marriage group. Even after the tenth generation, he may not enter God's marriage group" (Deuteronomy 23:3). A child born out of wedlock is *not* a bastard according to Jewish law, but a child born without his mother having a proper Jewish divorce *is*.

Obtaining a Jewish divorce (*get*) is a relatively simple and inexpensive procedure. Therefore, if it is necessary, every effort should be made to obtain one, so that the status of the future marriage will not be questionable, and so that the children will not be stigmatized.

4. See *Yevamoth* 23a.

In a case where either the bride or groom must undergo conversion to Judaism, the matter should be referred to a qualified rabbinical court (*beth din*). Although some Orthodox rabbis perform conversions, not all are univerally accepted. In Israel, there is a list of rabbinical courts whose conversions are universally accepted. Preferably, the conversion should be performed by a rabbinical court consisting of three rabbis, all of whom are expert in the laws of conversion.[5]

If a man's wife dies, he must wait until three of the festivals, Pesach, Shavuoth and Sukkoth pass, before remarrying.[6] A woman, whether widowed or divorced, must wait 90 days before remarrying.[7] In some cases, if a woman has a child, she may not remarry until the child is two years old.[8] In all such cases, the question should be referred to a rabbi expert in Jewish law.

If a woman is widowed, and her husband never had any children, then, if the husband has any surviving brothers, she must undergo the ceremony of *chalitzah* ("removing the shoe," Deuteronomy 25:9). This ceremony consists of her removing a specially made chalitzah shoe from the foot of her late husband's brother. The symbolic meaning of this is to release any claim that the brother may have to the dead husband's inheritance.[9] In such cases, the widow may not remarry until the chalitzah ceremony has been completed. This ceremony can be done only under the auspices of a rabbi who is expert in all the pertinent laws.[10]

If a woman has been widowed twice, there are some cases

5. The laws of conversion are found in *Yoreh Deah* 268.

6. *Yoreh Deah 392:2. However, in many cases, he may be permitted to marry after only thirty days; see Rabbi Yitzchak Tzvi Leibowitz, Shulchan HaEzer* 11:5 (Des. 1929; Beregszasz, 1932) 11:5.

7. *Evven HaEzer* 13:1; *Yevamoth* 41a. For details, see *Shulchan HaEzer* 1:26.

8. *Yevamoth* 42a; *Evven HaEzer* 13:11; *Shulchan HaEzer* 1:28.

9. See Rashbam, Chizzkuni, on Deuteronomy 25:9. Cf. Ruth 4:7.

10. The laws of *chalitzah* are found in *Evven HaEzer* 157. See *Shulchan HaEzer* 1:24.

where she is not permitted to remarry at all. Such a question must be brought to a rabbi expert in Jewish law.[11]

When a man is a *cohen* (a member of the Jewish hereditary priesthood), there are also other rules that he must observe.

A *cohen* is forbidden to marry a woman who has been divorced, but he may marry a widow.[12]

A *cohen* is forbidden to marry a convert to Judaism.[13]

A *cohen* may not marry a girl who has had sexual intercourse with a gentile. Similarly, if a woman has ever engaged in adultery, she is forbidden to a *cohen*. In other cases where a girl has engaged in premarital or extramarital intercourse, a rabbi expert in Talmudic law must be consulted before she marries a *cohen*.[14]

A *cohen* may not marry a *chalalah*. A *chalalah* is defined as the daughter of a *cohen* from a marriage forbidden to him. If a *cohen* marries any of the above mentioned women, who are forbidden to him, any daughters of such a marriage are also forbidden to marry a *cohen*. Therefore, if a *cohen* wishes to marry a *cohen*'s daughter, he must be sure that the father's marriage was permitted by Jewish law. In such cases, a rabbi should be consulted.[15]

These rules regarding a *cohen* are found in the Torah itself, as it is written, "[A *cohen*] may not marry a woman who is sexually defiled, who is a *chalalah*, or who has been divorced from her husband, since he is sanctified to God" (Leviticus 21:7). The *cohen* has a permanent hereditary status as being "holy to God." This imposes additional duties and restrictions upon him. There is absolutely no way in which a *cohen* can relinquish or put aside his status to marry a woman forbidden to him. He is born with the status of *cohen*, and it remains with him all his life.

11. *Yevamoth* 64b; *Evven HaEzer* 9:1; *Shulchan HaEzer* 1:31.

12. The laws are detailed in *Evven HaEzer* 6. See *Shulchan HaEzer* 1:17.

13. *Yevamoth* 61a; *Evven HaEzer* 6:8; *Shulchan HaEzer* 1:18.

14. *Ibid.*

15. *Evven HaEzer* 7:12; *Shulchan HaEzer* 1:23.

Some circles maintain the custom of not permitting a marriage where the bride has the same name as the groom's mother, or where the groom has the same name as the bride's father.[16] Most authorities, however, are inclined to permit such marriages.[17]

Some of these laws may seem harsh and restrictive. But, on the other hand, they are necessary. It has been Jewish marriage, and the Jewish family, that have enabled the Jews to survive as a people for over three thousand years. Any tampering with these laws can therefore cause the weakening and demise of large elements of the Jewish people. It is an observable fact that in circles where these laws are not observed, intermarriage and assimilation are rife.

Every Jewish marriage is a link in a chain that goes back to Abraham, Isaac and Jacob — and to the great revelation at Sinai. It is a chain that has endured until this day, and has changed the face of this entire planet. But a chain is only as strong as its weakest link. Judaism therefore strives to make every marriage as strong as possible, so that every link in the chain will be firm.

16. The source of this custom is the ethical will of Rabbi Yehudah HaChasid (1148 — 1217); see *Tzavaath Rabbi Yehudah HaChasid* 22; *Sefer Chassidim* 477. Also see Rabbi Emanuel Chai Rikki, *Mishnath Chassidim* (Livorno, 1722), *Mesekhta Chathunah U'Milah* 1:5, p. 64b; Rabbi David Fardo, *Mizmor LeDavid* 179 (Livorno, 1818); *Ben Ish Chai, Shoftim* 28; Rabbi Menachem Mendel of Lubavitch, *Piskey Dinim* (Vilna, 1884), p. 213b, end; *Pith'chey Teshuvah, Yoreh Deah* 116:6; *Teshuvoth Divrey Chaim, Evven HaEzer* 8. For discussion, see Rabbi Chaim Chizkiyahu Medini, *Sedey Chemed* (Warsaw, 1894 — 1911), *Chathan VeKallah* 5; *Shulchan HaEzer* 1:11.

17. See *Chokhmath Adam* 123:13; *Teshuvoth Modah BeYehudah Tinyana, Evven HaEzer* 79; *Teshuvoth Chatham Sofer, Evven HaEzer* 1:116; Rabbi Moshe Feinstein, *Igroth Moshe, Evven HaEzer* 4.

Chapter 4

ENGAGEMENT

There comes a time when a couple realizes that they are right for each other. At this time, the man usually proposes marriage. If the girl accepts, they consider themselves engaged.

In Jewish practice, this marriage proposal is actually the first step of formal engagement. The Talmud refers to the marriage proposal as *shidukhin* (שִׁידוּכִין).[1] To marry without first proposing was considered an immoral act.[2]

Even in ancient times, couples often met on their own and made their own decision to marry. Jacob met Rachel on his own, without going through his or her parents (Genesis 29:10,11). The Talmud similarly relates that Rabbi Akiba married his wife Rachel secretly, against the will of her parents.[3]

Of course, it was a widespread Jewish custom — and still is in many circles — for parents to arrange the marriages of their children. But even when marriages were arranged, both the boy and the girl had to give their full consent. Stories about couples being forced to marry against their will are nothing but myths.

This is seen in the Torah. Although Laban and Abraham's agent had agreed that Rebecca would marry Isaac, before they could complete the agreement, they had to say, "Let us call the

1. This definition of *shidukhin* is found in Rashi, *Kiddushin* 13a, s.v. *BeDeShadikh; Arukh*, s.v. *Shadakh* 4; *Evven HaEzer* 28:2 in *Hagah*. Also see *Kiddushin* 44b; *Teshuvoth Rashba* 558; Teshuvoth HaRosh 27:5, 34:1. Cf. Rashi, *Kiddushin* 50b s.v. *Chosheshin; Tosafoth, Kiddushin* 52a s.v. *VeHilkhathah; Pith'chey Teshuvah, Evven HaEzer* 28:10; *Likutey Maharich* 3:129a; *Chazon Ish, Evven HaEzer* 39:1.

   The word *shidukh* denotes rest and tranquility; see *Targum* on Judges 3:11. This is the tranquility that a person finds in marriage (Ruth 1:9); see Ran, *Shabbath*, Rif 5b, s.v. *Ain*.

2. *Kiddushin* 12b, *Yevamoth* 52a; *Yerushalmi, Kiddushin* 3:10; *Yad, Issurey Biyah* 21:14; *Evven HaEzer* 26:4.

3. *Kethuboth* 62b.

girl and ask her what she says about it" (Genesis 24:57). From this is derived the rule that neither a man nor a woman can be married without their full consent.[4]

Very often matches are made without any intermediary. In other cases, there is a go-between. This intermediary may be a relative or friend, or he may be a professional matchmaker. In either case, since he (or she) makes the *shidukhin*, he is known as a *shadkhan* (שַׁדְכָן).[5] In some Jewish circles, marriages are still arranged through a *shadkhan*, and in the case of a professional, a matchmaker's fee is paid.[6] Nevertheless, there is nothing particularly Jewish or "traditional" about using a matchmaker.

Before formally announcing their engagement, it is customary for the couple to meet with both sets of parents, where practical. It is also customary for both sets of parents to meet each other. This is only proper, since they are planning to become related by marriage.

It is important for the couple to have the blessings of both sets of parents.[7] Nevertheless, if the parents do not agree to a marriage, the couple is not obliged to obey them. The law is that if a man and woman want to marry, they are permitted to marry over parental objections.[8] It does not make any difference whether the objections come from the groom's side or the bride's.[9]

4. Rashi *ad loc; Evven HaEzer* 2:1; *Beth Shmuel* 37:11; *Shulchan HaEzer* 2:1. Also see Rashi, *Kiddushin* 44a, s.v.*Kiddushin, Yevamoth* 19b, s.v. *Kiddushin.*

5. One of the earliest uses of the word is by Rashbam (1080—74), *Bava Bathra* 174b s.v. *Mitzvah.* Also see *Teshuvoth Rivash* 193; Rabbi Yitzchak Lipitz, *Mataamim* (Warsaw, 1889), s.v. *Chathan VeKallah* 60; Rabbi Shemtob Gaguine, *Kether Shem Tov (London, 1934), note 695.*

6. *See Teshuvoth Rabbi Meir of Rothenberg* 498, 499 (Budapest, 1895); *Teshuvoth HaRosh* 105:1; Mordechai, *Bava Kama* 173 (Vilna edition) p. 52d; *Terumath HaDeshen, Pesakim U'Kethavim* 85, quoting *Or Zerua; Choshen Mishpat,* in *Hagah* 87:39, 185:10, 264:7.

7. See *Beth Shmuel* 35:2.

8. *Yoreh Deah* 240:25 in *Hagah; Teshuvoth Maharik* 166:3; *Teshuvoth Rashgdam, Yoreh Deah* 95; *Sefer Chassidim* 561.

9. *Teshuvoth Tashbatz* 3:130; *Teshuvoth rabbi Akiva Eiger, Pesakim* 68;

It is true that the Torah considers honoring one's parents to be a most important commandment. Indeed, it is the fifth of the Ten Commandments (Exodus 20:12). Nevertheless, it is not an absolute mandate, as the Torah says, "Every man shall fear his mother and father, but keep My Sabbaths" (Leviticus 19:3). The Talmud explains that the Torah is teaching that keeping the Sabbath takes precedence over honoring one's parents. This is also the reason that in the Ten Commandments, the commandment regarding the Sabbath (Exodus 20:8) comes before the commandment to honor one's parents.

Therefore, if a parent tells a child to do anything that would involve a violation of the Sabbath, the child is forbidden to obey his parent. The same is true if the parent tells the child to violate the Torah in any other way.[10]

When a couple marries, the Torah places overriding importance on their being suited to each other.[11] Therefore, when a person finds a suitable mate, he or she is forbidden to break the match because of the objections of others. To marry and have children is a commandment of the Torah, and when a person finds a suitable mate, he has the opportunity to fulfill the commandment in the best possible way. He can never be sure that the opportunity will arise again. Therefore, when parents object to a marriage, it is tantamount to their demanding that a commandment be violated. In such cases, there is no obligation to obey the parent.[12] As a paradigm, Rabbi Akiba married Rachel against her father's wishes.[13]

Of course, this is not the best possible situation. No matter how strong the parental objects are, every effort should be made to get the parents to agree to the marriage.[14] The blessing of

Rabbi Pinchas (ben Tzvi Hirsch) Horowitz, *Teshuvoth Giva'ath Pinchas* 3 (Lvov, 1838); Rabbi Chaim (ben Mordechai Ephraim) Sofer, *Teshuvoth Machaneh Chaim* 1:32 (Munkatch, 1872).

10. *Yevamoth* 6a; *Yoreh Deah* 240:15.
11. See *Tosefta, Sotah* 5:6 (in Vilna Talmud).
12. *Teshuvoth Maharik* 166:3.
13. *Kethuboth* 62b.
14. Rabbi Yekuthiel Yehudah Teitelbaum, *Teshuvoth Avney Tzedek, Yoreh Deah* 99 (Lvov, 1885); *Shulchan HaEzer* 1:1:8.

both sets of parents is very important if the marriage is to get off to a good start.

Once the parents have been informed, the couple will want to inform their closest friends. This is often done even before there is any formal engagement announcement or party.

It is an ancient custom for the groom to give his bride an engagement present. In Talmudic times, such a gift was known as a *sivlon* (סִבְלוֹן).[15] Nowadays, following the general custom, the man usually gives his bride a diamond engagement ring.[16]

The custom of giving a diamond is so ingrained that many couples feel that they are not engaged without one. This, of course, is nonsense. In many of the best marriages, the bride was never given a diamond engagement ring. The main thing is that she should be as precious to her husband as a diamond, and not that she wear one on her finger.

Even when a diamond ring is bought, the groom should not go beyond his means to purchase it. At the beginning of a marriage, many things are needed, and to forgo them for the sake of a ring is ludicrous. There are times when lack of money (or even debt) resulting from the purchase of the engagement ring places serious strains on a marriage. Although it is nice to be able to show off a beautiful, expensive ring, this is not what a Jewish marriage is about.

According to many authorities, the engagement ring should not be given in the presence of witnesses. Since giving the

15. Other sources give the pronunciation as *savlan; Arukh HaShalem*. See *Kiddushin* 50b; *Evven HaEzer* 45:3; *Arukh HaShulchan* 45:16-18.

The word *sivlan* or *savlan* is derived from the root *saval* (סבל), denoting something that is passed from one person to another; Rambam on *Kiddushin* 2:6, *Bava Bathra* 9:5; *Tosefoth Yom Tov* on *Kiddushin* 2:6. Other sources state that the word has the direct connotation of a gift; *Arukh*, s.v. *saval; Sefer HaTishbi*. Others say that it is derived from the Greek word *symbolus*, a symbolic gift; *Mussaf HaArukh*. Also see *Zohar* 1:137a.

16. It was an ancient custom to give jewelry; Rashbam, *Bava Bathra* 145a, s.v. *HaShole'ach*; Bertenoro on *Bava Bathra* 9:5. It has a stone to denote that it is not a wedding ring, since a wedding ring may not have a stone; see below, Chapter 6, note 40.

engagement ring is considered a prelude to marriage, there is concern that if it is given in the presence of witnesses, the couple may be considered married. To break the engagement would then require a *get* (Jewish divorce).[17]

It is a custom to have some kind of formal party to announce the couple's engagement to the community. Originally, it was customary to make *tenaim* (תְּנָאִים)[18] and this is still prevalent in some Jewish circles today.[19] The word *tenaim* literally means "conditions." This was a formal ceremony, where a contract was signed, setting the wedding date and stipulating various prenuptial agreements.[20]

There are various forms that the *tenaim* contract takes.[21] However, most *tenaim* contracts begin in the following manner:

To good fortune.[22] לְמַזָל טוב

17. Rabbi Yosef Eliahu Henkin, *Ik'rey Dinim U'Minhagey Beth HaKenesseth* 45 in *Eduth LeYisrael* (New York, 1948), p. 141. See *Evven HaEzer* 45:1.

18. See *Yad, Mekhirah* 11:18; *Turey Zahav, Orach Chaim* 546:2, *Evven HaEzer* 50:12; *Shulchan HaEzer* 2:1.

19. This is true in many Chassidic circles.

20. In many sources this was also referred to as Shidukhin; see Rabbi Yehudah Barceloni (circa 1100), *Sefer HaShetaroth* 72 (Berlin, 1898), p. 128; *Teshuvoth HaRosh* 35:1; *Evven HaEzer* 50:5,6; Rabbi Chaim Yosef David Azzulai (Chida), *Avodath HaKodesh, Tziporen Shamir* 6:87. Also see *Terumath HaDeshen* 207; *Teshuvoth Rabbi Tam ibn Yachya* 301 in *Tummath Yesharim* (Venice, 1520), p. 110. In Talmudic times, this contract was known as a *Sh'tar Pesikta; Kiddushin* 9b; *Nimukey Yosef, Bava Bathra*, Rif 77b (Vilna Talmud); HaGra, *Evven HaEzer* 51:14. Also see *Evven HaEzer* 51:1 in *Hagah* (end); *Beth Shmuel* 51:12.

21. Various forms are found in *Nachalath Shiva* 8-11; Rabbi Asher Anshil Greenwald, *Kitzur Nachalath Shiva* 8 (Ungvar, 1926); Rabbi Yitzchak Ohlbaum, *Ezer LeYitzchak* 5:4 (Budapest, 1949); Rabbi Hyman E. Goldin, *HaMadrikh* (New York, 1939), p. 2. Older, obsolete forms are found in Rabbi Yehudah Barceloni, *Sefer HaShetaroth* 72, p. 128; *Sefer HaIttur*, s.v. *Tanai* (Warsaw, 1885), p. 40a; quoted in *Hagahoth Mordechai, Kethuboth* 293, p. 10b.

22. This is taken from the "last *tenaim*" in *Nachalath Shiva* 9. However, *Nachalath Shiva* only has *mazal tov*: "good fortune shall sprout and ascend."

יַעֲלֶה וְיִצְמַח כְּגַן רָטוּב. מָצָא אִשָּׁה מָצָא טוֹב וַיָּפֶק רָצוֹן מֵה׳ הַטּוֹב, הָאוֹמֵר לַדֶּבֶק טוֹב.

May [this match] flourish and grow like a verdant garden. He who finds a wife finds good, and obtains favor from God[23] who is good,[24] and who says the match is good.[25]

הַמַּגִּיד מֵרֵאשִׁית אַחֲרִית, הוּא יִתֵּן שֵׁם טוֹב וּשְׁאֵרִית, לָאֵלֶּה דִבְרֵי הַתְּנָאִים וְהַבְּרִית, שֶׁנִּדַּבְּרוּ וְהוּתְנוּ בֵּין שְׁנֵי הַצְּדָדִים....

May [God] who declares the end from the beginning[26] be the One to provide a [good][27] name and future[28] to these words of the agreement and covenant that was contracted and agreed upon by both parties...

It is a custom to make a meal for the engagement party.[29] This is usually held at the house of one of the parents, but it may be held at a friend's house or in a small hall. This meal is considered a religious event, and it is customary to invite the rabbi and other community leaders.[30]

23. From Proverbs 18:22.

24. This is not in the above verse.

25. Isaiah 41:7.

26. Isaiah 46:10. Actually, the standard, regular tenaim begins with this verse; *Nachalath Shiva* 9. This is a prayer that the marriage should be good from the beginning; *Nachalath Shiva* 9:1. Others see it as referring to the fact that matches are destined before the couple is born; Rabbi Naftali Tzvi Horowitz of Ropshitz, *Zera Kodesh* (Lvov, 1868) on 15 Av; quoted in Rabbi Avraham Yitzchak Sperling-Danzig, *Taamey HaMinhagim* 938 (first printed in Lvov, 1896; we used the Jerusalem, 1957 edition).

27. Not in *Nachalath Shiva* 8.

28. From 2 Samuel 14:7.

29. *Turey Zahav, Orach Chaim* 546:2; *Elyah Rabbah* 546:3; *Shulchan HaEzer* 2:1:21.

30. *Turey Zahav, Evven HaEzer* 50:11.

Where a formal *tenaim* is made, the community rabbi or another learned leader officiates. After the contract is signed, it is read aloud by this person.[31]

After the *tenaim* contract is read, it is a custom for the mothers of the bride and groom to break a china dish.[32] In some circles, pieces of this dish are made into jewelry and given to the bride's friends.

The reason for breaking the dish is to show that we mourn for Jerusalem and all the other martyred Jews even at the height of our joy.[33] A china dish is broken to show that, just as a china plate can never be fully repaired, a broken engagement is an irreparable breach. Even if the bride and groom are later reconciled, the breaking of a formal *tenaim* contract is considered very reprehensible.[34]

Because of this, since World War II, it has become a custom in many circles to make the formal *tenaim* just before the wedding. Many difficult problems arise when *tenaim* are broken, and in the confusion following the war, such broken engagements became a common occurrence. Therefore, the *tenaim* ceremony was shifted to just before the wedding, so that there would be no chance that it would be broken.[35]

31. *Teshuvoth Beth Chadash* 10; *Teshuvoth Nodah BeYehudah, Evven HaEzer* 68; *Shulchan HaEzer* 2:2:19.

32. *Elyah Rabbah* 560:7 (quoting *Maadney Yom Tov*); *Pri Megadim, Mishbetzoth Zahav, Orach Chaim* 560:4. Cf. *Darkey Moshe* 560:2; *Teshuvoth Avney Shoham* 51; *Teshuvoth Tirash VeYitz'har; Likutey Moharan* 60:8. This is not a custom among Sephardim; *Kether Shem Tov, Seder HaErusin VeHaNesuin* 23.

33. See *Orach Chaim* 560:2 in *Hagah; Taamey HaMinhagim,* p. 411. Regarding breaking the glass under the chupah, see below, Chapter 22, notes 89 — 91.

34. *Shaarey Rachamim* (Vilna, 1871) quoting Rabbi Eliahu, the Vilna Gaon, who writes that it is better to write a *get* than to tear *tenaim*. See *Taamey HaMinhagim* p. 411; *Mataamim* 6; *Likutey Maharich* 3:129a. See *Bereshith Rabbah* 14:7.

35. Rabbi Yaakov Kopel Pasternak, private communication. In any case, it was customary to make a second tenaim before the wedding; see *Sefer Meirath Eynayim (Sema)* on *Choshen Mishpat* 245:2; *Nachalath Shiva* 9:2. Also see *Shulchan HaEzer* 2:2:1.

In circles where formal *tenaim* are not made, it is customary to have a "word" (*vort*, וואָרט, in Yiddish). While this is considered a formal engagement, it is not as immutable as *tenaim*. The custom at a *vort* is to make a meal, and to have the rabbi or another officiant make a *kinyan* (קִנְיָן) with the bride, groom, and their parents.

A *kinyan* is a formal acceptance of obligation. The act of acceptance is usually done by taking the corner of a handkerchief, napkin, or other object that the officiant is holding. According to Jewish law, taking the object is a formal acceptance of an obligation. The practice is mentioned in the Bible: "This was the ancient practice in Israel... to confirm all things: a man would take off his shoe and give it to the other party. This, among the Israelites, would create an obligation" (Ruth 4:7).[36] While the Biblical custom may have involved a shoe, a handkerchief or other article can also be used.[37]

To some people, even such an obligation is considered too legalistic. Even a formal obligation involving a *kinyan* should not be broken except in the direst circumstances. To break a *kinyan* is almost as bad as breaking *tenaim*. Therefore, in some circles, the *vort* simply consists of making a party, and having the families drink *lechaim* (לְחַיִּים, "to life") to the forthcoming wedding.

It goes without saying that any engagement party (and certainly a wedding) must be treated as a religious affair. The meal should be kosher, and should be initiated with the *HaMotzie* (הַמּוֹצִיא) over bread, and closed with the Grace after Meals (*Birkath HaMazon*, בִּרְכַּת הַמָּזוֹן). Furthermore, either the groom or the rabbi should deliver a Torah lesson (*devar Torah*, דְּבַר תּוֹרָה) at the meal, since this makes it a "mitzvah meal" (*seudath mitzvah*, סְעוּדַּת מִצְוָה).[38]

Where families announce the couple's engagement with a *vort*, it is the custom to make the *tenaim* at the reception just

36. See *Bava Metzia* 47a. Also see below, Chapter 15, note 34.

37. See *Bava Metzia* 7b.

38. *Teshuvoth Chavath Yair* 70; *Shulchan HaEzer* 2:1:21.

before the wedding ceremony. According to Rabbi Moshe Feinstein שליט״א, the *tenaim* contract then takes a somewhat different form. Such *tenaim* contracts are available from most Jewish book stores.

Chapter 5

SETTING THE DATE

When a couple announces their engagement, the first question people usually ask is, "Have you set the date?" The question is simple, but the answer requires planning.

There are many practical considerations that must be taken into account before the date can be set. The bride or groom may want to finish a school term, or arrange the wedding when it is convenient for them to take off from work during the week after the wedding. In some areas, they might want to give themselves enough time to find an apartment or house and furnish it. This will provide a general idea of how long they want to wait.

A second factor will be the availability of a place for the wedding. Before the date can be set, the couple will have to decide what kind of wedding they want, and where they want to hold it. This is a decision that is usually made together with both families. This is a time when an atmosphere of cooperation should be developed between both sides. The manner in which the wedding is planned by both sides often has long lasting effects on the relationship between the families.

If the bride and groom are from different cities, they will have to agree about where the wedding will be held. Usually, it is held in the city of the bride, but this is not a hard and fast rule. Sometimes, the couple will decide on a point convenient to both families.

Nowadays, with easy air transportation available, the wedding is often held in the bride's city, while one or more of the *Sheva Berakhoth* (see Chapter 26) is held in the groom's community.

A primary concern is the cost of the wedding. This will determine what kind of wedding is planned, and how many guests will be invited. A wedding is (hopefully) a once in a lifetime affair, and both parties will want it to be as nice as possible. Still, it must be stressed that many of the happiest marriages begin with very simple, inexpensive weddings. There is absolutely no correlation between the lavishness of the wedding and the subsequent happiness of the couple.

Even where money is available, it can often be better used by the couple to begin their new life together rather than to make a lavish wedding. In many cases, huge debts are incurred to make a large, fancy wedding, and then the couple has severe marital problems because of lack of money. It takes wisdom to determine how much to spend on the wedding, and how much to save for the couple.

My friend, Rabbi Shmuel Mendelson, once gave a very good example. In the Talmud, there is a dispute as to how Chanukah candles are lit. The House of Shammai maintains that on the first day, we begin by lighting eight candles, and that each day we light one less, until on the eighth day, only one candle is lit. The House of Hillel, whose opinion is universally followed today, maintains that on the first day, only one candle is lit; then on each subsequent night an additional candle is added, until on the eighth night, all eight candles are lit.[1]

Rabbi Mendelson said that some couples begin their married life with the Shammai attitude. When they begin, they have everything. However, they have little to look forward to. Often, as each day passes, they find their lives diminishing.

Other couples start with the Hillel attitude. They can start off with one candle — with very little. But for the rest of their life they are adding.

The bride's parents usually pay for the bulk of the wedding.[2]

1. *Shabbath* 21b.

2. We thus find that Laban made a feast for Jacob's wedding (Genesis 29:22). Similarly, Rebecca's family made a feast for Eliezer when he came to take her for Isaac (Genesis 24:54); See Rabbi Avraham Eliezer Hirshovitz, *Otzar Kol Minhagey Yeshurun, Chathunah* 14 (St. Louis, 1918), p. 48. The custom is mentioned in the codes; *Turey Zahav* 57:4; *Ba'er Hetiv* 56:3; *Shulchan HaEzer* 9:1. Early sources also state that, "The Seven Blessings are said at the meal made by the bride's father"; *Sefer HaIttur* 2:4, 64b.

The bride's family originally made the meal only for the betrothal (*erusin*) as we find in the Mishnah; *Pesachim* 49a; *Orach Chaim* 444:7; Hai

There are certain things that the groom's family contributes, depending on local custom. There are, however, no hard and fast rules. Where the groom's family is in a better position to afford the wedding, and where they want a larger wedding, there is nothing wrong with the groom's family contributing, or even paying for it.[3] The most important thing, however, is that all this be done in a spirit of cooperation, without allowing the bride's family to feel that they are being put down.

A wedding can be held virtually anywhere. A small wedding may be held in the home. In many communities, the only large kosher facility may be the synagogue banquet hall. In larger cities, hotels and catering halls may have excellent kosher facilities.[4]

It is easiest to have a wedding where it can be professionally catered. It is a good idea for the prospective couple to see an example of the caterer's work before making a commitment, to determine whether or not they are satisfied with the atmosphere the caterer provides. Some catering halls are known to conduct weddings in the truest Jewish spirit, while others have been known to vulgarize the affair. It is therefore

Gaon, quoted in Rabbi Avraham ben Nathan HaYarchi (c. 1150 —1215), *Sefer HaManhig* (Jerusalem, 1978), p. 535; *Teshuvoth Rivash* 260; Rabbi Yitzchak Gayoth, p. 14. Later, when the *erusin* and *nesuin* were combined (see below), the entire feast became the responsibility of the bride's family; see Rashi, *Sefer HaPardes, Hilkhoth Birkath Chathanim* (Budapest, 1924), p. 74; Rabbi David Yehudah Leib Zilberstein, *Sheviley David, Evven HaEzer* 60 (Jerusalem, 1863).

Moreover, it is assumed that the bride's family will make a greater effort for the meal than the groom's; *Pachad Yitzchak,* s.v. *Chathan,* p. 60d, from *Chullin* 83a; *Kerem Shlomo, Evven HaEzer* 59. It is also taught that if people enjoy the *groom's* meal and do not make him rejoice, they are in violation; *Berakhoth* 6b. Therefore, in order to avoid the possibility of a violation, the bride's family made the feast; Rabbi Asher Anzel, *Korban Ani* (Lvov, 1872), quoted in *Taamey HaMinhagim* 980; *Mataamim* 42. There are also Kabbalistic reasons that the bride's father makes the meal; *Zohar* 2:169a; *Mataamim* 41. See next note.

3. It appears that the original custom was for the groom to pay for the wedding meal; *Berakhoth* 6b; *Evven HaEzer* 64:4. See Judges 14:10.

4. Among Sephardic Jews in Amsterdam, it was customary to hold weddings in special wedding halls; *Kether Shem Tov* 2, p. 597.

very important for the couple to make sure that their wedding lives up to their tastes and aspirations.

In Hebrew, the term for wedding is *kiddushin* (קדושין).[5] This word comes from the root *kodesh* (קודש), meaning "holy"; therefore, a wedding is considered a holy occasion.[6] Although it is a time for happiness and rejoicing, it should be remembered that the wedding is a religious ceremony, and even the party and dinner accompanying it are part of the sacred occasion.[7] As we shall see, a special set of "Seven Blessings" (*Sheva Berakhoth*) are said at the end of the wedding meal.

In many halls, the caterer or band leader acts as the master of ceremonies. In large cities, these individuals may be deeply religious in their own right, knowing how to maintain the balance of exuberance and sanctity that a Jewish wedding requires. However, some "masters of ceremony" have very vulgar ideas of what a Jewish wedding is. [Singing "The Bride Cuts the Cake" to the tune of "The Farmer in the Dell," is hardly consonant with the spirit of a Jewish wedding.]

It is therefore important to go over all details with the rabbi. The rabbi is well aware of the exuberance that is maintained in a traditional wedding, but he knows how to maintain it with a balance of holiness and Jewishness. Do not expect him to be severe or restrictive; in many cases, he will be able to make the wedding not only a more joyous affair, but also a much more meaningful one.

There are few hard and fast rules as to where the wedding ceremony should be held. Many authorities maintain that the wedding ceremony should not be held in a synagogue sanctuary — this being too reminiscent of a church wedding.[8]

5. See *Kiddushin* 2b; *Tosafoth ad loc.* s.v. *DeAssar.*

6. Rabbi Menachem HaBavli, *Taamey HaMitzvoth* (Lublin, 1571), quoted in Rabbi Yitzchak (ben Moshe Mendel) Zaller, *Yalkut Yitzchak* 552:3 (Warsaw, 1895). See *S'hnei Luchoth HaBrith, Shaar HaOthioth* (Lvov, 1860) 1:164b, quoted in *Mataamim* 74.

7. See Below, Chapter 24.

8. *Teshuvoth Chatham Sofer, Evven HaEzer* 98; *Teshuvoth Sho'el U'Meshiv,* Third Edition 1:182; *Teshuvoth Kethav Sofer, Evven HaEzer* 47; *Levushey*

However, a good number of authorities do permit it.[9] There is also an ancient custom of having the ceremony outdoors, weather permitting.[10] This should be taken into account when choosing the place. Many halls have facilities where the ceremony can be held outdoors, or where there is an opening in the roof, allowing the sky to be visible.

It goes without saying that the wedding must be a completely kosher affair. The wedding is the foundation of the couple's future married life. If the wedding is to have the aura of holiness and meaningfulness that most modern couples want today, it must be kosher. Even if neither family keeps kosher, there is nothing hypocritical about having a kosher wedding. This is a time of special blessing for the bride and groom, where everything should be as traditional as possible.

In any case, a place for the wedding should be booked well in advance. This is especially important if the couple wishes to get everything they want.

There are certain times when a wedding cannot be held. Obviously, a wedding cannot be held on the Sabbath, or on such major holidays as Rosh HaShanah, Yom Kippur,

Mordechai, Evven HaEzer 47; *Teshuvoth Chatham Sofer* 85; *Tifereth Yisrael* (beginning of *Moed*), *K'leley Simchoth, Gezeroth, Lamed* 2, in note; *Sedey Chemed, Chathan VeKallah* 1; *Shulchan HaEzer* 7:2:3; *Shaarim Metzuyanim BeHalakhah* 147:1; *Teshuvoth Yehudah Yaaleh, Orach Chaim* 38; *Teshuvoth Maharam Shick, Evven HaEzer* 87; *Otzar Kol Minhagey Yeshurun* 16:6.

9. If the couple wish to have the wedding in the synagogue sanctuary, and there is no intent to make it like a "church wedding," it is not actually forbidden.There is also no reason that a rabbi should not participate in such a wedding; *Igroth Moshe, Evven HaEzer* 93.

Actually, in Germany and some parts of Poland, between the 14th and 17th centuries, it was the custom to hold weddings in the synagogue sanctuary; *Teshuvoth Rabbi Moshe Mintz* 107; *Maharil* (Jerusalem, 1969), p. 64b; *Nachalath Shiva* 12:9. Even today, Sephardim in London and Germany have an established custom of holding weddings in the synagogue; *Kether Shem Tov* 2, note 698. Some permit it, since men and women do not mingle at the ceremony; *Otzar Kol Minhagey Yeshurun* 16:6.

10. See below, Chapter 18.

Sukkoth, Shemini Atzereth, Simchath Torah, Pesach or Shavuoth. Marriages may not be held even during the intermediate days (*chol ha-moed*) of Pesach or Sukkoth.[11]

It is also customary not to have weddings on the day immediately preceding a major holiday.[12] On Friday morning or early afternoon, however, it is permitted.[13]

It is also a custom not to have a wedding on Purim, except in a case where no alternative is possible.[14] On Chanukah, however, it is permissible to have a wedding.

It is a universal custom not to have weddings during the period between Pesach and Shavuoth, when the Omer is being counted. Known as *Sefirah* (סְפִירָה), this is a time of national mourning, because Rabbi Akiba's students died during this period, virtually wiping out all Jewish leadership.[15] On Lag

11. *Orach Chaim* 546:1; *Evven HaEzer* 64:6.

12. *Magen Avraham* 546:4 (end).

13. *Evven HaEzer* 64:3; *Shulchan HaEzer* 4:6:12. In some places, it was actually an ancient custom to have weddings on Fridays; *Rokeach* 353; *Kol Bo* 75 (Lvov 1860), 44c; *Maharil* 64b; *Nachalath Shiva* 12:1. This was so that the poor would not have to spend money on a wedding meal, but would be able to combine it with the Friday night, Sabbath meal; Mordechai, *Kethuboth* 129; Bertenoro on *Kethuboth* 1:1. Another reason for this may have been that Adam and Eve were created on a Friday (the sixth day), and were married on that day; *Teshuvoth Tashbatz* 3:301. Hence, the first wedding in the world was held on a Friday. See below, Chapter 11, note 13.

According to Jewish law, a wedding can be held on any weekday; Rabbenu Yerocham, *Toledoth Adam VeChavah* 23:2 (Venice, 1553), p. 184d; *Piskey Tzemach Tzedek, Yoreh Deah* 192:6.

14. *Magen Avraham* 696:18; see *Shulchan HaEzer* 4:6:6. Some authorities, however, permit it; *Orach Chaim* 696:8.

15. *Orach Chaim* 493:1. This custom is mentioned by Hai Gaon (998 c.e.); see Rabbenu Yerocham 23:2, 186d. Also see *Teshuvoth HaGeonim, Shaarey Teshuvah* 278, quoting Netrunai Gaon (858 c.e.); *Halakhoth Pesukoth* 92; Rashi, *Sefer HaOrah* 92 (Lvov, 1905), p. 107; Rabbi Yitzchak Gayoth 2:109; *Meiri* on *Yevamoth* 62b; *Kaftor VaFerach* 78 (Berlin, 1851), p. 23a; *Rokeach* 354; *Sefer HaManhig*, p. 538. Also see *Teshuvoth Shevuth Yaakov* 2:38; *Teshuvoth Imrey Yosher* 186.

Some sources state that weddings are not held during this period because it is a time when the wicked are judged; *Ezer LeYitzchak* 14:3, quoting Rabbi Yaakov Weil.

B'Omer, however, weddings are permitted.[16] There are also other times during *Sefirah* when some groups have the custom of permitting weddings; where questions arise, a rabbi should be consulted.

It is also a universally accepted custom not to have weddings during the "Three Weeks," the period between the fast of the Seventeenth of Tammuz (*Shiva Asar BeTammuz*) and Tisha B'Av (the Ninth of Av). This is also a time of national mourning for all Israel, since it marks the time during which Jerusalem was invaded and put to the sword, and the Temple destroyed. Both the first and second Temples in Jerusalem were destroyed on Tisha B'Av.[17]

Weddings should also not be held on *Asara BeTeveth* (the Tenth of Teveth), which commemorates the date when Nebuchadnezzar lay siege to Jerusalem prior to the destruction of the first Temple.[18] Weddings are generally not held on other minor fast days.

Besides being times of mourning, the above mentioned periods are considered inauspicious times. Since the wedding begins the couple's life together, it should be held at the most auspicious time possible.

It is also customary not to set the wedding date for the Ten Days of Repentance, the period between Rosh HaShanah and Yom Kippur.[19] These are solemn days, when the exuberance at a wedding is considered out of place.

In the case of a second marriage, weddings are permitted during some of the periods mentioned above. Since the laws are fairly detailed, a rabbi should be consulted.

It is an ancient custom, whenever possible, to set the

16. Some have a custom of marrying on Lag B'Omer. Regarding the proper procedure, see *Igroth Moshe, Evven HaEzer* 97. Sephardim do not marry on Lag B'Omer, but they do marry after Lag B'Omer.

17. *Orach Chaim* 551:2; *Kol Bo* 75.

18. *Pri Megadim, Eshel Avraham* 551:10.

19. *Matteh Ephraim* 602:5; *Hagahoth Chokhmath Shlomo* 606; Rabbi Avraham Frisco, *Berakh Eth Avraham* (Salonica, 1862), p. 107a top; *Sedey Chemed, Chathan VeKallah* 23; *Shulchan HaEzer* 4:6:13.

wedding date during the first half of the lunar cycle, when the new moon is waxing. This symbolizes that the couple's happiness and fortune should increase, just as the new moon is increasing.[20]

While this is not a hard and fast custom, it should be followed wherever possible. Some authorities maintain that, under this custom, weddings can be held until the 18th of the Hebrew month.[21] Others maintain that they can be held until the 22nd of the Hebrew month.[22]

Some authorities also maintain that this custom need not be observed during the Hebrew month of Elul.[23] Others hold that it also does not apply during the months of Adar[24] and Tishrei.[25] In any case, this custom is not a hard and fast rule; when there are other important considerations it can be ignored.[26]

There is also one other point that should be taken into account when the wedding date is set. Whenever possible, it should be set so that the bride can be purified from her menstrual period. This means that the wedding date should be set for at least seven days after her period ends. Besides being a consideration with regard to the marriage itself, the marriage can then be consummated without any problems.

20. *Yoreh Deah* 179:2; *Evven HaEzer* 64:3 in *Hagah; Teshuvoth Ramban* 283; *Nemukey Yosef, Sanhedrin,* Rif 16b. See *Tikkuney Zohar* 69, 101b, 102a.

21. Rabbi Yisrael Binyamin Feivelson, *Segulath Yisrael* (Zolkiev, 1839, Kovna, 1929).

22. Rabbi Shlomo Kluger, *Nedarey Zerizim* (Zolkiev, 1839, 1855); quoted in *Likutey Maharich* 3:129b; *Shulchan HaEzer* 4:5:6.

23. *Darkey Teshuvah, Yoreh Deah* 179:18; *Shulchan HaEzer* 4:5:8. However, Rabbi Nachman of Breslov was careful of this even in Elul; see his letter to his future father-in-law, Yechezkel Trachtenberg, in 1807, in *Alim LeTerufah* (unnumbered page at beginning of volume, Jerusalem, 1968).

24. *Sedey Chemed, Chathan VeKallah* 21:7.

25. *Arukh HaShulchan* 64:13. See *Sefer Minhagim* (Lubavitch; New York, 1972), p. 76.

26. *Tav Yehoshua,* quoting Rabbi Yehudah Assad, *Yehudah Yaaleh* (Lvov, 1873; Pressberg, 1880); *Shulchan HaEzer* 4:5:8.

Once the date is set, there are many other things to arrange. The first is a rabbi to officiate at the wedding. If the couple is close to a particular rabbi, he will be asked to officiate. If the marriage is held in a synagogue, it is a courtesy to consult with the rabbi of the synagogue before asking another rabbi to officiate. In many ways, the synagogue is the rabbi's domain, and the synagogue rabbi would naturally be the one to perform the marriage.[27] If the rabbi will not allow a colleague to officiate (an extremely rare occurrence), the couple will want to be aware of it before making final plans.

If the wedding is held in a hotel or a hall, it is not a good idea to let the caterer choose a rabbi at the last minute. Rather, if the couple does not have a rabbi of their own, they should meet with the rabbi of the community where the wedding will be held, and ask him to officiate. Sometimes a close relative will recommend a rabbi to whom the couple can relate.

In some communities it is the practice for both the rabbi and the cantor to officiate. A cantor is not required for the ceremony, although, if his chanting is tasteful, it will enhance the ceremony. There are also chants at the beginning of the ceremony that are very beautiful when sung by a good cantor.

In any case, the couple should make every effort to make sure that the rabbi officiating at their wedding is God-fearing and a true Torah scholar.[28] The Talmud says, "One who is not

27. Where a community has a rabbi, only he can perform the marriage, unless he gives permission to another rabbi; *Teshuvoth Mahariv* (Rabbi Yaakov Weil) 85; quoted in *Pith'chey Teshuvah* 49:3; *Teshuvoth Shevuth Yaakov* 3:123. Also see *Teshuvoth Rivash* 399; *Teshuvoth Tashbatz* 2:8; *Teshuvoth Sho'el U'Meshiv* 1:239; *Teshuvoth Maharsham* 1:160; *Teshuvoth Chatham Sofer, Yoreh Deah 230; Minchath Eliezer* 3:39; *Teshuvoth Divrey Chaim, Yoreh Deah* 51; *Maharam Shick, Orach Chaim* 312, *Yoreh Deah* 396; *Ezer LeYitzchak* 17:4; *Shulchan HaEzer* 6:7; *Kether Shem Tov,* note 702.

28. The officiating rabbi should be one who has a reputation as a Torah scholar; *Yoreh Deah* 242:14 in *Hagah; Pith'chey Teshuvah, Evven HaEzer* 49:3; *Nohag KeTzon Yosef, Nesuin* 11; *Eduth LeYisrael* (Henkin) 45, p. 141. He must also be an expert in the laws of the kethubah; *Teshuvoth Mahari Bruna* 81; *Taamey HaMinhagim* 964 in note.

It is a custom to get the greatest rabbi available to perform the wedding; Rabbi Aaron Alfandari, *Yad Aaron* 62:9 (Izmir, 1762). The Talmud states that a Torah scholar must know the wedding blessings; *Chullin* 9a.

expert in the laws of marriage and divorce should not officiate."[29] There are many important points of law that not every rabbi is familiar with.

The officiating rabbi is known as the *mesader kiddushin* (מְסַדֵר קִדוּשִׁין, "arranger of the marriage"). In many circles, it is customary to divide the wedding blessings and other honors among the guests. This will be discussed further in Chapters 21 and 22.

At the meeting with the rabbi, he will ask some questions about family background, as outlined in Chapter 3. He will also check out the proposed wedding date to make sure that there are no problems. He will have to know the Hebrew names of both the bride and groom, as well as the names of their fathers, since this information is necessary for the *Kethubah* (marriage contract).[30] Since it may take some time to ascertain this information exactly, the meeting with the rabbi should take place as early as possible.

Once the initial arrangments are made, the normal preparations for the wedding can be begun.

As soon as the date is set, invitations are usually ordered.[31] It is a custom that, where possible, the invitations be printed both in Hebrew and in English. When there is enough time, such invitations can be ordered from larger communities, especially from New York, without any trouble. Many printers specialize in Jewish wedding invitations, and can produce invitations that are both traditional and beautiful.

It is a custom to pay the rabbi; *Choshen Mishpat* 185:10 in *Hagah; Ezer LeYitzchak* 17:2; *Shulchan HaEzer* 6:7.

29. *Kiddushin* 6a, 13a; *Evven HaEzer* 49:3.

30. The rules for spelling names and the like are found in *Evven HaEzer* 129. It is important to realize that Yiddish names, such as Golda or Hinda, end with an *alef* and not with a *heh*; *Evven HaEzer* 129:34. A rabbi must be expert in all the laws of names before writing a kethubah.

31. See *Kether Shem Tov* 29. Also see *Zohar* 1:149a.

Music plays a very important role in setting the mood of a wedding.[32] Obviously, since the wedding is a sacred occasion, care must be taken that the music is appropriate. The wedding should be an expression of the deepest spiritual commitment between the bride and groom, and the music should be appropriate.[33] It is taught that proper music can have a

32. The custom of having music at a wedding dates back to Biblical times; Cf. Psalms 78:63, Radak *ad loc*; Psalms 45:15,16; Genesis 31:27. Throughout Jewish history it has remained a custom to play before the bride and groom with drums and other instruments; 1 Maccabees 9:39; *Zohar* 3:230b; *Perush HaTefilloth VeHaBerakhoth leRabbi Yehudah ben Yakar* (circa 1170; Jerusalem, 1979), part 2, p. 38, from *Pirkey Rabbi Eliezer* 12.

Some authorities maintain that music is an essential part of the wedding; *Maharil, Eruv Chatzeroth* 31b; *Ibid.* 64b; *Otzar HaGeonim, Ketuboth,* p. 24, quoting Hai Gaon. Music is played before the bride and groom just as it is before a king and queen; *Midrash Talpioth,* s.v. *Chathan VeKallah.*

It is true that when the Temple was destroyed, it was legislated that music be avoided; *Sotah* 48a; *Gittin* 7a; *Orach Chaim* 560:3. However, for a wedding, it is permitted; *Tosafoth, Gittin 7a, s.v. Zimra; Orach Chaim* 560:3 in *Hagah.* This is especially true if the songs contain praise to God; Rabbenu Yerocham 23:2, 186c. A wedding is called a *hilula* because people sing songs of praise to God *(hallel)*; *Arukh* s.v. *Hilula; Kol Bo* 75, p. 44c; *Taamey HaMinhagim* 965; *Otzar HaGeonim, Kethuboth,* p. 24.

Some authorities write that the highest joy can be attained only through musical instruments: *Maharil loc. cit.*; Rabbi Nathan of Namirov, *Likutey Halakhoth, Peru U'Revu* 3:4. Others, however, preferred that only vocal music be used; *Teshuvoth Radbaz* 4:132 (1202), quoted in *Elyah Rabbah* 338:4; *Likutey Maharich* 3:130b, quoting Maharam Shick; *Chupath Chathanim* 6:8; *Sedey Chemed, Chathan VeKallah* 13. Also see *Shulchan HaEzer* 9:2:8, 9:8:3; *Eduth LeYisrael* 7:7; *Teshuvoth Shevuth Yaakov* 2:85.

33. When the music at a wedding is of a sacred, rather than a secular nature, it makes the entire wedding a sacred occasion; Mordechai, *Pesachim* 604; *Magen Avraham* 670:4.

In many circles, effort is made that all the musicians at a wedding be religious Jews; *Darkey HaChaim VeHaShalom* 1051. Furthermore, it is highly preferable that the music have been composed by a religious Jew; *Igroth Moshe, Evven HaEzer* 96. Music from an immoral person can have a negative influence on those who hear it; *Likutey Moharan* 3.

powerful spiritual effect on the couple's future happiness.[34]

In larger communities, religious Jewish bands and orchestras that specialize in weddings can be found. Many of them know the best music to set the tone of a wedding, both spiritually and emotionally. It is not unheard of to import such bands to smaller communities. Although the expense may be considerable, it may represent only a small fraction of the cost of a larger wedding, and may well be worth the investment.

Where such a band is not available, good sheet music can be obtained for use by local bands. Here again, a cooperative rabbi can be of immeasurable help. He has seen many traditional weddings, and knows the type of music that is most appropriate. A younger rabbi may also be familiar with the new wave of Jewish music, which is deep, rich, spiritual, and at the same time, very contemporary. He will be able to suggest good sheet music that can be used by a local band. There is nothing more beautiful than an authentic Jewish wedding with true Jewish music.

Most couples will want to look back at their wedding as the high point in their lives. They will therefore want a good professional photographer to record the event. In larger communities, there are professional photographers who specialize in Jewish weddings, and know exactly when and where to position themselves to record every key moment. Most general photographers also have experience with Jewish weddings.

The photographer should be instructed to be as unobtrusive as possible. Of course, in some circles, the photographer is considered almost an integral part of the wedding party, with all the associated rights and privileges. On the other hand, there does not seem to be any reason that the photographer must have three assistants under the chupah, where unobtrusive candid shots would be more in order. I have also

34. Music is associated with the Levites, and it was Levi who brought Jacob and Leah together (Genesis 29:34); *Likutey Moharan* 237. Furthermore, song is a powerful rectification for the couple's future sexual life; *Likutey Halakhoth, Peru U'Revu* 3:4; *Likutey Moharan* 205.

seen some photographers push aside rabbis and members of the wedding party, and that is certainly going far beyond their authority.

There is absolutely no objection in Jewish law to having pictures taken of the wedding ceremony. It is true that some rabbis have objections, but there is nothing in Jewish teachings to support their contention. I have been at weddings of some of the greatest rabbis in the world, where pictures were taken of the entire ceremony, from beginning to end. As long as the photographer remains unobtrusive, his presence will not in any way detract from the sanctity and spirit of the occasion.

Chapter 6

THE RING

The groom should buy the wedding ring well in advance of the wedding. In a Jewish wedding, the ring is much more than a mere symbol; it is an integral part of the ceremony. It is the giving of the ring, and not any blessings said by the rabbi, that makes the couple man and wife.

In order for the marriage to be binding, the ring must be the legal property of the groom. To take an extreme example, if the groom stole a ring and used it for the ceremony, the wedding would be invalid.[1]

Sometimes, there may be a desire to use a family ring, with sentimental value, for the ceremony. However, if such a ring is merely loaned to the groom, serious problems may arise.[2] The law requires that the ring that the groom gives to the bride be his unconditional property at the time.[3] If it is not, the validity of the entire wedding ceremony may be questionable.[4]

1. *Evven HaEzer* 28:1.

2. The law is that if the groom tells the lender that he will be using the ring to contract a marriage, it is assumed that the lender is actually giving him the ring as a gift, on the condition that it be returned, and not merely lending it to him; Rosh, *Kiddushin* 1:20; *Evven HaEzer* 28:19. Also see *Teshuvoth HaRosh* 35:2; *Teshuvoth Rivash* 170; *Terumath HaDeshen* 210. Even if he does not say why he wants the ring, some are lenient as long as it is understood; *Chelkath Mechokak* 28:33; *Beth Sh'muel* 28:48.

   A woman can, similarly, lend her own wedding ring to the groom to use; *Teshuvoth Maharsham* 1:29. However, if one borrows a ring from a woman without her husband's knowledge, there may be serious questions regarding the validity of the marriage; *Evven HaEzer* 28:19 in *Hagah; Teshuvoth Ramban* 144; *Teshuvoth Rashba* 1241. Some authorities, however, are also lenient in this case; *Chelkath Mechokak* 28:35; *Arukh HaShulchan* 28:83.

3. If the groom wants to use another person's ring, he should make sure that the person gives it to him as an unconditional gift; *Nethivoth Shalom, Evven HaEzer* 13:7.

4. See *Teshuvoth Rashba* 6:2; *Teshuvoth Tashbatz* 3:240; Rabbenu Yerocham

The prevalent custom, therefore, is for the groom to perform the ceremony with a ring that is unconditionally his own.[5] Some authorities maintain that if the groom does not have a ring of his own, he should preferably use a coin of his own for the ceremony, rather than a ring.[6]

This is because using a ring *per se* for the ceremony is only a custom, as we shall see. The main part of the ceremony is the groom giving *something* of value to the bride.[7] In theory, then, the marriage could be contracted with a potato or an article of clothing. The requirement that the article used in the ceremony belong to the groom is a clear point of law.

In order to understand this, one must understand what is accomplished when something of value is given. There are two ways of purchasing something in Jewish law: by cash (*kesef*) or by barter (*chaliphin*). When something is purchased by barter, what has transpired is simply an exchange of property. However, when a transaction is made for cash, the transaction can also effect a change of status.

Therefore, when the groom gives the bride something of value, he is not "buying her." Rather, he is changing her status from that of a single woman to that of a married one.[8] Obviously, a woman is not a chattel, and cannot be purchased for money. The money is merely a legal "consideration" that makes the woman's new status binding.[9] The Talmud states

23:1, 182c; Abudarham p. 359; *Nachalath Shiva* 12:12,13. There are also kabbalistic reasons that the ring should belong to the groom; *Shoshan Sodoth* (Koretz, 1784), p. 60b; Rabbi Asher [Margolies] *Siddur HaAri* (Jerusalem, 1970), p. 149b. If the ring is borrowed from a gentile, the marriage is invalid; *Meshiv Davar* 2:34.

5. *Teshuvoth HaRosh* 35:2, 35b; quoted in *Ba'er Hetiv* 28:36; *Teshuvoth Mahari Bruna* 94 end.

6. *Shulchan HaEzer* 8:1:18; *Eduth LeYisrael* (Henkin) 45, p. 141. Cf. *Chokhmath Adam* 129:16.

7. *Kiddushin* 2a. See Hosea 3:2.

8. Cf. *Kiddushin* 2b; *Tosafoth ad loc.* s.v. *DeAssar*.

9. Actually, the marriage can also be contracted with a document (*sh'tar*) or with intercourse; *Kiddushin* 2a. However, the general custom is to use the

emphatically that a woman cannot be married through a barter transaction, because this would imply a change in ownership, and would give the woman the status of a chattel.[10]

However, for a "cash" transaction, one does not actually have to use cash. Any article of value can be used, whether a coin, a vegetable, an article of clothing, a ring, or anything else. However, it must be given for its monetary value, and not as barter.

It is significant that God's taking of Israel as His nation is likened to a marriage.[11] God was, so to speak, the Groom, and Israel was the bride. Before the Israelites left Egypt, God gave them all the wealth of the Egyptians (Exodus 12:36). It is taught that this wealth was the "cash" used to seal the betrothal between God and Israel.[12] Here, too, God was not "buying" the Israelites, but transforming their status to that of the Chosen People.[13]

"cash" (*kesef*) transaction; *Yad, Ishuth* 3:21. Some authorities maintain that the "cash" transaction of a marriage is only derived from rabbinical interpretation; *Yad, Ishuth* 3:20; Ramban on *Sefer HaMitzvoth, Shoresh* 2 (Jerusalem, 1947), p. 19b. Some hold it is only valid by rabbinical legislation; Rabbenu Yerocham 23:1, 181a. The general opinion, however, is that it is a transaction defined by the Torah itself; Raavad on *Yad, Ishuth* 3:20; Rabbenu Yerocham, *loc. cit.; Halakhoth Gedoloth* 70 (Warsaw, 1875), p. 81a.

10. *Kiddushin* 3a. Rashi writes that it is denigrating for her; *Kiddushin* 3b, s.v. *Lo Makania*. Others maintain that it is not the type of transaction that can make a marriage; *Tosafoth, Kiddushin* 3a, s.v. *VeIshah*. See Rashba *Ibid., Sefer HaKaneh* (Cracow, 1894), p. 90a.

    Rabbi Elchanan Wasserman taught that in contracting a marriage there is a monetary transaction (*mamon*) as well as a marital transaction (*ishuth*). Rashi maintains that since there is no monetary transaction, the marital transaction also cannot take place. *Tosafoth* maintains that here there is only a question of the marital transaction.

11. *Taanith* 26b. See Ezekiel 16:8 ff.

12. Radbaz (Rabbi David ibn abu Zimra), *Metzudoth David* 125 (Zolkiev, 1862), p. 25d.

13. The Israelites were thus "purchased" by God as His "bride"; see Exodus 15:16. Marriage is also called a kinyan; *Kiddushin* 2a.

It is an ancient custom to use a ring for the wedding ceremony. The main function of the ring, however, is that it is the article of value that binds the marriage.

According to many authorities, a ring was the normal means of binding a marriage even in the times of the Patriarchs.[14] There is also some evidence that when the Israelites returned from Babylon to the Holy Land with Ezra and Nehemiah over 2300 years ago, a ring was used for the wedding ceremony.[15]

It is also taught that the Torah itself was like the "wedding ring" with which God married Israel.[16] The revelation at Sinai, where God gave the Torah to Israel, is said to be like a wedding.[17] The Torah is like a ring; it is endless, and as soon as one finishes, one must begin again. Each time one studies a Torah lesson, one gains new insights. The Torah is therefore like a wedding ring, a circle without beginning or end.[18]

The Torah is also likened to a ring because, just as a ring is endless, so is the Torah bond between God and Israel. God thus told the Israelites, "I will betroth you to Me forever" (Hosea 2:21). Thus, when the groom gives his bride the ring, it symbolizes that, just as the bond between God and Israel is endless, so is the bond of love between husband and wife.

14. *Daath Zekenim (Baaley Tosafoth)* on Genesis 38:18.

15. *Beney Tabaoth* (children of rings) are mentioned in Nehemiah 7:46. They are given this appellation because they married with rings; Saadia Gaon *ad loc* (Oxford, 1882), p. 50.

16. See Rabbi Barukh Tolidano ed., Rabbi Avraham ben Nathan HaYarchi (Raavan) on *Mesekhta Kallah Rabathai* (Jerusalem, 1906), p. 19; *Machzor Vitri* (Berlin, 1889), p. 336. Also see *Targum Yonathan* on Ezekiel 16:11. It is also taught that Rabbi Akiba made the Torah into "rings"; *Avoth DeRabbi Nathan* 18:1. This could have been the "cash" transaction, since the "great wealth" that God promised Abraham (Genesis 15:14) is interpreted to denote the Torah; *MeAm Lo'ez/The Torah Anthology* 4:147, quoting Alshekh; *Yad Yosef; Kli Chemdah, BeShalach.* Also see *Tashbatz (Katan)* 466.

17. See note 11.

18. *Mataamim* 135. See *Zohar* 1:96a from Isaiah 5:2; *Kether Shem Tov* 18, note 714.

It appears that the ring was used for marriages among the Jewish mystics as early as 2000 years ago.[19] Around the eighth century, it began to be used almost universally in the Holy Land.[20] In Babylon, where the leadership of world Jewry was then centered, the ring came into use about a century later.[21] Today, the custom of using a ring is almost universal.[22] However, there are some Jewish communities in the Middle East that still use a coin rather than a ring for marriage.[23]

There are a number of reasons for the ring. The simplest is

19. It is thus mentioned in a second century Kabbalistic source; *Tikkuney Zohar* 5 (19a), 10 (25b), 21 (55b); *Tikkuney Zohar Chadash* (Margolies edition, Jerusalem, 1978) 100b.

 Significantly, Pliny mentions that it was a Roman custom to use an iron ring for betrothal (circa 70 c.e.). By the second century, the gold wedding ring came into use among the Romans. See below, note 27.

20. Writings from around this time indicate that the ring was used in the Holy Land, but not in Babylonia; Rabbi Chaim Modai ed., *Teshuvoth HaGeonim, Shaarey Tzedek* (Salonika, 1792), p. 19b; Harkevey, *Teshuvoth HaGeonim*, p. 395; Rabbi Chaim Sathhon, *Eretz Chaim* (Jerusalem, 1908), p. 124a; *Maharshal, Differences between Babylonia and Eretz Yisrael*, 25, in *Yam Shel Sh'lomo*, end of *Bava Kama; Otzar HaGeonim, Kiddushin*, p. 9; *Kether Shem Tov* 18, note 714; *Otzar Kol Minhagey Yeshurun* 16:9, quoting *Ma'asef Bikkurim* 1865.

21. Around 980, Hai Gaon wrote that for over one hundred years it was a custom in Kherson to use a ring; Simcha Assaf, ed.; *Teshuvoth HaGeonim* 1:113; *Teshuvoth HaGeonim, Shaarey Tzedek* 12, 18b; *Otzar HaGeonim, Kethuboth*, p. 118. See next note.

22. *Evven HaEzer* 27:1 in *Hagah*; *Darkey Moshe* 27:3. Cf. *Evven HaEzer* 31:2; *Metzudoth David* 125; *Shulchan HaEzer* 8:2:1.

23. This is a prevalent custom in the Syrian Jewish community today. It was also a custom in Baghdad; see *Ben Ish Chai, Shoftim* 8. Saadia Gaon was familiar with the custom of using a ring (see above, note 15), but in his time the general custom was to make the *kiddushin* with the cup over which the wine blessing was said; *Siddur Rav Saadia Gaon* (Jerusalem, 1979), p. 97; *Otzar HaGeonim, Kiddushin* p. 11; Rashi, *Sefer HaOrah* 14, p. 182; Cf. *Kiddushin* 48b. In other places it was the custom to place the ring in a cup; *Sefer HaIttur* 2:1, p. 63a. This custom still exists in Georgia, U.S.S.R.

 Some authorities maintained that *kiddushin* should not be made with a coin; *Beth Shmuel* 27:1; *Avney Melu'im* 27:2; *Arukh HaShulchan* 27:3. See below, note 42.

that it is something that is worn at all times. The article through which the marriage is bound should be worn by the bride as a constant reminder of this most important moment in her life. Instead of giving her just any article, the groom gives her something that she can wear on her person at all times.[24]

The ring also has the form of a link from a chain. This symbolizes that in the marriage, the couple becomes a link in the chain of humanity that extends from the beginning of creation until the end of time.[25]

The ring is a circle that has no beginning or end. As such, it represents the cycle of life. The three main points in the cycle of life are birth, marriage and death. Since marriage is the point where a new generation is about to begin, it is a key point in the cycle. The ring thus represents the place of marriage in the cycle of life.[26]

The giving of a ring also symbolized the giving over of authority. Thus, when Pharaoh transferred authority to Joseph, he gave him his ring (Genesis 41:42). Similarly, Achashverosh gave his ring of authority first to Haman (Esther 3:10), and later to Esther (Esther 8:2). In giving his new wife a ring, the husband is symbolically giving her authority over his household and everything else that is his. From that moment on, everything in their lives will be shared.[27]

The ring also symbolizes the protection that the husband gives his wife. Just as the ring surrounds the finger, the aura of the husband's protection surrounds his wife.[28] This is closely related to the spiritual aura that comes to the wife from her

24. *Sefer HaChinukh* 552; *Metzudoth David* 125; Rabbi Menachem HaBavli, *Taamey HaMitzvoth*, quoted in *Yalkut Yitzchak* 552:3.

25. *Mataamim* 31. Cf. *Zohar* 2:136b. A ring is also used to join two things; *Likutey Maharich* 3:132b.

26. *Kether Shem Tov* 18, note 714, from *Zohar* 1:96a end; *Derekh Emeth ad loc.* 4. See *Mataamim* 135.

27. *Kether Shem Tov Ibid.*; *Pirkey DeRabbi Eliezer* 13; Radal *ad loc.* 13:22. The Romans used to give the wife a signet ring at betrothal, symbolizing that all his property was at the wife's disposal.

28. *Or HaChamah* on *Zohar* 1:96a end.

husband, providing her with an entirely new consciousness.[29]

The ring also represents the faith that the couple has in each other.[30] The husband gives authority to his wife over all his possessions, while at the same time offering her his protection. He has faith in her, and she has faith in him. The ring surrounding the finger thus symbolizes the aura of faith that will surround the couple for the rest of their lives.

When a man puts on tefillin, he winds the strap threee times around his left middle finger and says, "I will betroth you to Me forever. I will betroth you to Me in justice, love and kindness. I will betroth you to Me in faith, and you shall know God" (Hosea 2:21,22). The strap is thus a renewal of the "marriage" between God and Israel, and it is therefore wound around the finger just like a wedding ring. Then, just as the strap binds man to God, the wedding ring binds the bridegroom to his bride.[31]

There is also a much deeper significance to the ring. It is taught that at the very beginning of creation, God created the empty space in which He would then create the universe.[32] At that time, all the forces of creation surrounded this space like a ring, so that creation was able to take place.[33]

29. This is the "surrounding light" (*or makif*) that a woman gets when she is married, Ari, *Shaar HaMitzvoth, Ki Thetze* (Ashlag edition; Tel Aviv, 1962), p. 142; *Naggid U'Metzaveh* (Lublin, 1929), p. 34a; *Mishnath Chassidim* 1:5, 64b; *Ben Ish Chai, Shoftim* 8. Psychologically, women can experience higher states of consciousness during intimacy than men.

The ring is also said to represent Wisdom (*Chokhmah*); *Pardes Rimonim* 23:9; Rabbi Yehudah Chait, *Minchath Yehudah* on *Maarekhheth Elokuth* 4 (Mantua, 1558), p. 75a; *Sh'nei Luchoth HaBrith, Shaar HaOthioth* 1:63a.

30. *Likutey Moharan* 7:1, from Psalms 89:9.

31. *Tikkuney Zohar* 47 (84a); *Tikkuney Zohar Chadash* 100b; *Mataamim* 135. Also see *Zohar* 3:230b top.

32. *Etz Chaim, D'rush Egolim VeYashar* 2.

33. *Zohar* 1:15a; *Zohar HaRakia ad loc.*; *Mikdash Melekh ad loc.*; *Shefa Tal* 3:5; *Kissey Mekleh* on *Tikkuney Zohar* 5 (32b). The forces of creation are seen as a ring, since the "beginning is embedded in the end"; *Shefa Tal* 6:1 (Lvov, 1859), p. 91c; see *Sefer Yetzirah* 1:7. The Midrash also speaks of the forces of creation as being a ring; *Bereshith Rabbah* 11:9. This is the ring of the bride; Maharzav *ad loc.* See Rabbi Shneur Zalman of Liadi, *Torah Or* (Zhitomer, 1862), p. 44d.

When man and wife come together, they also have the power to create — new life. In this respect, their union is God-like. The Torah thus says, "God created the human in His image, in the image of God He created them, male and female He created them" (Genesis 1:27). Since they can emulate His power of creation, man and woman together form the image of God the Creator.

The ring then represents the circle of creative force that surrounded the world at the very beginning of creation. In contracting the marriage, the man and wife are emulating God, and beginning a new creative cycle. Out of their union, an entire world can be created.[34]

Before the ring is bought, the couple should be aware of the general requirements and customs.

The general custom is to use a gold ring for the wedding ceremony.[35] This is because gold is considered the most noble of metals.[36] The groom presents his bride with a gold ring to show that she is as precious to him as gold.

Some sources maintain that it is preferable to use a silver ring. It is taught that silver represents love, while gold represents strength. It is written, "The world is built on love" (Psalms 89:3). Since the bride and groom are building a new world of love, these sources maintain that silver is more appropriate.[37]

34. *Tikkuney Zohar* 5 (19a). See *Zohar* 3:256b.

35. Mordechai, *Kiddushin* 488; *Hagahoth Maimonioth, Ishuth* 7:8 #5; *Shulchan HaEzer* 8:1:22, 8:2:1; *Kissey Melekh* 7, p. 32b.

36. Gold is also a metal associated with the Garden of Eden, see Genesis 2:11, 12. Gold therefore represents a link to Eden, where Adam and Eve had a perfect marriage.

37. *Sefer HaKaneh* 90a: *Shoshan Sodoth* 63a; *Metzudoth David* 125 (25d). [It is significant that all three of these works appear to come from the same Kabbalistic tradition.] Also see *Mataamim* 47, 48: *Ben Ish Chai, Shoftim* 8; *Eduth LeYisrael* (Henkin) 45, p. 141.

However, there are some authorities who maintain that a silver ring should not be used; *Beth Yosef, Evven HaEzer* 30, p. 56b.

In any case, it is important that the true metal out of which the ring is made not be disguised, and be readily apparent. Therefore, for example, the ring should not be gold plated or the like.[38] The true value of the ring should be perfectly obvious.

This is because the marriage is contracted, not with the ring itself, but with the monetary value of the ring.[39] Therefore, the bride must be able to ascertain the monetary value of the ring at a glance. If it is a simple metal, this is relatively easy. However, if the ring is plated, or if it is made of a type of metal that is not easily identified, then the validity of the marriage might be called into question.

For the same reason, it is a long established custom not to use a ring that has any kind of stone in it.[40] A stone is a blind item, whose value is not readily apparent. In many cases, only a trained jeweler or gemologist can determine the value of a stone. Therefore, the bride might assume that the stone is worth more than it really is, and this can call the entire marriage into question.[41]

Kabbalistically, silver represents love; see *Bahir* 136. The Hebrew word for silver, *kesef* (כסף) is associated with the word *kissufin* (כסופין) meaning longing and desire.

38. *Teshuvoth Radbaz* 467; *Teshuvoth Mahari Bruna* 94 end. The ring also may not be made of brass that looks like gold; *Hagahoth Maimonioth, Ishuth* 8:1 #2. If it is silver and the bride thinks it is gold, or vice versa, the marriage is not valid; *Kiddushin* 48b; *Yad, Ishuth* 8:1. Also see *Kol Bo* 143:10.

39. See above, note 10.

40. This was first mentioned by Rabbenu Yaakov Tam (circa 1100—1171); *Tosafoth, Kiddushin* 9a, s.v. *VeHilkhatha*. Also see Mordechai, *Kiddushin 488; Hagahoth Maimonioth, Ishuth 7:18* Teshuvoth Rashba 1186; Rabbenu Yerocham 23:1, p. 182a; *Sefer HaManhig,* p. 536; Rosh, *Kiddushin* 1:8; *Orachoth Chaim, Hilkhoth Kiddushin* 2:55: *Evven HaEzer* 31:2; *Ezer LeYitzchak* 18:2. Some say that the woman may anticipate an expensive ring, and if its value is less, she may be disappointed enough to invalidate the wedding; *Kol Bo* 75, 44b; Abudarham, p. 359. Some say that the reason for this custom was so as not to embarrass the poor; *Kether Shem Tov* 46, note 742.

41. However, in an emergency, if the bride knows how much the ring is worth, it may be used; *Eduth LeYisrael* (Henkin) 45, p. 142; Rabbi Avraham (ben Shmuel) Alkelai, *Zekher LeAvraham* (Salonika, 1793), p. 22; *Teshuvoth Lechem Rav.* 20; *Yeshuoth Yaakov, Perush HaKatzar* 31:3; *Shulchan HaEzer* 8:1:19.

For a very similar reason, in some circles it is customary to use a very simple ring. Engraving or design can add to the ring's value, but the additional value is not easily ascertainable.[42]

There are also kabbalistic reasons for this. The perfectly smooth ring represents the perfectly smooth, untroubled cycle of life.[43] In some circles, the custom is that the ring not have any design or pattern on it, neither on the inside nor on the outside.[44]

Nevertheless, this is by no means a hard and fast custom.[45] Even in ancient times, extremely elaborate wedding rings were very often used.[46]

Knowing the facts, the bride and groom can choose the type of wedding ring they prefer. They should discuss it with the rabbi who will perform the ceremony, and he will be able to offer advice. Although the engagement ring may be more expensive, the wedding ring is the one that counts.

43. *Otzar Kol Minhagey Yeshurun* 16:9, p. 46.

44. *Sefer HaMinhagim* (Lubavitch), p. 76.

45. In some areas it was a custom to engrave the letter *heh* on the ring; *Ben Ish Chai, Shoftim* 8. Other sources indicate that the ring was to be round on the insid and square on the outside; Rabbi Moshe Zakout, *Kithevey HaRamaz,* p. 30d; *Zohar Chai* 1:4a, 1:20d; Rabbi Yeshia Asher Zeleg Margolies, *Yashiv Rucho;* quoted in *Taamey HaMinhagim* p. 412 note; *Shulchan HaEzer* 8:2:1.

46. In the 17th and 18th centuries, it was a common practice to make wedding rings in the form of a house, indicating that the couple was establishing a new home. The wedding ring of Samson Wertheimer (1658-1724) had the house opening to show a cup, bread, and books.

Chapter 7

THE TALLITH

Another item that is usually purchased before the wedding is the groom's tallith. This is the traditional gift that the bride gives the groom.[1] In some ways, the tallith is even more important than the wedding ring.

The tallith dates back more than three thousand years to the Torah itself. The Torah states that God told Moses, "Speak to the Israelites and tell them to make themselves tassles (*tzitzith*) on the corners of their garments" (Numbers 15:38). The tassled garment that is worn in keeping with this commandment is the tallith. It is worn in the synagogue at all morning services.

The tassles on the tallith are made in a very special way. Examining them closely, one will notice that each tassle consists of eight strings (four strings doubled over). They also contain five double knots, and four sets of windings. There are a total of 39 windings in each tassle.

Throughout Eastern Europe, and in most American communities, it is customary for a man to begin wearing a tallith when he gets married.[2]

This is based on an interesting juxtaposition of verses. The Torah says, "You must make tied tassles (*gedilim*) on the four corners of the garment with which you cover yourself.... When a man takes a wife..." (Deuteronomy 22:12,13). Some say that this indicates that the tallith is worn only after a man is married.[3]

1. The earliest mention of this custom is in Rabbi Zeev Wolf of Zhitamar, *Or HaMaor*, first published in Koretz 1798 (see note 6); and in Rabbi Nachman of Breslov, *Likutey Moharan* 49:7, published in Ostrog, 1806. Also see *Likutey Etzoth, Chitun* 3; Rabbi Rachamim Yitzchak Palaggi, *Yeffe LaLev* (Izmar, 1893), p. 39; *Sedey Chemed, Chathan VeKallah* 11; *Otzar Kol Minhagey Yeshurun* 16:1. Some sources mention the custom of the bride giving the groom both a tallith and a kittel; *Shulchan HaEzer* 9:9.

2. See *Sefer HaManhig*, p. 539, from *Kiddushin* 29b; Cf. *Magen Avraham* 8:3; *Beney Yessachar, Tishrei* 13:2. Even though the man does not wear a tallith before marriage, he must wear a tallith katan; *Elyah Rabbah* 17:3. The custom among German Jews is to wear the tallith from the time of Bar Mitzvah; *Likutey Maharich* 1:13b. This is also the custom among Sephardic Jews; *Sedey Chemed, Chathan VeKallah* 11.

3. *Tashbatz* 465; Maharil 65a; *Taamey HaMinhagim* 966. Other sources,

Just as the wedding ring represents the surrounding aura (*or makif*) that the groom gives the bride, the tallith represents the aura that the bride gives the groom.[4] This is the aura of love that the groom has when he marries. Just as the bride will wear her ring for the rest of her life, so will the groom use his tallith for the rest of his.

The tallith represents protection against outside sexual temptation. In giving the commandment for the tzitzith-tassles, God said, "They shall be tassles for you, and you shall look at them, and not be tempted after your hearts and after your eyes" (Numbers 15:39). The Talmud states that this is speaking specifically about sexual temptation.[5] Now that the man is marrying, the tallith will protect him against being tempted by any woman other than his wife.[6]

This is one reason for the custom that the bride sends the groom a tallith on the day of the wedding.[7] Just as the wedding ring symbolizes that she is bound to him to the exclusion of all other men, the tallith symbolizes that he is bound to her to the exclusion of all other women.

Each of the tassles on the tallith contains eight strings. Since there are four such tassles, there are a total of 32 strings. In Hebrew, the number 32 is written *lamed beth* (לב), which spells out the word *lev* (לֵב), meaning heart. In sending her groom the tallith, the bride symbolizes that she is giving her whole heart over to him.[8]

On a deeper level, the tallith contains an allusion to the marriage between God and Israel at Sinai. It is taught that at Sinai, the Israelites saw a vision of God wrapped in a tallith.[9]

however, use this juxtaposition to derive the teaching that the groom wears the tallith *on* the day of his wedding; *Rokeach* 353; *Sefer HaManhig*, p. 539.

4. *Beney Yessachar, Tishrei* 13:2; *Korban Ani*, quoted in *Taamey HaMinhagim* 967.
5. *Berakhoth* 12b.
6. *Or HaMaor, Sukkoth* (Lvov, 1875), p. 293a; *Mataamim* 12.
7. *Ibid.*
8. *Ibid.; Taamey HaMinhagim* 947. See *Bahir* 92, 98.
9. *Mekhilta;* Rashi, on Exodus 20:2; *Yad, Yesodey HaTorah* 1:9. See *Rosh HaShanah* 17b.

Of course, this was not a physical tallith. God has no body, shape, or form, and the concept of a physical garment cannot apply to Him at all. Nevertheless, the fact that the Israelites saw this in a vision has important significance.

God's "tallith" is said to be the first light of creation. It is written that at creation, God "wrapped Himself in light as with a garment" (Psalms 104:2). This "garment" was the tallith, representing the light that contained the power of creation. Indeed, the 32 strings in the tallith represent the 32 times that God's name occurs in the account of creation. Thus, in a sense, God's "tallith" represents the creative power with which He made the world.[10]

Until the Torah was given, creation was not complete. The Torah was the blueprint of the world, and it was inextricably tied to the deepest purpose of creation.[11] Without the Torah, the world could not have endured, as God said, "If not for My covenant day and night, I would not have set forth the principles of heaven and earth" (Jeremiah 33:25).[12]

The Israelites therefore saw God wearing His "tallith" at Sinai. This indicated that the act of creation was now complete. With the giving of the Torah, creation could endure.[13]

In a sense, since the time of Sinai, God and Israel have been partners in creation. Thus, Sinai is seen as the wedding between God and Israel. When a man and woman marry, they release their creative force and begin a family. Similarly, when God and Israel "married," they were able to liberate the creative forces of all the world.

The groom begins to wear a tallith at his wedding just as God was seen as wearing a tallith at His "wedding" with Israel at Sinai, when the Torah was given. Many other wedding customs are also derived from the experience at Sinai.

10. *Tikkuney Zohar* 10 (55b). This is discussed at greater length in my book, *A Thread of Light, the Mystery of the Tallith.*

11. *Bereshith Rabbah* 1:2. See *The Handbook of Jewish Thought* 4:3.

12. See Commentaries on *Avoth* 1:2.

13. *Lamed* and *beth are also the last and first letters of the Torah respectively.*

In another sense, the tallith represents the light of creation. Since the couple will be emulating God in their ability to create a family, the groom begins to wear the tallith at this time.

In many circles, it is a custom for the groom to wear a tallith at the wedding ceremony itself.[14] He wears the tallith, just as God did when He married Israel.

In other circles, it is the custom to place the tallith over both the bride and groom during the ceremony.[15] This also represents the light of creation. Although masculine words are often used for God, the true image of God is androgynous, with man and woman together. It is thus written, "God created the human in His image, in the image of God He created them, male and female He created them" (Genesis 1:27). A man and a woman together can create new life, just as God is the Creator of life. Thus, just as the light of creation surrounded God when He made the world, so the tallith surrounds the bride and groom on their wedding day.

The tallith is therefore one of the most important purchases that the couple will make before the wedding. They should be careful to buy a proper tallith.

The most important consideration is that the tallith be large enough. The tallith is meant to be worn like a cape, not like a scarf. When it is worn, it should cover at least the upper part of the body. Unfortunately, unscrupulous manufacturers make tallithes that are not valid under Jewish law, and some congregations unknowingly use them. The knowledgeable couple, however, will be careful to buy one that is large enough to satisfy the requirements of Jewish law.

It is preferable to have a tallith made of wool. In Biblical times, the tallith was almost always made of wool; it is thus the traditional material. Of course, a silk tallith is also valid, and in some communities it was a general custom to use a silk tallith.[16]

14. *See above, note 3. Also see Kol Bo* 75, 44b; *Sheyarey Kenesseth HaGedolah, Orach Chaim* 8:5; *Halakhoth Ketanoth, Teshuvoth* 1:22; *Pachad Yitzchak,* s.v. *Chathan,* p. 61b; *Ben Ish Chai, Shoftim* 12.

15. See Chapter 18, note 37.

16. See *Kether Shem Tov,* p. 5.

However, care must be taken to buy such a tallith from a reliable source.

In many ways, the tallith is an item of tremendous spiritual power. If it is made according to the rules set down by the Torah, wearing it can be a great spiritual experience. Since it is intimately associated with marriage, it can also lend an important spiritual dimension to the couple's married life.[17]

17. For more information, see my book, *A Thread of Light, the Mystery of the Tallith.*

Chapter 8

THE WEDDING GOWN

One of the most exciting of the wedding preparations for the bride is choosing her wedding gown. The wedding is the bride's day, and she is bedecked like a princess. Every bride is beautiful, and she is dressed to display her beauty.

It is taught in the Midrash that God Himself adorned Eve for her wedding with Adam.[1] At the first wedding in the world, God made sure that the bride would be perfectly beautiful.

Female beauty is one of God's great gifts to the world.[2] When a husband has pleasure in his wife's beauty, it gives him a better and broader outlook on life.[3] The Torah specifically tells us that Rachel was very beautiful, and that this was one of the things that attracted Jacob to her (Genesis 29:17).[4] And, of course, every bride is beautiful to her groom. It is said that beauty is in the eyes of the beholder — but love makes the beholder's eyes appreciate beauty.

As noted in the Talmud, even two thousand years ago, brides were made up and perfumed so as to enhance every aspect of their beauty.[5] The Midrash speaks of 24 adornments with which the bride was beautified.[6] Everything was done to make the bride as lovely as possible.

1. *Bereshith Rabbah* 18:1. Also see*Bereshith Rabbah* 8:13; *Berakhoth* 61a.
2. *Taanith* 31a; *Kethuboth* 59b.
3. *Berakhoth* 57b; *Yevamoth* 63b.
4. See Radak *ad loc.*
5. *Shmoth Rabbah* 23:5. Cf. *Yevamoth* 34b; *Yoma* 38a, 39b. Also see Isaiah 3:24.
6. *Bereshith Rabbah* 18:1. These are the 24 adornments mentioned in Isaiah 3:18-24; Rashi on *Bereshith Rabbah loc. cit.* The last item mentioned in Isaiah, perfume, is not counted (*Matnath Kehunah* on *Bereshith Rabbah*). These 24 adornments are seen as paralleling the 24 books of the Bible; *Shmoth Rabbah* 41:5; *Shir HaShirim Rabbah* 4:22; *Tanchuma, Ki Thisa* 16; *Tanchuma B, Ki Thisa* 11; Rashi on Exodus 31:18.

   In speaking of Eve, the Torah says, "God *brought her* to Adam" (Genesis 2:22). The Hebrew for "brought her" is *vay-vi-eha* (וַיְבִאֶהָ), which has a numerical value of 24; *Zohar* 1:48b; *Matnath Kehunah*. Also see Isaiah 41:18, 61:10.

The traditional color of the wedding gown today is white.[7] Unlike other traditions, Judaism does not see the white gown as denoting virginity. Rather, it suggests purity from sin, since all the couple's sins are forgiven on their wedding day (see below, Chapter 12).[8] No matter what her past experience, on the day of her wedding, every bride is as pure and as innocent as a newborn child.[9]

There are no requirements as to the style of the wedding gown. To a large degree, it depends on the tastes of the couple. It can be knee length (but not shorter) or long, depending upon the circumstances.

However, there are some minimal requirements of modesty required by Jewish law, and these will affect the design of the gown. The sleeves of the gown should reach at least to the elbows.[10] Also, it should not be cut low in front or in back.[11] It should not be made of a sheer material through which the bride's body would be visible.

One must remember that a wedding is considered one of the most holy of all Jewish ceremonies. The very name, *kiddushin,* implies holiness. The bride and groom represent Adam and Eve beginning a new world, and they also represent God and Israel at the giving of the Torah. The couple's modesty should reflect the spirit of the ceremony.

This is also true of all the other people in the wedding party. Where mothers and bridesmaids choose gowns, these gowns should also conform to the Torah standards of modesty. The skirts should be at least knee length, the sleeves should come to

7. Some Chassidic leaders have the custom of having their daughters married in light pastel shades. See Chapter 17, note 37; Chapter 12, note 10.

8. *Kol Bo* 75, 45c. The groom also wears the *kittel*, a white garment; see Chapter 17.

9. White can thus be worn even for a second marriage.

10. *Kethuboth* 72b; *Yad, Ishuth* 24:12; *Evven HaEzer* 115:4; *Zohar* 1:142a; *Rokeach* 324; *Ben Ish Chai, Bo* 8; *Kaf HaChaim* 75:2. This follows local custom, see *Lechem Chamudoth* on *Berakhoth* 24a. Also see *Tifereth Shmuel* on Rosh 2:37; *Pith'chey Olam* 3.

11. *Berakhoth* 24a; *Orach Chaim* 75:1.

the elbow, and the neckline should be modest. Married women should wear hats or the like that cover their hair completely. Single girls, however, need not wear any head covering.[12]

There is another very important reason for this modesty requirement. The Torah says, "There shall not be seen an immodest word with you" (Deuteronomy 23:15). The Talmud teaches that an "immodest word" is a word of prayer spoken in the presence of immodesty.[13] Therefore, if anyone under the wedding canopy is dressed immodestly, there is a question as to whether the blessings pronounced over the bride and groom are valid.[14]

Tradition also calls for the bride to be veiled. According to some authorities, the veiling of the bride is an integral part of the ceremony. The various customs regarding the veil will be discussed in Chapter 17.

After the wedding, many brides put their gowns away as a keepsake. However, it is a very fine custom to make the gown available to brides who cannot afford to buy their own. In some communities, there is a registry of such bridal gowns, along with their sizes, so that girls who wish to borrow a gown will have ready access to those available. In traditional Jewish communities, there is absolutely nothing wrong with being married in a borrowed gown.

Other brides choose to donate their gowns to institutions (*hakhnasath kallah*) in Israel who make them available to poor brides. The names of such institutions can usually be obtained from a local rabbi. Doing this is an act of charity and a holy deed on the part of the bride. When such plans are made before the wedding, the merit enhances the spiritual nature of the wedding itself.

12. *Orach Chaim* 75:2. In some Sephardic communities, unmarried girls do cover their hair in synagogue.

13. *Berakhoth* 25b.

14. *Mishneh Berurah* 75:2. Some say that it is permitted in the case of uncovered hair of a married woman; *Arukh HaShulchan* 75:7.

Chapter 9

THE WEDDING PARTY

One of the important preparations for the wedding is choosing the wedding party.[1] The wedding party will include the best man, the maid or matron of honor, the ushers, the bridesmaids, and all those who walk the bride and groom down the aisle.

In ancient times, a member of the wedding party was known as a *shoshvin* (שׁוֹשְׁבִין).[2] We thus find that when Samson was married, he took thirty young men to be members of his wedding party (Judges 14:11).[3]

In general, the word *shoshvin* denotes a close friend.[4] In more specific cases, it refers to a special constant companion.[5] In Talmudic times, the wedding feast was often made as a communal meal, and the people who participated were known as *shoshvinin*[6]

1. Attendants (*shoshvinin*) are chosen before the wedding; *Targum Yonathan* to Deuteronomy 32:50.

2. *Sanhedrin* 3:5 (27b), Rashi, Bertenoro, *ad loc.* See *Tosefta, Shabbath* 17:4. A Jew should not be a *shoshvin* for a gentile; *Tosefta, Avodah Zarah* 1:9.

3. Rashi, *Mezudoth, ad loc.*

4. See *Targum* on 2 Samuel 13:3, 15:37, 16:16, 18:37, 1 Kings 4:5, 1 Chronicles 27:33; Rashi on 1 Chronicles 27:33; Rashbam, *Bava Bathra* 144b, s.v. *Shoshvinin*; *Arukh* s.v. *Shoshvin*; Rambam on *Sanhedrin* 3:5. Some say that the word *shoshvin* comes from the Greek *syskenos,* denoting a friend or companion; *Mussaf HaArukh.* Most authorities, however, maintain that it is from a semitic root.

5. Radak on 2 Samuel 15:37, 1 Kings 4:5.

6. The communal meal was known as *shoshvinuth; Bava Bathra* 144b, 145a, b. Some sources indicate that the *shoshvinin* were the ones who made the *shoshvinuth; Yad, Zekhiyah U'Mattanah* 7:1, but see Rambam on *Sanhedrin* 3:5. Other sources, however, indicate that the word *shoshvinuth* comes from the word *shoshvin;* Rashbam, *Bava Bathra* 144b. Also see *Eruvin* 18b; *Tur, Evven HaEzer* 60; *Tosafoth, Bava Bathra* 145b, s.v. *HaAchin*; Rambam on *Bava Bathra* 10:4.

More specifically, the *shoshvinin* were special attendants for the bride and groom.[7] These attendants could be either male and female.[8] In modern times, they would be the ushers and bridesmaids at the wedding.

At every wedding, there would be a special *shoshvin* for the groom;[9] he would be at the groom's "right hand," and take care of all his needs.[10] In modern terms, this is the best man.

The best man may be a close friend or relative of the groom. Some of his functions may also be performed by the groom's father. The best man acts as the groom's secretary and valet, seeing to details of the wedding. He often announces the honors at the ceremony, and makes sure that the ceremony and dinner run smoothly. This is done under the direction of the *mesader kiddushin*, the rabbi performing the wedding.

The bride also has a special attendant.[11] In modern terms, she is the maid or matron of honor. She may hold the *kethubah* (marriage contract) for the bride after the bride accepts it.[12] She may also be the one to lift the bride's veil when the bride drinks

7. See Rashi, *Berakhoth* 61a, s.v. *Shoshvin; Machzor Vitri* 488, p. 599; Radal on *Pirkey Rabbi Eliezer* 12:57. Such attendants were given to the bride and groom to make sure that there was no cheating in determining the virginal status of the bride; *Kethuboth* 12a; *Tosefta, Kethuboth* 1:4. The *shoshvinin* brought the groom to the bride's house; *Teshuvoth HaGeonim* (Harkevey) 65. They would also bring him to yichud; *Mataamim HaChadash* 55.

8. Female attendants are mentioned in *Machzor Vitri,* p. 602. Also see *Kiddushin* 81a; *Rashi ad loc.* s.v. *Shoshvintey.* The feminine of *shoshvin, shoshvinah* (שׁוֹשְׁבִינָה) has the same letters as *sos binah* (שׁוֹשׂ בִּינָה), meaning, "Understanding rejoices;" Rabbi Yaakov Kopel, *Siddur HaAri, Kol Yaakov* (Slavita, 1804), p. 121b.

9. Radak, *Metzudoth* on Judges 14:20. Kabbalistically, this *shoshvin* was also Binah; Rabbi Naftali ben Yaakov Elchanan of Frankfort, *Emek HaMelekh, Shaar Kiryath Arba* (Amsterdam, 1652), p. 84d.

10. *Machzor Vitri* 488, p. 599.

11. Often this was a male attendant; *VaYikra Rabbah* 20:10; *BeMidbar Rabbah* 2:15; *Machzor Vitri* 489, p. 599. This attendant would often take care of the bride's interests even after the wedding; *Shmoth Rabbah* 31:10, 44:4, 46:1; *Tanchuma, Mishpatim* 11.

12. See *Shmoth Rabbah* 46:1. See Chapter 21, note 58.

the wine, although in many circles, the mother of the bride or groom does this.

There are also special attendants[13] who bring the groom to the *chupah* (wedding canopy).[14] Other special attendants then bring the bride to the groom.[15] These are usually the parents of the bride and groom.[16] This shall be discussed in detail in Chapter 19, where we speak about the processional.

Many of these wedding customs have their roots in the first wedding between Adam and Eve. It is written that after God created Eve, "He brought her to Adam" (Genesis 2:22). The Talmud teaches that God Himself acted as Eve's attendant, bringing her to Adam.[17] God also gave Adam the two archangels, Michael and Gabriel, to be his own attendants.[18] Other angels were attendants all around the canopy.[19]

Similarly, at Sinai, Israel was the bride and God was the Bridegroom. The Torah says, "Moses led the people out of the camp to meet God" (Exodus 19:17). The Midrash teaches that Moses brought forth the Israelites just as the attendant brings

13. The ones who walk the bride and groom down the aisle are known as *unterfirers*. These are identified as the *shoshvinin* in *Teshuvoth Beth Shaarim, Evven HaEzer* 5:246.

14. Rabbi Moshe (ben Avraham) Mat, *Matteh Moshe* (Cracow, 1591), *Amud Gemiluth Chesed, Hakhnasath Kallah* 3:2; *Likutey Maharich* 3:131a; *Shulchan HaEzer* 7:4.

15. See *Berakhoth* 61a; *Eruvin* 18a; *Tanchuma, Chayay Sarah* 2. It is taught, "Happy is the city whose king brings the bride to the groom"; *Bereshith Rabbah* 18:3. See Chapter 19, note 19.

16. *Zohar* 1:49a. See Chapter 19, note 24.

17. *Berakhoth* 61a; *Tanchuma, Chayay Sarah* 2; *Avoth deRabbi Nathan* 4:3. Other sources, however, state that God provided angels to bring Eve to Adam; *Midrash Lekach Tov (Pesikta Zatratha) ad loc.*

18. *Bereshith Rabbah* 8:13. In general, Gabriel and Michael are angels who watch over Israel; *Shmoth Rabbah* 18:5. They took the birthright from Esau and gave it to Jacob; *Bereshith Rabbah* 63:19. See below, note 25.

19. *Pirkey Rabbi Eliezer* 12; Radal *ad loc.* 12:57.

the bride to the groom.[20] Moses was joined by Aaron, and together they brought the Israelites to the wedding canopy.[21] God Himself was accompanied, as it were, by the two Tablets of the Ten Commandments, as His attendants.[22]

The groom's two attendants stand to his right and left as they accompany him to the canopy. The same is true of the bride's attendants.

It is taught that the right hand represents love and kindness, while the left represents strength and firmness. The two attendants symbolize the relationship that the bride and groom must maintain toward each other. It must be a balanced relationship, with both love and firmness, giving and taking.[23] Each one must be able to maintain his own identity, while at the same time, fully recognizing the identity of the other.[24]

In a sense, this dual relationship was symbolized by Moses and Aaron at the wedding between Israel and God.[25] Moses was the lawgiver, and he represents the part of the relationship where certain rules and guidelines must exist between husband and wife. Although the rules and guidelines are often unspoken, without them, the relationship cannot endure.

Aaron, on the other hand, represents the pure love between the couple. It is taught that Aaron loved peace, pursued peace,

20. *Pirkey Rabbi Eliezer* 41 (Warsaw, 1852), p. 96b.

21. *Raya Mehemna, Zohar* 3:20a; *Mataamim* 87. Elsewhere it is taught that Moses was the king, and Aaron was *shoshvin* to the king; *Zohar Chadash* 42c.

22. *Shmoth Rabbah* 41:6; *Tanchuma, Ekev* 10.

23. The two attendants of the groom thus represent Chesed and Gevurah; *Shoshan Sodoth* 60b. They also represent the lower spiritual worlds, Beriyah, Yetzirah and Asiyah; *Siddur HaAri* (Rav Asher), p. 149a; Rabbi Shabbathai of Roshkov, *Siddur HaAri* (Lvov, 1866), p. 102b.

24. In this respect, the *shoshvinin* represent Netzach (dominance) and Hod (submissiveness); *Kehilath Yaakov,* s.v. *Shoshvinin*; see above, notes 21, 22. Moses and Aaron personify Netzach and Hod, as do the two Tablets. See above, note 9.

25. They also represent the archangels, Michael and Gabriel, who represent the two Sefiroth, Chesed and Gevurah; see above, notes 18, 23.

loved people and brought them close to the Torah.[26] Aaron thus represents the spirit of love, peace and compromise that must exist between husband and wife.[27] It is taught that one of Aaron's main tasks was to reconcile couples who were having marital problems.[28] Although there must be rules and guidelines in a marriage, both spoken and unspoken, they must always be ameliorated by a spirit of love and compromise.

26. *Avoth* 1:12.

27. He sought peace even in making the Golden Calf; Exodus 32.

28. *Avoth deRabbi Nathan* 12:4.

Chapter 10

THE WEEK BEFORE

The week before the wedding is the time during which anticipation begins to build steadily.[1] This week is traditionally called the "Golden Week."[2] It is the final preparation for the most important moment in the couple's life.

It is customary for orphans to visit their parents' graves during this week. It is taught that deceased parents and grandparents are present at the wedding.[3] The bride and groom therefore go to the cemetery to invite them.[4]

In many circles, it is a custom for the couple not to see each other during the week before the wedding.[5] Of course, if it is necessary for the wedding preparations or for other reasons, it is permitted. In other circles, the custom is merely for them not to see each other on the day of the wedding.

On the Sabbath before the wedding, it is the custom for the

1. See Rashba, *Mishmereth HaBayith,* on *Torath HaBayith, Beth Nashim* 2 (Josefof, 1883), p. 6b; *Piskey Tzemach Tzedek, Yoreh Deah* 192:6.

2. Some say that without a wife, one does not have access to the Torah (*Yevamoth* 62b), and the Torah is likened to gold (Psalms 19:11); therefore the week before marriage is golden; *Mataamim* 21; *Otzar Kol Minhagey Yeshurun* 16:1. Others say that the numerical value for *ha-zahav* (הַזָּהָב), Hebrew for "the" gold, is 19. This is one above 18, which is the age for marriage (*Avoth* 5:21); *Mataamim* 22. In some places it was the custom to send food to the bride and groom during this week; this was called *mest vach*; *Minhagey Mattersdorf* 109, in Rabbi Yisrael Toisig, *Beth Yisrael Telitha'ah* (Jerusalem, 1969).

3. An orphan's parents attend the wedding spiritually; *Zohar* 3:220a; *Yalkut Yitzchak* 552:21. Grandparents and great-grandparents are also present; *Sefer HaMinhagim* (Lubavitch), p. 75.

4. In some places, it was customary to hold an orphan's wedding in the cemetery; *Or Zarua, Aveluth* 448, from *Moed Katan* 23a; *Teshuvoth Maharsham* 4:40; Rabbi Yekuthiel Yehudah Greenwald, *Kol Bo Al Aveluth* (New York, 1956), p. 167 #12.

5. *Sefer HaMinhagim* (Lubavitch), p. 75; Rabbi Chaim Uri Lipshitz, *Betrothed Forever* (New York, 1979), p. 9. See *Yoreh Deah* 192:1.

groom to be called to the reading of the Torah.[6] This is called an *Aufruf*, which literally means "calling up."

The source of this custom is the Midrashic teaching that, when King Solomon built the Temple, he made two special gates, one for mourners, and one for bridegrooms, so that mourners would be consoled and bridegrooms would be blessed. When a bridegroom would enter, the people near the gate would say, "May He who dwells in this Temple bless you with good children." Later, when Solomon's Temple was destroyed, it became the custom to have the bridegroom come to the synagogue so that the people would be able to bless him.[7]

The bridegroom is called to the Torah reading in the synagogue because, when a man marries, his commitment to Torah increases and deepens.[8] Judaism and Torah are not the same for a single person as they are for one who is married. The groom is called to the Torah to denote his new commitment to Judaism and Torah.[9]

Also, a bridegroom is like a king.[10] Just as Adam was king over all creation when he married, so is every bridegroom who stands in Adam's place. However, a king must have a special commitment to the Torah, so as not to become corrupted by his power. It is for this reason that a king has a special obligation to write his own Torah scroll, as it is written, "When he sits on his royal throne, he must write a copy of this Torah scroll"

6. *Levush* 282:7 in *Hagah; Magen Avraham* 282:18 in *Hagah; Rabbi Yosef Yozfa Cashman, Nohag KeTzon Yosef* 2 (Hanau, 1718; Tel Aviv, 1969), p. 112, *K'riath HaTorah* 9, p. 137; *Shulchan HaEzer* 6:1; *Eduth LeYisrael*, p. 4.

7. *Pirkey Rabbi Eliezer* 17; Radal *ad loc.* 17:74; *Mesekhta Sofrim* 19:12; Rosh, *Moed Katan* 3:46; *Tur, Yoreh Deah* 393; *Menorath HaMeor* 216 end; *Kaftor VaFerach* 6, p. 17a; *Taamey Haminhagim* 939; *Otzar Kol Minhagey Yeshurun* 16:4.

8. See *Yevamoth* 62b.

9. He is called up before and after the wedding to distinguish between the Torah that he has before and after; Rabbi Yaakov Hager and Rabbi Yisrael Berger, *Atereth Yaakov VeYisrael* (Lvov, 1881), quoted in *Mataamim* 20; *Yalkut Yitzchak* 552:6.

10. *Pirkey Rabbi Eliezer* 12 end; Abudarham p. 361: *Sefer HaIttur Birkath Chathanim* 63b; *Tanya Rabathai* 90 (Warsaw, 1873), p. 97d.

(Deuteronomy 17:18). The groom is called to the Torah to indicate that he has a similar status.[11]

The family of the groom (and the family of the bride, if they live in the same area) come to the synagogue for the Aufruf, dressed in their finest clothes.[12] In some circles, the groom wears the clothes that he has bought for the wedding.[13] Some have the custom that the groom's friends come to his house and walk him to the synagogue. The groom is then like a king followed by his retinue.[14]

In most synagogues, an Aufruf is a major affair, almost like a Bar Mitzvah. The cantor calls the groom to the Torah with a special chant, clearly indicating his status:

יַעֲמֹד הֶחָתָן... מַזָּל טוֹב!

Let the bridegroom rise... Mazal Tov!

The bridegroom then recites the first blessing over the Torah. He should say it loud enough for everyone to hear. He begins:

בָּרְכוּ אֶת יְיָ הַמְבוֹרָךְ.

Bless God who is praised.

The congregation responds:

בָּרוּךְ יְיָ הַמְבוֹרָךְ לְעוֹלָם וָעֶד.

Blessed is God who is praised forever and ever.

11. *Midrash Talpioth*, s.v. *Chathan VeKallah.*

12. Maharil, *Tisha B'Av* 33a; *Orach Chaim* 551:1 in *Hagah; Magen Avraham* 551:6. This is also true of the couple's parents; *Atereth Zekenim* 551.

13. In Chassidic communities the groom wears his *shtreimel* (fur hat) and *bekeshe* (silk coat); *Shulchan HaEzer* 6:1; *Darkey HaChaim VeHaShalom* 1045.

14. See note 10. Some say that this is because, "In the way he wants to go, he is led;" *Makkoth* 10b; *Mataamim* 18. It is a custom to walk slowly; *Atereth Yaakov VeYisrael; Mataamim* 19.

The groom then continues:

בָּרוּךְ יְיָ הַמְבוֹרָךְ לְעוֹלָם וָעֶד.

Blessed is God who is praised forever and ever.

בָּרוּךְ אַתָּה יְיָ אֱלֹהֵינוּ מֶלֶךְ הָעוֹלָם אֲשֶׁר בָּחַר בָּנוּ מִכָּל הָעַמִּים וְנָתַן לָנוּ אֶת תּוֹרָתוֹ. בָּרוּךְ אַתָּה יְיָ נוֹתֵן הַתּוֹרָה.

Blessed are You, O God our Lord, King of the Universe, who chose us from all peoples, and gave us His Torah. Blessed are You, O God, Giver of the Torah.

The regular Torah portion is then read. After the Torah reading, the groom recites the final blessing:

בָּרוּךְ אַתָּה יְיָ אֱלֹהֵינוּ מֶלֶךְ הָעוֹלָם אֲשֶׁר נָתַן לָנוּ תּוֹרַת אֱמֶת וְחַיֵּי עוֹלָם נָטַע בְּתוֹכֵנוּ. בָּרוּךְ אַתָּה יְיָ נוֹתֵן הַתּוֹרָה.

Blessed are You, O God our Lord, King of the Universe, who gave us a true Torah, and planted eternal life in our midst. Blessed are You, O God, Giver of the Torah.

It is a custom to sing for the groom after he finishes the blessing.[15]

In some circles, it is customary to sing a special song for the groom:[16]

אֶחָד יָחִיד וּמְיוּחָד
אֵל נִדְרַשׁ לְבַר לֵבָב
אֲשֶׁר שׁוֹאֵל
אַךְ טוֹב לְיִשְׂרָאֵל
הַלְלוּיָהּ.

One, unitary and unique
Is God sought out by the pure in heart,
Who desires only good for Israel
Halleluyah!

15. *Levush* 282:7 in *Hagah.*

16. *Nohag KeTzon Yosef* 2, p. 112; *Darkey HaChaim VeHaShalom* 1045; *Taamey HaMinhagim* 939; *Shulchan HaEzer* 6:1.

While the congregation is singing, it is customary for the women to throw bags filled with nuts, raisins, and candy at the groom.[17] In general, this symbolizes that the new couple should have a sweet, fruitful life.[18] It especially symbolizes that the bridegroom should have a sweet life with his bride.[19]

The nuts that are thrown are alluded to in the verse, "I went down to the nut garden..." (Song of Songs 6:11). Before one can enjoy the kernel of a nut, one must first break away the shell. Similarly, before two people can know one another intimately, they must break away the shells that surround them. In marriage, the barriers between husband and wife gradually disappear.[20]

It is also taught that the Hebrew word for nut, *egoz* (אֱגוֹז), has a numerical value of 17. This is the same as the numerical value for *tov* (טוֹב), meaning good. This indicates that the bridegroom

Some say that this song is sung because the bridegroom has all his sins forgiven, and he is like a king, so he can "request good for Israel"; Rabbi David Dov Reifman, *Shulchan HaK'riyah* (Vilna, 1864), quoted in *Mataamim HaChadash* 33; *Shulchan HaEzer* 6:1:4. Also see *Maagley Tzedek,* quoted in *Shulchan HaEzer loc. cit.*

17. *Shulchan HaEzer* 6:1:5; *Eduth LeYisrael* p. 5. The Talmud speaks of throwing nuts and toasted wheat; *Berakhoth* 50b; Cf. *Tosefta, Shabbath* 8:8. There was a later custom of throwing wheat; Maharil 64b.

18. Cf. Rashi, *Berakhoth* 50b, s.v. *Mamshichin; Rokeach* 352.

19. *Mataamim* 57.

20. Cf. Rabbi Mordechai Kahanah, *Divrey Tzadikim* (Sighet, 1874, 1876); quoted in *Mataamim* 58.

Eve is referred to as a "nut" or "nut tree" as stated in the "Blessing for Virgins" (*Birkath Bethulim*) that was once said after a marriage was consummated: "Who raised up a nut in the Garden of Eden;" *Sheiltoth* (not in our editions), quoted in *Or Zarua* 1:341 end; *Halakhoth Gedoloth, Hilkhoth Kethuboth* 36, p. 66d; *Siddur Rav Amram Gaon* (Jerusalem, 1971), p. 182; *Rokeach* 353; Abudarham, p. 365; Rosh, *Kethuboth* 1:15; *Evven HaEzer* 63:2; *Machzor Vitri* 586; *Sefer HaOrah* 178. We no longer say this blessing; *Evven HaEzer* 63:2 in *Hagah.*

The bride is referred to as a "nut," because she is chaste and closed to all men like a nut; Philo, *De Opificio Mundi* (On the Creation) 15:24; *Otzar HaGeonim, Kethuboth* 44:6; *Tolaath Yaakov,* quoted in *Shnei Luchoth HaB'rith, Shaar HaOthioth* 1:163b.

is forgiven all his sins, and has been transformed from a state of sin to a state of good.[21]

It is customary for the little children to gather up these bags and enjoy the sweets.[22] The new generation is thus able to see how sweet marriage can be.

After this, the cantor chants a special *Mi SheBerakh* (מִי שֶׁבֵּרַךְ "May He who Blessed...") prayer for the bride and groom.[23] The families make a donation to the synagogue, so that the merit of charity will be a blessing to the new couple.[24] It is also a custom for the families to make a "Kiddush," where cake and the like is served to the congregation.[25]

On that Sabbath, in the afternoon,[26] it is a custom for the friends of the groom to come to his house and make a *fahr-shpiel*, literally, a "pre-celebration."[27] Cake and fruit are served, and the groom is subjected to good-natured chiding, as well as serious words of Torah. The bride's friends similarly make a *fahr-shpiel* in her house.[28] The *fahr-shpiel* is a time of singing and rejoicing for both families.

In some circles, the bridegroom does not go out alone during the week before the wedding.[29] In other circles, this is observed

21. *Mataamim* 56; *Yalkut Yitzchak* 552:7; *Taamey HaMinhagim* 940.

22. Cf. *Yerushalmi, Kethuboth* 2:10 (15a); *Yerushalmi, Kiddushin* 1:5 (16b); *Ruth Rabbah* 7:9. Also see *Bava Metzia* 4:12 (60a); *Pesachim* 109a.

23. *Shulchan HaK'riyah; Mataamim HaChadash* 33; *Shulchan HaEzer* 6:1:4.

24. *Betrothed Forever,* p. 10. It was once a custom to donate mantles for the Torah scrolls; *Tashbatz* 466; *Segulath Yisrael.*

25. See Rabbi Yisrael Klapholtz, *Minhagey Belza* (1974), p. 86.

26. *Likutey Maharich* 3:129b; *Shulchan HaEzer* 6:1:6; *Betrothed Forever,* p. 10. An older custom was to go to the groom's house on Friday night; Maharil, Tisha B'Av, p. 33b; *Nohag KeTzon Yosef* 2, p. 112.

27. The word is first found in *Machatzith HaShekel* 551:6. Originally, it was called a *shpin-holtz*; Maharil, *Tisha B'Av*, p. 33a; *Magen Avraham* 551:6. Some interpret this word as *she-ben alatz* (שֶׁבֵּן עָלַץ), "the son rejoices"; *Nohag KeTzon Yosef* 2, p. 112.

28. *Nohag KeTzon Yosef* 2, p. 112; *Shulchan HaEzer* 6:1.

29. *Eduth LeYisrael* p. 6. See Chapter 26, note 7.

only on the day of the wedding, where both the bride and groom are given *shomrim* or "watchers" for the day.[30]

During this week, the couple will be receiving presents from their friends and relatives, especially from those invited to the wedding. It is an ancient custom to give presents to the newlyweds. In ancient times, people would often give them gifts of food or cash to help offset the cost of the wedding.[31] In those times, the wedding was often celebrated with a communal meal.

All those invited to the wedding usually bring a gift.[32] One reason is because the bridegroom is like a king. Just as people bring gifts and tribute to a king, so they bring presents to the groom and his bride.[33]

30. *Betrothed Forever*, p. 10.

31. *Bava Bathra* 144b, 145a; *Tur, Evven HaEzer* 60. See Chapter 9, note 6.

32. *Zohar* 1:149a; *Kether Shem Tov* 29.

33. *Midrash Talpioth,* s.v. *Chathan VeKallah.*

Chapter 11

SPIRITUAL PURIFICATION

Before the marriage can be consummated, the bride must immerse in a mikvah. This is a very important requirement of Jewish law. In many ways, immersion in a mikvah is even more important than the wedding ceremony itself.

The usual custom is for the bride to immerse the night before the wedding.[1] If this is not possible, she may immerse earlier. In any case, it is best that she do so as close to the wedding as possible.[2] If necessary, she can even immerse on her wedding day.[3] In such a case, however, some authorities maintain that the ceremony should not be held until after sunset.[4]

This immersion is directly related to the woman's menstrual cycle. As we see in the Torah, such immersion is one of the most important aspects of marriage.

According to the Torah, a woman has the status of *niddah* (נִדָּה) from the time she has her period until she immerses in a mikvah. The Torah says, "When a woman has a discharge of blood, where blood flows from her organ, she shall be a *niddah* for seven days" (Leviticus 15:19). However, even after the seven days are over, the woman does not lose the status of *niddah* until she immerses in a mikvah built according to the dictates of Torah law.

It is important that the concept of *niddah* be understood. The word *niddah* has no implication of dirtiness or uncleanness. Rather, it comes from the root *nadad* (נָדַד), meaning "removed" or "separated."[5] The status of *niddah*

1. *Teshuvoth Shaarey Deah.* 2:145; *Shulchan HaEzer* 8:5:5.

2. *Yoreh Deah* 192:2 in *Hagah.*

3. *Yoreh Deah* 197:3 in *Hagah*; Maharil, *Niddah.* 82b.

4. *Dagul Marvava* on *Yoreh Deah* 197:3; *Teshuvoth P'ath HaSadeh, Evven HaEzer* 17.

5. Rashi on Leviticus 15:19; *Targum* on Leviticus 12:12; Rashbam, Bachya, Hirsch on Leviticus 12:12; Ibn Ezra on Numbers 19:19; Radak on Isaiah 30:22; Rashi, *Shabbath* 64b, s.v. *BeNida-tha.*

therefore means that the woman must be "removed" and "separated" from her husband, and that they must forgo all physical contact during this period. Thus, the word *niddah* does not even have the connotation of menstruation, but of the need for separation.

This explains the Torah's attitude toward menstruation. When a woman menstruates, it is a sign that the time has come for her to separate from her husband. The Torah understands that if the couple were intimate without any period of separation, their relationship would become dull and jaded in the course of time. But when the couple is separated several days a month, they experience a monthly renewal in their relationship.[6]

A woman's monthly period can therefore be seen as one of God's many gifts to humanity. Rather than something negative, it is a means of preserving the close love between man and wife. It affords the couple a monthly honeymoon, where their marriage is constantly renewed.

Nevertheless, it is important to realize that the Torah forbids sexual contact between a man and a woman who has the status of *niddah*. One of the Torah's commandments is, "You shall not approach a woman who is forbidden as a *niddah* to be intimate with her" (Leviticus 18:19).[7]

Sexual relations between a man and a woman who has the status of *niddah* is considered a most serious sin. The Torah states, "If a man lies with a woman who is a *niddah* and is intimate with her, both of them shall be [spiritually] cut off from their people" (Leviticus 20:18).

The penalty of being spiritually cut off (*kareth*, כָּרֵת) is one of the worst penalties in the Torah, reserved for the most serious sins. It means that the individual is cut off from his spiritual source.[8] He loses the ability to feel and appreciate the spiritual

6. *Niddah* 31b. Of course, this is not the only reason; therefore, the rules of niddah apply equally to unmarried women; *Chinukh* 95; *Torath HaShelamim* on *Yoreh Deah* 183:4; *Kerethi U'Pelethi, Tifereth Yisrael* 183:3; *Darkey Teshuvah* 183:13.

7. See *Sefer HaMitzvoth*, Negative Commandment 348.

8. *Zohar* 2:142b; *Nefesh HaChaim* 1:18; *Tanya, Shaar HaTeshuvah* 5 (95b);

and the Godly; hence, he becomes "cut off" from the most important elements of life as a Jew. The only way for such a person to undo this, and re-attach himself to his spiritual source, is for him to repent and express his remorse to God.[9]

Once a woman has the status of *niddah*, she retains it until she immerses herself in a mikvah built according to Torah law. The Torah says of a *niddah*, "She must count seven days, and she must then purify herself" (Leviticus 15:28). This means that the woman must count seven days after her period ends, and then she must undergo the usual process of purification. As known from many other sources, the universal means of purification is the mikvah. This means that to remove the status of *niddah*, the woman must immerse in a mikvah.[10]

Monthly attendance at the mikvah is one of the most important aspects of Jewish married life. If a woman does not immerse after her period, she retains the status of *niddah*, and intimacy with her husband is considered a serious sin. In many ways, it is even worse than premarital relations. A couple may be married by the greatest of rabbis, but if the wife does not

Or HaChaim on Leviticus 7:10. Also see *Emunoth VeDeyoth* 9:9 (Warsaw, 1913), p. 88a; Ramban on Leviticus 15:31; *Shaar HaGamul* (in *Torath HaAdam*, Jerusalem, 1958), p. 78a, from *Rosh HaShanah* 17a; Bachya on Genesis 18:25; Abravanel on Numbers 15:23; *Shemonah Shaarim, Shaar HaMitzvoth*, Introduction, s.v. *Derush* (Ashlag edition, Tel Aviv, 1962), p. 5.

9. *Sanhedrin* 90b; *Makkoth* 13b; *Yad, Teshuvah* 6:2; Rashi on Numbers 15:31; *Pri Megadim, Introduction to Orach Chaim* 3:19.

10. *Targum Yonathan ad loc.; Torah Temimah* on Leviticus 15:33. Cf. *Yad, Issurey Biyah* 4:3, 11:16, from Leviticus 15:18; see *Sifra ad loc.* A niddah is in the same category as a *zav* (Leviticus 15:13), and hence the purification is the same; Ramban on Leviticus 15:23. According to the Geonim, there is also another compelling, logical reason for immersion. Even things that a niddah touches require immersion (Leviticus 15:27); hence, she herself certainly has this requirement for purification; *Teshuvoth HaGeonim* (Lyck, 1864) 45 (18a); *Torathan Shel HaRishonim* 2:8; *Halakhoth Pesukoth* 77; *Otzar HaGeonim, Chagigah*, p. 9; *Tosafoth, Yevamoth* 47b, s.v. *BaMakom, Chagigah* 11a, s.v. *Lo Nitzracha, Yoma* 78a s.v. *MiKan; Sefer Mitzvoth Gadol*, Positive Commandment 248; *Hagahoth Maimonioth* on *Yad, Issurey Biyah* 4:3; Bachya on Leviticus 15:19; *Sefer HaManhig*, p. 548; *Sefer HaEshkol* 1:119; *Orachoth Chaim* 2:138.

attend the mikvah, they are considered to be living in sin.[11]

It is important to realize that although the mikvah is often referred to as "purification," it is really much more than that. Immersing in the mikvah is considered spiritual rebirth. We thus see that after going into the Holy of Holies on Yom Kippur, the High Priest (*Cohen Gadol*) had to immerse in a mikvah before changing his vestments. The High Priest was obviously not defiled in any way by entering the Holy of Holies. Rather, his status was completely altered at that moment, and to regain his normal status, he had to immerse in a mikvah.

The reason for this is that the mikvah has the power to change a person completely. This is also the reason that when a person converts to Judaism, the most important part of the conversion ritual is immersion in a mikvah.

In many ways, the mikvah represents the womb. When a person immerses, it is as if he has momentarily returned to the womb. Then, when he emerges, it is as if he were reborn. He is then like a completely new person.[12]

This is related to the woman's immersion just before marriage. On the day of their marriage, every couple is like Adam and Eve. However, it is taught that Adam and Eve were married on the same day they were created.[13] Similarly, the bride is born anew through her immersion just before her wedding.

It is very significant that the woman's menstrual cycle parallels the cycles of the moon. Indeed, in ancient times, it was the custom to have weddings on Wednesday (the fourth day of the week), the day that the sun and moon were created.[14] Every month, when it begins a new phase, the moon is "born anew."[15]

11. See *The Waters of Eden*, p. 3, p. 20 ff.

12. *Reshith Chokhmah, Shaar HaAhavah* 11 (Munkatch, 1896), p. 92b; *The Waters of Eden*, p. 81, note 20, p. 12 ff.

13. *Sanhedrin* 38b. See above, Chapter 5, note 13.

14. *Kethuboth* 2a. See *Zohar Chadash* 69c top.

15. Therefore, the new moon is called the *molad*. In the blessing of Kiddush HaLevanah, we also say, "A crown of beauty to [Israel] concealed in the womb, who will be renewed like [the moon]."

Similarly, every month when a woman goes to the mikvah, she is as if born anew.

Beyond that, the marriage itself is also born anew. In the course of a marriage, many problems arise and tensions begin to develop. But each month, the couple separates physically, and learns to communicate on a non-physical basis. Then, when the woman goes to the mikvah, they experience their monthly honeymoon. It is as if their marriage is reborn, and they are making a new start. Whatever problems may have existed last month have no effect on their life this month.

In a deeper sense, the mikvah represents the water of Eden.[16] When Adam and Eve lived in the Garden of Eden, they had the most perfect relationship between man and woman imaginable. Their love was perfect, without any flaw, blemish, or inhibition. By immersing, the woman brings the entire marriage back to the Edenic state, where such love exists.[17]

The bride and groom also represent God and Israel at Mount Sinai. Before the Torah was given at Sinai, all the Israelites had to immerse in a mikvah.[18] At that time, every Israelite was like a convert to Judaism, who must immerse as part of his conversion. Indeed, the law that a convert must immerse is derived from the fact that the Israelites immersed before the revelation at Sinai.[19]

Speaking of His marriage to Israel at Sinai, God said, "I swore to you, and entered into a covenant with you... and you became Mine. Then I immersed[20] you in water..." (Ezekiel 16:8,9). The immersion refers to that of the Israelites before receiving the Torah.[21] In the metaphor of the Israelites as the

16. See *The Waters of Eden*, p. 31ff.

17. However, only the woman must immerse, since the upper waters (Genesis 1:7) are masculine, while the lower waters are feminine; *Yerushalmi, Berakhoth* 9:2, 65b, *Taanith* 1:3, 4b, from Psalms 42:8; *Bereshith Rabbah* 13:13. The mikvah represents the feminine waters (Genesis 1:9).

18. See Exodus 19:10, *Mekhilta*, Ramban *ad loc.; Yevamoth* 46b; *Yad, Issurey Biyah* 13:1.

19. *Kerithoth* 9a; *Yad, loc. cit.*

20. The Hebrew *rachatz* denotes immersion; see *The Waters of Eden*, p. 58.

21. Radak, *Metzudoth David ad loc.*

bride, however, it also refers to the immersion of a bride before marriage.[22]

In any case, this premarital immersion is not something to be taken lightly. It is true that many Jews are ignorant of the rules of mikvah and may even tend to denigrate them. But anyone knowledgeable in Jewish teachings knows that mikvah is the most important pillar of Jewish married life.

As mentioned earlier, the wedding day should be planned so that the bride will be able to count the seven days after her period and immerse before the wedding. If it is impossible for her to immerse, the rabbi performing the wedding should be consulted, and he will advise the couple.

More important than going to the mikvah before the wedding, however, is the commitment to make it a monthly ritual. This, much more than even the wedding ceremony, is what makes a Jewish marriage.

22. *Abravanel ad loc.*

Chapter 12

THE WEDDING DAY

As the time of the wedding approaches, the preparations increase. In many circles, it was a custom to provide the bride and groom with special attendants for twenty-four hours before the wedding, to watch over them. When a person is about to do something particularly important in his life, it is felt that the forces of evil are particularly apt to harm him.[1]

In many groups, it was also customary to make a prenuptial meal for the bride and groom the night before the wedding.[2] This was usually made in the bride's house.[3] In some communities, it was the custom for the bride and groom to exchange gifts before this meal.[4] Some would make this into an elaborate feast, with music.[5]

1. *Betrothed Forever,* p. 10. See *Berakhoth* 54b; Radal on *Pirkey Rabbi Eliezer* 12:58; *Eduth LeYisrael,* p. 6.

2. This custom is mentioned over one thousand years ago, where the *shoshvinin* would bring the groom to the bride's house the night before the wedding; *Teshuvoth HaGeonim* (Harkevey) 65. Also see *Teshuvoth Maharam Mintz* 109; *Magen Avraham* 444:9; *Machatzith HaShekel* 444:9; *Beth Shmuel* 35:2; *Nohag KeTzon Yosef* 3:4; *Likutey Maharich* 3:129b; *Shulchan HaEzer* 6:2; Rabbi Moshe Yehudah Katz, *VaYaged Moshe* (Brooklyn, 1969) p. 14 (Printed at end of *Shulchan HaEzer*).

   This was called the *seudath kinyan; Magen Avraham.* 444:9. In Oriental communities, the women would go to the bride's house and perform the *chinna* ceremony.

   In some communities, there was also a custom to make a feast two nights before the wedding, known as the *maniza mahl,* but only the wealthy were permitted to do it; *Nohag KeTzon Yosef* 3.

3. *Shulchan HaEzer* 6:2. See *Teshuvoth HaGeonim* (Harkevey) 65.

4. *Teshuvoth Moshe Mintz* 109; *Magen Avraham* 444:9. When gifts were sent, the feast was called the "*sivlonoth meal.*" It is also mentioned that the gifts were sent through the head of the rabbinical court (*av beth din*) or the rabbi performing the ceremony. Eliezer also gave gifts and had a meal the day before he took Rebecca for Isaac (Genesis 24:53, 54).

5. *Nohag KeTzon Yosef* 3.

In many circles, however, this meal is not made, since it is a custom for the bride and groom not to see each other during the week before the wedding.[6] In some Chassidic circles, a meal is made only for the groom.[7]

In most communities,[8] it is a custom that the groom fast on

6. See above, Chapter 10, note 5. In general, some authorities were against the custom; Rabbi Aryeh Leib Tzinz, *Tiv Kiddushin* 35:1 (Warsaw, 1856). However, other authorities were in favor of this meal, since it gave the couple a last minute look at each other before the ceremony; *Beth Shmuel* 35:2.

7. This was called the "*chathan mahl*"; *Minhagey Belza*, p. 85.

8. This is primarily an Ashkenazic custom. In many Sephardic communities the custom was not to fast; *Magen Avraham* 559:11, quoting *Kenesseth HaGedolah*. Thus, in Constantinople, it was the custom not to fast; *Kenesseth HaGedolah* 562. The same was true in the rest of Turkey, as well as in Egypt, Syria, and the Sephardic community of London; *Kether Shem Tov* 7. The Sephardim in the Holy Land also did not have a custom of fasting; Rabbi Meyuchas Raphael ben Shmuel, *Mizbe'ach Adamah* (Salonika, 1777), p. 23; *Birkey Yosef, Orach Chaim* 470:2. However, the Sephardim in Safed did fast; Rabbi Chaim Sathhon, *Eretz Chaim, Evven HaEzer* (Jerusalem, 1908), p. 128. In some Sephardic communities in the Holy Land, the groom was not permitted to fast, even if he wanted to; Rabbi Chaim (ben Yitzchak) HaLevi, *Siddur Imrey Phi* (Jerusalem, 1975), p. 415.

However, in some localities, Sephardim did have the custom of fasting; *Kenesseth HaGedolah* 562; Rabbi Avraham (ben Sh'muel) Alkelai, *Zekhor LeAvraham* (Salonika, 1798), Volume 1, p. 158. The Sephardic community in Amsterdam also had the custom to fast; *Kether Shem Tov* 7. In Baghdad, it was a prevalent, but not a universal custom; *Ben Ish Chai, Shoftim* 13.

Some authorities would have preferred to abolish the custom of fasting entirely, since it weakened the bridal couple; *Sedey Chemed, Chathan VeKallah* 4. Rabbi Yitzchak Hutner, Rosh Yeshiva of Chaim Berlin, was also opposed to the fast.

Other sources preferred to have the couple fast a day or two earlier, so as not to be weakened on their wedding night; *Sedey Chemed, Chathan VeKallah* 4; Cf. Rabbi Menachem (ben Shimeon Mordechai) of Adrianopolis, *Divrey Menachem* (Salonica, 1866), end of 562; quoted in Rabbi A.L. Horowitz, *Harey Besamim* (Lvov, 1883), p. 76c. This was the custom in Algiers; Rabbi Eliahu Gig, *VaYigash Eliahu*, in *Zeh HaShulchan* 104:15 (Algiers, 1889).

his wedding day;[9] in most circles, the bride also fasts.[10]

This is because, on the day that a person is married, all of his or her sins are forgiven.[11] Before a person is married, it is very easy to fall into sexual temptation, both in thought and in deed. However, on a person's wedding day, God gives him a completely new chance. The slate is wiped clean, and he can start anew.[12]

The simplest reason for this is that, with marriage, one is

9. This custom is first mentioned by Rabbi Eliezer of Worms (circa 1165-1230); *Rokeach* 353. Also see *Evven HaEzer* 61:1 in *Hagah*; *Orach Chaim* 573:1 in *Hagah*; *Teshuvoth Maharam Mintz* 109; *Nachalath Shiva* 12:15; *Chupath Chathanim* 6:1; *Kitzur Shulchan Arukh* 146:1; *Sedey Chemed, Chathan VeKallah* 4; *Shulchan HaEzer* 6:3; *Ezer LeYitzchak* 15:1; *Eduth LeYisrael* 2.

10. Most sources indicate that the bride must also fast; *Evven HaEzer* 61:1 in *Hagah*; *Elyah Rabbah* 573; *Teshuvoth Yad Yitzchak* 2:103; *Teshuvoth Maharam Mintz* 109; *Sedey Chemed, Chathan VeKallah* 4; *Nachalath Shiva* 12:15; *Levush, Evven HaEzer* 60:1; *Nohag KeTzon Yosef* 8; *Chupath Chathanim* 6:1; *Shulchan HaEzer* 6:3; *Eduth LeYisrael* 2:2.

    However, some authorities maintain that the bride does not fast; *Matteh Moshe* 3:2; *Likutey Maharich* 3:130a; *Pri Megadim, Eshel Avraham* 571. Some sources state explicitly that the bride eats; Marahil 65b. In some Sephardic communities, even where the groom did fast, the bride did not; *Sedey Chemed, Chathan VeKallah* 4; *Ben Ish Chai, Shoftim* 8.

11. *Yerushalmi, Bikkurim* 3:3 (11b), from Genesis 28:9; *Bereshith Rabbah* 67:13; Rashi, Ramban, on Genesis 36:3; Midrash on Samuel 17; *Teshuvoth Maharam Mintz* 109; *Magen Avraham* 573:1; *Beth Shmuel* 61:5; HaGra 61:9; *Teshuvoth Mahari Bruna* 93; *Bayith Chadash, Orach Chaim* 429 end, 562 end; *Midrash HaItamri* 1. It is also taught that when a person marries, his sins are taken away; *Yevamoth* 63b; *Sedey Chemed, Chathan VeKallah* 4.

    This day is thus like Yom Kippur for the couple; *Nohag KeTzon Yosef* 8. Fasting makes the heart contrite; *Ben Ish Chai, Shoftim* 13.

    All the people attending the bride and groom are also forgiven all their sins; *Degel Machaneh Ephraim* on Exodus 10:23, quoted in *VaYaged Moshe*, p. 17.

12. This, however, is only true if the marriage itself is permitted; Rabbi Moshe Sofer, *Torath Moshe, VaYetze*; quoted in *VaYaged Moshe, loc. cit.*

beginning a new phase of life.[13] Marriage involves a complete change in lifestyle, and the person is given a chance to start it with a pure soul.[14] The love that the couple has for one another on their wedding day can annul any misplaced passion that they had in the past.[15]

Furthermore, on their wedding day, every bride and groom is like Adam and Eve on the day they were created and married. In the Torah, we clearly see that Adam and Eve were married before they sinned (Genesis 2:22). Thus, every bride and groom begins with a clean slate, just as Adam and Eve did when they were married.[16]

Besides being a sign of repentance and atonement, the fast is an act of contrition, where the bride and groom pray to God that they be spared any problems in their marriage.[17] As much as a couple may be in love on their wedding day, once the honeymoon is over, problems are bound to arise. In a successful marriage, however, problems can be dealt with in a mature manner. The couple fasts and prays for divine guidance that they may be able to overcome problems as they arise.

Another possible reason why the couple fasts is that the first sin involved eating — eating from the Tree of Knowledge. Therefore, on the day that the bride and groom are seeking forgiveness from sin, they refrain from eating. It is almost a statement that they want nothing to do with the sinful eating of the Tree of Knowledge.[18]

Furthermore, as we see in the Torah, before Adam and Eve ate from the Tree of Knowledge, they were "one flesh" (Genesis

13. Maharal, *Gur Aryeh* on Genesis 36:3; quoted in *Yalkut Yitzchak* 552:13.

14. Rabbi Eliahu HaCohen of Izmir, *Midrash HaItamri* 1 (Warsaw, 1900), p. 10a.

15. *Ibid.*

16. Original. Just as Adam was lord over all creation, so is the groom, since he is like a king. Therefore, he has all his sins forgiven; *Midrash Talpioth*, s.v. *Chathan VeKallah*.

17. *Teshuvoth Mahari Bruna* 93. See *Shabbath* 130a.

18. Original.

2:24). They were in the most perfect state of harmony imaginable. It was only after they had eaten from the Tree of Knowledge that elements of disharmony began to creep into their relationship. By fasting, the couple demonstrates that they have no association with the eating from the Tree of Knowledge, and are therefore pledged to a totally harmonious relationship.[19]

Marriage involves both spiritual and physical elements. While the physical is the most immediate, unless the couple have spiritual harmony, their physical desire for each other will rapidly fade. A physical relationship without an emotional bond may be exciting at first, but without the emotional, the excitement rapidly vanishes. But, on a deeper level, even the emotional bond depends on the spiritual.

This is another reason that the bride and groom fast. By fasting, they show that they are not that closely bound to the physical. In Hebrew, the word for bread is *lechem* (לֶחֶם). This root is closely related to *lacham* (לָחַם) which means to wage war. Thus, a *milchamah* (מִלְחָמָה) is a war. Eating is seen as the battleground between the physical and the spiritual. A person may want to be totally spiritual, but as long as he must eat, he must contend with the physical. Only someone who could reach the spiritual heights of Moses when he received the Torah would be able to go without food for forty days.[20]

The bride and groom thus fast to dissociate themselves from the physical. In this manner, they are better able to direct their consciousness toward the spiritual aspects of their marriage. This in itself will serve to preserve the bond of love that exists between them.[21]

This is also reflected in the fact that the bride and groom are like Israel and God at the giving of the Torah. Before the Torah was given, it is said, "The people had a vision of God, and they ate and drank" (Exodus 24:11). The Zohar explains that they

19. Original. See *Sefer Hafla'ah, Kethuboth* 8a.

20. Original. See Hirsch on Genesis 3:19.

21. Thus they fasted as the First Saints (*Chassidim Rishonim*) did before they did a virtuous deed; *Rokeach* 353; *Matteh Moshe* 3:2.

did not eat physical food; rather, their very vision of God was their nourishment, and to them it was just like food and drink.[22]

Thus, the Israelites actually fasted before receiving the Torah. The bride and groom emulate this fast on their wedding day.[23] On the day the Torah was given, the love between God and Israel was so strong that the Israelites could not even think about food. The same is true of the bride and groom on this, their wedding day.[24]

At the afternoon Mincha service, which is usually said before the wedding ceremony,[25] it is customary for the bride and groom to add the prayer *Anenu* (עֲנֵנוּ, "Answer Us") to the Amidah, as we do on every fast day.[26] In most communities, it is also a custom for the bride and groom to say the entire confession (*Viduy*), just as it is said in the Mincha service before Yom Kippur.[27] According to many authorities, this confession is said even if they do not fast.[28]

22. *Zohar* 1:135a; Cf. *VaYikra Rabbah* 20:10; *Berakhoth* 17a; *Targum, Midrash Lekach Tov,* on Exodus 24:11. This occurred before the giving of the Ten Commandments; Rashi on Exodus 24:1; *Mekhilta* on Exodus 19:10.

23. *Tashbat* 465.

24. *Midrash HaItamri* 1, p. 10a.

25. See below, Chapter 17, note 4. If Mincha is said after the wedding ceremony, there is a question as to whether *Anenu* is said; see *Shulchan HaEzer* 6:3:7.

26. As part of the blessing *Sh'ma Kolenu* in the Amidah. This is first mentioned in *Terumath HaDeshen* 157; *Teshuvoth Mahari Bruna* 93. Also see *Orach Chaim* 562:2 in *Hagah*; *Kitzur Shulchan Arukh* 146:1; *Shulchan HaEzer* 6:3:6; *Eduth LeYisrael* 2:3.

    If the groom does not plan to fast until nightfall, he should leave out the words *be-yom taanith-enu* (בְּיוֹם תַּעֲנִיתֵנוּ, "on the day of our fast") in this prayer; *Turey Zahav, Orach Chaim* 562:1.

27. That is, the prayer *Al Chet* (עַל חֵטְא, "For the Sin..."). This custom is first mentioned in Rabbi Yehudah Leib (ben Yosef) Puchavitzer, *Daath Chokhmah, Shaar Teshuvah* 3 (Hamburg, 1692), quoted in *Nohag KeTzon Yosef* 8. Also see Rabbi Shlomo Amarillio, *Kerem Shlomo* (Salonika, 1719); quoted in *Pith'chey Teshuvah, Evven HaEzer* 61:9; *Shulchan HaEzer* 6:3:7; Rabbi Yaakov Lorberbaum of Lisa, *Siddur Derekh Chaim*; *Kitzur Shulchan Arukh* 146:4.

28 *Kerem Shlomo*; quoted in *Pith'chey Teshuvah* 61:9. See *Sedey Chemed, Chathan VeKallah* 4, *Viduy* 3 (6:458). See note 44.

Of course, merely reciting the words of the confession is not enough. As on Yom Kippur itself, the confession must be accompanied by repentance and spiritual purification.[29] The bride and groom should also pray to God in their own words, asking Him to forgive all their previous sins, and also asking that He grant them a happy, successful marriage.[30]

Another, more prosaic reason for the fast is that the bride and groom should not over-indulge in drink during the prenuptial celebrations. The marriage ceremony is one of the most important moments in their lives, and they must enter into it in a perfectly clear and sober state of mind.[31]

If the wedding occurs during the day, the fast is broken when the bride and groom sip the wine under the chupah.[32]

29. *Shnei Luchoth HaB'rith, Shaar HaOthioth* 1:162b; *Tosafoth Chaim,* 132:55; *Kitzur Shulchan Arukh* 146:4; *Shulchan HaEzer* 6:3:7; *Eduth LeYisrael* 2:9.

In Frankfort, it was the custom for the groom to cover his head like a mourner; *Nohag KeTzon Yosef* 8. In some communities, the bridegroom also attended the mikvah as a sign of purification; *Chupath Chathanim* 6:1, p. 28; *Shulchan HaEzer* 6:5:3.

30. There are also a number of regular prayers for the bridegroom; *Chupath Chathanim* 6. Some also have the custom of reciting Psalms on the wedding day; *Sefer HaMinhagim* (Lubavitch), p. 75.

31. This is the second reason given in *Teshuvoth Maharam Mintz* 109, quoted in *Magen Avraham* 573:1; *Beth Shmuel* 61:5. Also see *Teshuvoth Mahari Bruna* 93.

32. *Terumath HaDeshen* 157; *Orach Chaim* 562:2 in *Hagah*; *Teshuvoth Mahari Bruna* 93; *Levush* 573; *Minhagim* at end of *Levush, Orach Chaim,* 53; *Pri Megadim, Eshel Avraham* 573:8; *Kitzur Shulchan Arukh* 146:1; *Kether Shem Tov* 703; *Sefer HaMinhagim,* (Lubavitch), p. 75.

The fast may be broken before nightfall, even if no such condition was originally made; *Atereth Zekenim* 562. Still, it is best that such a condition be made; *Mishneh Berurah* 562:12.

Some authorities maintain that the fast must be formally accepted; *Chupath Chathanim* 5. Others, however, do not require it; *Arukh HaShulchan* 61:21; HaGra on *Orach Chaim* 562:2; *Eduth LeYisrael* 2:5.

According to some authorities, the primary reason for the fast is so that the couple will not get drunk; thus, they must fast until the ceremony, even if it is late at night; *Beth Shmuel* 61:5; *Likutey Maharich* 3:129b.

Although the fast is like that of Yom Kippur, unlike Yom Kippur, the fast need not be kept until nightfall.[33] As soon as the marriage ceremony begins, their sins are forgiven, and they are permitted to eat and drink.[34]

However, if the wedding ceremony is not held until nighttime, then the bride and groom are permitted to break their fast at nightfall.[35] Since this day is like Yom Kippur for them, there is no reason that the fast should be kept more strictly than Yom Kippur itself, which ends at nightfall. However, when the fast is broken, the couple should be very careful not to drink anything intoxicating, so that they have perfectly clear minds at the ceremony.[36]

The fast of the bride and groom is considered a "private fast" (*taanith yachid*), and there are certain days upon which a private fast may not be held.[37] Therefore, they do not fast on the New Moon festival (*Rosh Chodesh*),[38] the day after a festival (*Isru Chag*),[39] Chanukah,[40] Purim,[41] Tu B'Shevat (the New

33. After the ceremony, it is like a festival for the bride and groom, when fasting is not appropriate; *Sedey Chemed, Chathan VeKallah* 4.

34. *Nachalath Shiva* 12:15.

35. *Chokhmath Adam* 129:2.

36. *Ibid.* The couple must be careful of this even on days when they do not fast; *Kitzur Shulchan Arukh* 146:3.

37. See *Magen Avraham* 473:1; *Chokhmath Adam* 129:2; *Kitzur Shulchan Arukh* 146:2; *Shulchan HaEzer* 6:4; *Eduth LeYisrael* 2:8; *Ezer LeYitzchak* 16. Also see *Orach Chaim* 570:1-3, 572:2.

38. In some places it was the custom to fast on Rosh Chodesh Nissan; *Orach Chaim* 573:1; Cf. *Orach Chaim* 480:2. Some dispute this, however, and maintain that the couple should not fast; *Sedey Chemed, Chathan VeKallah* 4. In some places it was the custom to fast part of the day even on Rosh Chodesh; *Nohag KeTzon Yosef* 8.

39. Some maintain that the day after Shavuoth is a festival with respect to fasting, according to Torah law; *Misgereth HaShulchan* 146, quoted in *Ezer LeYitzchak* 16. Others, however, maintain that it is merely custom; for discussion, see *Eduth LeYisrael* 2:8.

40. *Orach Chaim* 573:1.

41. *Orach Chaim* 697.1.

Year for Trees),[42] and 15 Av.[43] However, even though the couple does not fast on these days, they should still repent, and, according to many authorities, recite the confession at the Mincha service.[44]

42. *Rosh HaShanah* 2a; *Hagahoth Maimonioth, Shofar* 1:1 #1; *Orach Chaim* 572:3.

43. For the significance of this day, see *Taanith* 30b.

44. See Note 28. Also see *Levushey Mordechai, Evven HaEzer* 49; *Taamey HaMinhagim* 941; *Ezer LeYitzchak* 16; *Siddur Derekh Chaim.*

Some authorities, however, maintain that it should not be said on days when one does not fast, especially on Rosh Chodesh; *Sheviley David, Orach Chaim* 576; *VaYitzbor Yosef* 66. According to this opinion, Psalm 51 should be substituted; *Yalkut HaGirshuni, Hashmatoth* 3:20, quoting Rabbi Yehudah Assad.

Chapter 13

OUTLINE OF THE WEDDING

Before discussing the wedding ceremony in detail, it would be useful to give an outline of the wedding as a whole. Later, we will discuss each step in detail.

Before the ceremony, it is customary to have a reception for the bride and groom, usually separately. The bride's reception is usually accompanied by music and a buffet. The groom's is more subdued, attended by the rabbi performing the ceremony.

At the groom's reception, the *kethubah* (marriage contract) is signed. Without the *kethubah*, the couple is not permitted to live together.

After the *kethubah* is written, it is customary to hold the afternoon Mincha service. As we have seen, at this service the groom (and the bride, separately) recite the Yom Kippur confession. In some circles, the Mincha service is conducted after the bride is veiled.

The veiling consists of the groom being led to the bride and covering her face with the veil, reciting a special verse. The couple then prepares for the actual ceremony.

The ceremony is conducted under a marriage canopy, known as a chupah. It begins with the rabbi reciting the blessing over wine and the prenuptial blessing (*Birkath Erusin*). This is the first part of the wedding ceremony, after which the bride and groom sip from the cup. The groom then places the ring on the bride's finger, completing the betrothal.

To separate the two parts of the ceremony, the *kethubah* is then read.

After this, the Seven Wedding Blessings (*Sheva Berakhoth*) are recited over a second cup of wine. This is the second part of the ceremony, which is the actual marriage (*nesuin*). When the seven blessings are completed, the groom breaks a cup, and everyone responds "Mazal Tov."

The couple then goes to a special room, where they are entirely alone — separated from all the guests. Besides the fact that this may be their only chance to be alone together at the wedding, this *yichud*, as it is called, is an integral part of the marriage ceremony.

While the couple is alone together, the guests sit down for the main wedding meal. In the middle of the meal, usually just before the main course is served, the couple comes in together. This is a signal for everyone to get up and dance in honor of the bride and groom.

At traditional weddings, the dancing and celebration is anything but morose or serious. A good time is had by all, with all sorts of little dancing games. But even in the midst of the wildest exuberance, there is still an atmosphere of holiness.

After the meal, the traditional Grace after Meals is recited, just as it is after every meal where bread is eaten. At the end of the Grace (*Birkath HaMazon*), the Seven Wedding Blessings are recited for the couple a second time. It is very important that the bride and groom not leave the wedding until after the Grace.

This is an outline of the entire wedding. Each step will now be discussed in detail.

Chapter 14

THE PRENUPTIAL RECEPTION

It is customary to have a prenuptial reception for the bride and groom in the wedding hall as the guests gather for the wedding ceremony.[1]

The larger reception is held for the bride.[2] The band usually plays, and a smorgasbord is served.[3] Some say that this custom is derived from Eliezer, since before taking Rebecca to Isaac, he gave her family delicacies.[4] Although this reception is primarily for the women, many men come in to partake of the smorgasbord before going in to the groom's reception.

This is the bride's day, and she is treated accordingly. It is a very ancient custom, dating back to early Talmudic times, for the bride to sit on a "throne" at her reception.[5] Nowadays, this is usually a beautiful chair filled with cushions.[6] She is

1. *Eduth LeYisrael* 8:1. In some circles, it is customary for the groom's parents to pay for this reception; *Mataamim HaChadash* 42; *Otzar Kol Minhagey Yeshurun* 16:14. Some sources merely state that the groom's parents serve cake and the like; *Shulchan HaEzer* 6:6.

2. *Shulchan HaEzer* 6:6. This reception was originally held in the bride's home; she would meet the groom in the synagogue, and then hold a reception in her parents' house; Maharil 64b; Cf. *Rokeach* 353. It was then the custom to bring the bride from her home to the place of the wedding, accompanied by music; *Minhagey Mattersdorf* 111. It was considered a virtuous act (mitzvah) to accompany the bride; Rashi, *Megillah* 29a, s.v. *LeHakhnasath Kallah*; see *Mataamim HaChadash* 36.

3. Some say that people should not eat while standing; *Taamey HaMinhagim*, p. 409. It is not considered proper to eat while standing; *Mesekhta Derekh Eretz Zuta* 5.

4. *Mataamim HaChadash* 42; *Otzar Kol Minhagey Yeshurun* 16:4.

5. *Kelim* 22:4; *Eduyoth* 1:11; *Teshuvoth Rashba* 1180; Rabbenu Yerocham 23:2, 183c. See *Yevamoth* 110a; *Bereshith Rabbah* 20; *Piskey Tosafoth, Sanhedrin* 4:97.

6. *Shulchan HaEzer* 6:6:7.

surrounded by family and friends, while the other girls dance before her.

The groom's reception is usually more subdued.[7] Unlike the bride's reception, only cake and beverages are usually served at the groom's (although in recent times it has become the custom to serve somewhat more). The groom sits at the head of the table, and is greeted like a king.[8] He is usually flanked by his father and future father-in-law, as well as the dignitaries invited to the wedding.

When the rabbi performing the wedding arrives, he usually sits next to the groom. In many circles, it is customary to have a member of the wedding party pick up the rabbi personally.[9]

Very strict instructions should be given to the photographers not to disturb the people sitting around the table with the bridegroom. There have been some cases of prominent rabbis forced into a corner so that the photographer would be able to get a "better shot." When the photographer is hired, he should be given careful instructions not to order the guests around.

It is a custom for the groom to deliver a sermonette or Torah discourse at the reception.[10] On the simplest level, this is meant to show that even at the happiest moment in his life, he does not forget God and the Torah. He is about to marry and begin a family, and he wants it to be founded on the basis of Torah.[11] Moreover, the groom wants to show that his bride has a Torah scholar for a husband.[12]

7. The groom was separate from the bride, as with ancient royalty; *Midrash Talpioth*, s.v. *Chathan VeKallah;* Cf. Esther 1:9. This was also a Sephardic custom; *Kether Shem Tov* 4.

8. *Mataamim HaChadash* 36; *Midrash Talpioth, loc. cit.* See below, Chapter 24, note 16.

9. *Shulchan HaEzer* 6:7. See *Kether Shem Tov* 4.

10. *Shulchan HaEzer* 6:6:6; *Eduth LeYisrael* 7:5. See *Teshuvoth Maharshal* 85; *Magen Avraham* 306:15.

11. Commentary on *Targum Yonathan*, Deuteronomy 1:19; quoted in *Mataamim HaChadash* 40.

12. *Otzar Kol Minhagey Yeshurun* 15:8; *VaYaged Moshe*, p. 19.

In many circles, it is a custom only to let the groom say a few sentences before interrupting him with singing. Sometimes, he will make several attempts to continue, being interrupted each time.

On a simple level, this is so as not to embarrass the ignorant. Since every groom is interrupted, one who is unlearned will not feel debased on this, the most joyous day of his life.[13] Every bridegroom is interrupted, even a scholar, to show that no one can know the entire Torah; even the scholar is in many ways ignorant.[14]

There is also a deeper meaning to this interruption. As we have mentioned a number of times, the bride and groom represent Israel and God at the giving of the Torah at Mount Sinai. Thus, just as God gave the Ten Commandments at Sinai, the groom delivers a discourse on the Torah. However, just as the Tablets bearing these commandments were broken, the discourse is also interrupted.[15]

In some circles, the groom is interrupted by the *badchan*, a professional wedding jester, who recites comedy in rhyme. It is a venerable custom to have a *badchan* at a wedding.[16] Some say that this is because in rhyming he pairs words, just as the bride and groom have been paired together.[17] In many circles, he teaches the bride and groom important lessons in his rhymes.[18]

13. *VaYaged Moshe,* p. 20. See Rabbi Eleazar Spiro of Munkatch, *Divrey Torah* (Munkatch, 1929). Some, however, maintain that the groom should not be interrupted if he is a Torah scholar; Rabbi Avraham (ben Eliezer) HaCohen, *Uri VeYeshi,* End of *D'rush* 13 (Berlin, 1714); *VaYaged Moshe,* p. 20.

14. *VaYaged Moshe,* p. 19.

15. *Sichoth HaRan* 96; quoted in *Darkey HaChaim VeHaShalom* 1056. A similar idea is found in Rabbi Yehoshua Avraham ben Yisrael of Zhitomer, *Geulath Yisrael* (Ostrog, 1821), quoted in *Shulchan HaEzer* 6:6:6; *Mataamim* 66; *Yalkut Yitzchak* 552:16.

16. *Ramatayim Tzofim,* part 2, quoted in *Mataamim* 146; *Minhagey Belza,* p. 86.

17. I heard this from Mr. Raphael Dembitzer on the way to the Holy Land in 1955.

18. *Shulchan HaEzer* 6:6. Some sources indicate that he also recites before the bride; *Ibid.; Mataamim HaChadash* 43.

If the *tenaim* (the formal engagement) has not been made earlier, it is usually made as part of the groom's reception, before the *kethubah* is signed.

Chapter 15

THE KETHUBAH

The most important procedure at the groom's reception is the completing and signing of the *kethubah*.[1]

The word *kethubah* (כְּתוּבָּה)[2] literally means "that which is written." It is a contract that a man makes with his wife, declaring that he will carry out his obligations as a husband according to Jewish law and custom. It also stipulates the amount that the husband is bound to give his wife in the event that the marriage is dissolved.

The *kethubah* is closely related to the *mohar* (מֹהַר) or dowry mentioned in the Bible.[3] The *mohar* was the amount that a man would agree to pay his bride in the event that the marriage was terminated. The Torah thus speaks of a case where a man must pay "the *mohar* of a virgin" (Exodus 22:15). This indicates that a virgin would receive a special *mohar*.[4] It also shows that in ancient Israel, it was the custom to provide a bride with a *mohar*.[5] Indeed, in ancient times, this custom existed among

1. *Eduth LeYisrael* 3:5.

2. The word is *kethubah* (with a dagesh in the *beth*) rather than *kethuvah*; Rabbi David de Pomos, *Tzemach David* (Venice, 1587), s.v. *Kethubah*.

3. See Genesis 34:12, *Targum Yerushalmi*, Rashi, *ad loc*; 1 Samuel 18:25; *Bereshith Rabbah* 80:7; Rashi, Maharzav *ad loc.*; *Mekhilta* on Exodus 22:15; *Yerushalmi, Kethuboth* 3:5, 19b.

   The word *mohar* is related to the root *mahar* (מהר), meaning to move quickly. This was because the dowry would speed the marriage process; see Ramban on Exodus 22:16.

4. Rabbi Yaakov (ben Tzvi) Emden (Maharibatz), *Kethuboth* 56b.

5. Hirsch on Exodus 22:15. It is thus taught that Joseph gave his wife a kethubah; *Mesekhta Kallah Rabathai* 3; Rashi, *Midrash HaGadol* (p. 720) on Genesis 49:9.

   Also see Rashi, *Mekhilta, Adereth Eliahu*, on Exodus 22:15. Others, however, dispute this opinion; Ramban *ad loc.* Also see *Kol Bo* 143:2; *Tosafoth, Sotah* 27a, s.v. *Ish*.

gentiles as well.[6]

According to most authorities,[7] the *kethubah* is required by rabbinical legislation rather than by Torah law.[8] Although

Even if the Torah did not require a kethubah or *mohar*, it did recognize the custom; *Yad, Naarah Bethulah* 1:3; *Mishneh LaMelekh Ibid.* s.v. *U'Ra'ithi*; *Nodah BeYehudah Tinyana, Evven HaEzer* 33; Malbim on Exodus 22:15; *Igroth Moshe, Evven HaEzer* 101.

The word *ke-mohar* (כַּמֹּהַר) in Exodus 22:15 is seen as spelling out *kamah resh* (כַּמָה ר), meaning, "How much? 200," alluding to the 200 zuzim required for the kethubah; *Lekach Tov, Hadar Zekenim*, on Exodus 22:16; *Machzor Vitri* p. 593.

6. See *Kethuboth* 90a; *Chullin* 92a. Also, Shechem offered a *mohar*, even though he was not Jewish; see Genesis 34:12; above, note 3.

7. Some authorities, maintain that it is a Torah law. In the Talmud, this is the opinion of Rabban Shimon ben Gamliel; *Kethuboth* 10a; also see *Kethuboth* 110b. It is also the opinion of Rabbi Meir; *Kethuboth* 56b.

Many later authorities maintain that this is the accepted opinion, especially since it is a universal custom to write in the kethubah that it is due the bride "from Torah law" (*mi-de-Oraitha*); *Tosafoth, Kethuboth* 10a, s.v. *Amar, Yevamoth* 89a s.v. *Taamah; Sefer Mitzvoth Gadol*, Positive Commandment 48 (Venice, 1546), p. 126a; *Torah Temimah* on Exodus 22:16. Some Geonim were of this opinion; *Sefer HaMakhria* 42.

Some authorities state that, according to Rabbi Meir, even a widow requires a kethubah by Torah law; Rashba; Rabbi Yaakov Emden (Maharibatz) on *Kethuboth* 56b; Cf. *Tosafoth Ibid.*

Also see *Yerushalmi, Yevamoth* 7:3; *Peney Moshe* and *Korban HaEdah ad loc.* For general discussion, see *Teshuvoth Binyamin Ze'ev* 54; *Hagahoth Maimonioth, Ishuth* 10:7 #6; *Tur, Evven HaEzer* 66; *Eduth LeYisrael* 3:4. Also see below, Chapter 16, notes 43—46.

8. In the Talmud, this is the opinion of Rav Nachman and the majority of the sages; *Kethuboth* 10a; see *Chidushey HaRan, Sanhedrin* 31b. It was also the opinion of all the Geonim; Rosh, *Kethuboth* 1:19. Most later authorities hold that it is the accepted opinion; Rif 3b; *Yad, Ishuth* 10:7; Ran, *Kethuboth* Rif 65b s.v. *U'LeInyan; Teshuvoth Rivash* 67; Meiri, *Kethuboth* 10a; *Sefer HaIttur* p. 30a. Cf. *Yerushalmi, Kethuboth* 4:11.

More recent authorities maintained that it was the accepted opinion; *Chelkath Mechokak* 66:26; *Beth Shmuel* 66:14.

Other authorities maintain that the main idea of the kethubah is Torah law, but that the amount was fixed by rabbinical legislation; Rashba

there may have been a custom of giving a *kethubah* even before the Torah was given, this custom was not formalized as law until much later.[9] The Torah gives the Sanhedrin the power to legislate religious law, as it is written, "You shall go to the place that God shall choose, and you shall come to the [court administered by] the priests, Levites, and the chief justice at the time... You must obey whatever they teach you...." (Deuteronomy 17:8-10). Such legislated law is as binding as Torah law.[10]

Originally, the man could simply put aside an amount of money, and that would be his wife's *kethubah*. However, this money could easily be lost or hidden, thus depriving the wife of her rights. Therefore, around 100 b.c.e., the Sanhedrin, under the leadership of Shimon ben Shetach, legislated that a man's entire estate would be mortgaged to the *kethubah*. The woman would thus be able to collect her *kethubah* just as she would any other contracted debt.[11]

(actually Ramban), *Kethuboth* 110b, s.v. *Nasa;* Ritva, *Kethuboth* 110a, s v. *VeChakhamim; Shitah Mekubetzeth Ibid.* (Lvov, 1861), Volume 2, p. 167a; *Teshuvoth Rivash* 66; *Nachalath Shiva* 12:32:3; *Chelkath Mechokak* 66:24; *Torah Temimah* on Exodus 22:16. Also see Ramban on Exodus 22:16.

Some say that even those who maintain that it is Torah law, hold that it is "a law to Moses from Sinai" (*halakhah le-Moshe miSinai*), and is not required by the written Torah; Rashba, *Kethuboth* 110b, s.v. *Nasa*.

9. See Hirsch on Exodus 22:15. Also see note 5.

10. See *The Handbook of Jewish Thought* 11:26.

11. *Shabbath* 14b; *Kethuboth* 82b. Some sources indicate that Shimon ben Shetach's legislation also required a written kethubah; *Tosefta, Kethuboth* 12:1. It seems that at least part of the wording of our present kethubah was in existence by the first century b.c.e.; see below, Chapter 16, notes 2, 24.

In the Apocrypha, there is also a reference to the kethubah. At the marriage of Tobit and Sarah, "they took paper, wrote a contract and signed it; then they began to eat" (Tobit 7:14). In the original (?) Greek, the word for "paper" is *biblion,* which denotes a paper, scroll or letter. The word for "contract" is *syggraphon,* which means "that which is written," a literal translation of the word *kethubah*. This is also the translation given in Avraham Kahanah, *Sefarim HaChitzonim*. In the long version of Tobit in Kahanah, it is called, "the kethubah, the book of nesuin." Since Tobit (Tovia in Hebrew) lived in the time of the exile, this is an indication that the concept of the written kethubah existed even at that time. Moreover, the book of Tobit was written around 130 b.c.e.

It appears that the original legislation did not require the *kethubah* to be a written document; a duly witnessed oral agreement also sufficed.[12] As late as 360 c.e., there is evidence that, at least in some areas, the custom was not to put the *kethubah* in writing.[13] Even today, in emergencies, a man can give his bride cash or goods as her *kethubah*.[14] However, since it is possible for the woman to be left destitute if there is no written document as proof, it was legislated that, under normal circumstances, a written contract is required.[15]

According to this legislation, it is forbidden for a man to live with his wife unless a *kethubah* has been executed and signed.[16] The *kethubah* must be in the possession of the wife or her agent. If the *kethubah* is lost, a substitute *kethubah de-irkasa* (כְּתוּבָּה דְאִירְכָסָא, "kethubah for one lost") must be written.[17] Without a *kethubah*, the couple may not live together.

The *kethubah* was legislated chiefly to make it difficult for a man to divorce his wife.[18] In ancient times, a man was able to divorce his wife, even against her will, but the sages wanted to make it a costly process. A truly bad marriage could be dissolved, but the expense would motivate the man to do everything in his power to save it. Even today, under the excommunication ban (*cherem*) of Rabbenu Gershom (circa 960

12. *Kethuboth* 7a; Mordechai, *Kethuboth* 130; *Hagahoth Asheri, Kethuboth* 1:10:3. See *Evven HaEzer* 66:1.

13. *Kethuboth* 16a. This follows the opinion of the *Chakhamim; Kethuboth* 57a.

14. *Kethuboth* 7a; *Evven HaEzer* 66:1.

15. *Kethuboth* 56b. Some authorities hold that this was the legislation of Shimon ben Shetach; *Tosefta, Kethuboth* 12:1; *Chasdey David ad loc.*

16. According to Rabbi Meir; *Kethuboth* 57a. Also see *Kethuboth* 54b; *Yad, Ishuth* 10:10; *Evven HaEzer* 66:1. Some authorities maintain that without a kethubah the woman is forbidden as a *kedeshah*, as in Deuteronomy 23:18; *Chinukh* 570. Others maintain that she can be a *pilegesh* (common-law wife) without a kethubah; *Sanhedrin* 21a; *Yerushalmi, Kethuboth* 5:2.

17. *Kethuboth* 56a; *Evven HaEzer* 66:3. The form of the *kethubah de-irkasa* is in *Nachalath Shiva* 13.

18. *Kethuboth* 10a.

— 1028), when a man is forbidden to divorce his wife against her will, the *kethubah* is still required.[19]

In a sense, the *kethubah* is very much like alimony, except that, instead of being paid over a period of time, it is given to the wife in a lump sum. The amount was, at least in ancient times, enough for the woman to invest and to derive a steady income from it.[20] This would guarantee that the woman would be able to devote her full time to raising her children. Furthermore, in many societies where jobs were not available to women, the *kethubah* served as a financial safety net.

The *kethubah* also has a symbolic meaning. Since the bride and groom represent Israel and God at Sinai when the Torah was given, the *kethubah* represents the "Book of the Covenant" that Moses wrote prior to the revelation at Sinai (Exodus 24:4,7).[21] The Book of the Covenant spelled out the mutual obligations of God and Israel, just as the *kethubah* spells out the obligations between husband and wife.[22]

In most contemporary marriages, the *kethubah* consists of a printed form, with the date and other pertinent details to be filled in. Printed *kethuboth* have been used for a long time in a number of countries.[23] However, in many circles, it is a custom to have a beautiful, hand-lettered, illustrated *kethubah*, executed on parchment or paper, according to custom.[24] There

19. *Evven HaEzer* 66:3 in *Hagah; Chelkath Mechokak* 66:18; *Beth Shmuel* 66:11. This ban by Rabbenu Gershom is mentioned in *Teshuvoth Rabbi Meir of Rothenberg* 1121. Other sources, however, simply speak of it as a community enactment; *Sefer Raban* (Prague, 1610), p. 121b; or as a *Cherem HaYishuv; Hagahoth Asheri, Bava Bathra* 2:12.

20. This is spelled out in detail in Hirsch on Exodus 22:16. Also see *Teshuvoth Rivash* 153.

21. See *The Living Torah,* note *ad loc.* Some say that this was Leviticus 25—27; *Chizzkuni ad loc.*

22. See *Sefer HaKaneh* 99b; *Shoshan Sodoth* 61a. See below, Chapter 16, note 5.

23. This was the custom in Germany; *Kether Shem Tov* 41. In Holland, engraved kethuboth were known as early as the sixteenth century.

24. In the Holy Land, Syria, Turkey, Egypt, London and Amsterdam, the

are many artists and scribes today who can produce a *kethubah* that is a true work of art. This is part of an ancient tradition. Beautiful, artistic *kethuboth* from many centuries ago still exist.

Where possible, it is a nice custom for the couple to have a personalized *kethubah* hand-written especially for them.[25] The cost of writing the *kethubah* is usually borne by the groom or his family.[26]

Nevertheless, a printed *kethubah* is perfectly acceptable, as long as it conforms in all aspects to Jewish law.[27] Most printed *kethuboth*, however, are made for a girl who has never been married before. If it is a second marriage for the bride, the wording on most printed *kethuboth* is not correct. The wording cannot be rectified by crossing out the incorrect words or by changing them, since such alterations can render the document invalid.[28] There are, however, printed *kethuboth* with blanks for special cases.

The *kethubah* must be executed and signed prior to the wedding ceremony. The chupah symbolizes the couple setting up house together, and they are forbidden to live together without a *kethubah*. If the *kethubah* is not written beforehand, there may be questions regarding the validity of the

Sephardic Jews had the custom of writing the kethubah on paper; *Kether Shem Tov* 41. This was also the custom in Persia and elsewhere in the Near East. However, some communities in Amsterdam would use parchment; *Kether Shem Tov* 41. This was also the custom in Italy and southern Europe.

25. In the Sephardic community of Amsterdam, it was the custom for the kethubah to be written by a professional scribe. In London, it was written by the cantor, with permission of the secretary of the community. In the Holy Land, writing the kethubah was a hereditary privilege; *Kether Shem Tov* 3.

26. *Bava Bathra* 167b; *Devarim Rabbah* 3; *Evven HaEzer* 66:1.

27. Thus, no part of the date should be printed in. The word*ve-kanina* should also not be printed in (see below, note 38). See *Choshen Mishpat* 48:1; *Sifethey Cohen* 48:1; *Urim VeThumim* 48:1; *Nethivoth HaMishpat* 48:1; *Shulchan HaEzer* 6:8. Also see *Hagahoth Maimonioth, Ishuth* 10:7 #4.

28. See *Taamey HaMinhagim*, p. 409.

ceremony.[29] Furthermore, since the *kethubah* is normally read as part of the ceremony, it should be executed ahead of time.[30]

Great care must be taken in filling out the *kethubah*. The rabbi must be especially careful to get the precise names of the bride and groom, as well as their parents, and to spell them according to the law.[31] If there are any Yiddish names in the family, he should not Hebraicize them, unless this is indicated in the law.

Once the *kethubah* is filled out, it is customary for the rabbi or one of the witnesses[32] to make a *kinyan* with the bridegroom.[33]

The word *kinyan* (קִנְיָן) literally means purchase or acquisition, and it denotes a legal transaction based on the

29. *Yad, Ishuth* 10:7; *Maggid Mishneh ad loc.; Evven HaEzer* 55:3, 61:1 in *Hagah; Shulchan HaEzer* 6:8; *Eduth LeYisrael* 3:5. Cf. *Kethuboth* 7a; *Sefer HaIttur* 43b; *Tanya Rabathai* 98a; *Sefer HaManhig* p. 544.

This custom is also found in Geonic sources; see *Halakhoth Pesukoth (Halakhoth Re'u)* p. 84; David Sassoon, *Halakhoth Pesukoth* (Jerusalem, 1951), p. 109b; *Siddur Rav Saadia Gaon,* p. 96. It appears that, at least for a time, there was a decree from Rav Yehudai Gaon (757 c.e.) that the wedding ceremony could not be performed unless the kethubah was written previously; otherwise the ceremony would be invalid; *Teshuvoth HaGeonim* (Assaf) 1:113; *Otzar HaGeonim, Kethuboth* p. 18.

From the Apocrypha it also appears that the kethubah was written before the chupah; see Tobit 7:14.

30. *Arukh HaShulchan* 61:17.

31. *Teshuvoth Rama* 65; *Nachalath Shiva* 12:16.

32. The oldest sources state that the witnesses do it; see *Sefer HaOrah* 2:13; *Machzor Vitri* 470, p. 588; *Rokeach* 354. In most places, however, the custom is that the *mesader kiddushin* does it.

33. Rashi, *Sefer HaOrah* 2:13; *Machzor Vitri* 470, p. 588; *Rokeach* 354; *Teshuvoth Maharam Mintz* 109; *Evven HaEzer* 66:8 in *Hagah; Darkey Moshe* 66:3; *Nachalath Shiva* 12:69; *Shulchan HaEzer* 6:9; *Eduth LeYisrael* 3:5, p. 14f. See *Bava Metzia* 40a; *Teshuvoth Mahari Bruna* 94.

Other sources, however, indicate that a kinyan is not necessary; Hai Gaon, quoted in *Tur, Evven HaEzer* 66; *Teshuvoth Rivash* 345; Ritva, *Kethuboth* 54b; *Evven HaEzer* 66:8; HaGra 66:31. See *Chelkath Mechokak* 66:34.

rules of barter. This method of sealing a transaction is mentioned in the scripture, where it says, "This was the ancient practice in Israel... to confirm all things: a man would take off his shoe and give it to the other party. This, among the Israelites, would create an obligation" (Ruth 4:7). While the Biblical custom may have involved a shoe, a handkerchief or other article could have been used. Thus, if a person wanted to gain any right or obligation from another, he would give the person a handkerchief, napkin, scarf, or similar article.[34]

In this case, the groom must take upon himself the obligations of the *kethubah* through a *kinyan*. The rabbi or witness takes the place of the bride in making the *kinyan*.[35] The *kinyan* is done by giving the groom a handkerchief, napkin, or similar article. If none is available, the groom can grasp a corner or lapel of a garment worn by the person making the *kinyan*, provided that he grasps a section three fingerbreadths square.[36] As soon as he does that, he has taken the object in "barter" (*chaliphin*) for his obligation, and has thus obligated himself.

The witnesses who sign the *kethubah* should be very careful to see this transaction.[37] After the *kinyan* has been made, the rabbi writes in the *kethubah* the word *ve-kanina* (וְקָנִינָא, "I have made a *kinyan*), and the witnesses then sign. They should not sign until after the *kinyan*.[38]

In Jewish jurisprudence, a contract or other legal document is validated by the signature of two witnesses. In general, the witnesses must be virtuous, observant men, not related by blood or marriage to either party.[39] It is preferable that the witnesses know Hebrew and Aramaic well enough to understand the

34. *Bava Metzia* 47a; *Choshen Mishpat* 195. See above, Chapter 4, notes 36, 37.

35. *Sefer HaOrah* 2:13; *Machzor Vitri* 470, p. 588.

36. *Choshen Mishpat* 195; *Bava Metzia* 7a. Cf. Hai Gaon, *Teshuvoth HaGeonim, Shaarey Teshuvah* 49.

37. *Nethivoth HaShulchan* 20; *Shulchan HaEzer* 6:9:3.

38. *Shulchan HaEzer* 6:9; *Nachalath Shiva* 12:72.

39. See below, Chapter 21, notes 3 — 5.

document before signing it.[40] Some rabbis customarily explain the *kethubah* to the witnesses before they sign.

The witnesses sign the *kethubah* in Hebrew, just as they would sign any other legal contract in Jewish jurisprudence.[41] The two witnesses sign one under the other.[42] In some communities, it is also the custom for the groom to sign on the opposite side of the document.[43]

The general custom is that the witnesses to the *kethubah* not be the same as the witnesses to the wedding ceremony.[44] In some circles, however, the same witnesses are used for both.[45]

40. *Evven HaEzer* 66:13; *Nachalath Shiva* 2:7; *Shulchan HaEzer* 6:9:1.

41. Some say that they should write the word *ed* (עד), meaning "witness" after their name; *Nachalath Shiva* 2:12; *Shulchan HaEzer* 6:9:1; Cf. *Evven HaEzer* 130:11. However, in the Holy Land, Syria, Turkey and Egypt, the Sephardim did not write *ed*; *Kether Shem Tov* 1, p. 596.

42. Cf. *Evven HaEzer* 130:1 in *Hagah*.

43. Maharil 65b; *Teshuvoth Rabbi Yaakov Weil (Mahariv) 113; Terumoth HaDeshen, Pesakim* 229; *Nachalath Shiva* 12:73. Cf. *Teshuvoth Rabbi Meir of Rothenberg* 1003. In many Sephardic communities, the groom would sign *novio* ("bridegroom" in Ladino) after his name; *Kether Shem Tov* 1.

44. *Sefer HaOrah* 2:12; *Machzor Vitri* 469, p. 588; *Teshuvoth Maharam Mintz* 109; Maharil 65b.

45. This is the custom in Jerusalem; *Choshen Yeshuoth* 147:13; *Eduth LeYisrael* 3:5, p. 14, 6:6.

Chapter 16

UNDERSTANDING THE KETHUBAH

We will now discuss the wording of the *kethubah* and its meaning, as well as various details involved in writing it. Since this chapter may be somewhat technical, the reader may wish to skip it on the first reading.

The usual text of the *kethubah* is as follows:[1]

בְּ________ בְּשַׁבָּת, ________ יוֹם (יָמִים) לַחֹדֶשׁ________
שְׁנַת________ לִבְרִיאַת עוֹלָם לְמִנְיָן שֶׁאָנוּ מוֹנִין כַּאן ק״ק (עִיר).
________, אֵיךְ הֶחָתָן ________ בֶּן ________ (הַכֹּהֵן)
אָמַר לָהּ לַהֲדָא בְּתוּלְתָּא ________ בַּת ר׳ ________, הֲוִי לִי לְאִנְתּוּ
כְּדַת מֹשֶׁה וְיִשְׂרָאֵל, וַאֲנָא אֶפְלַח וְאוֹקִיר וְאֵיזוּן וַאֲפַרְנֵס יָתִיכִי (לִיכִי) כְּהִלְכוֹת
גּוּבְרִין יְהוּדָאִין דְּפָלְחִין וּמוֹקְרִין וְזָנִין וּמְפַרְנְסִין לִנְשֵׁיהוֹן בְּקוּשְׁטָא. וְיָהֵבְנָא
לִיכִי מֹהַר בְּתוּלַיְכִי כְּסַף זוּזֵי מָאתָן דְּחָזֵי לִיכִי מִדְּאוֹרַיְתָא, וּמְזוֹנַיְכִי וּכְסוּתַיְכִי
וְסִפּוּקַיְכִי, וּמֵיעַל לְוָתַיְכִי כְּאוֹרַח כָּל אַרְעָא. וּצְבִיאַת מָרַת ________
בְּתוּלְתָּא דָא וַהֲוַת לֵהּ לְאִנְתּוּ, וְדֵין נְדוּנְיָא דְהַנְעֲלַת לֵהּ מִבֵּי אֲבוּהָ בֵּין בִּכְסַף
בֵּין בִּדְהַב בֵּין בְּתַכְשִׁיטִין, בְּמָאנֵי דִלְבוּשָׁא, בְּשִׁמּוּשֵׁי דִירָה וּבְשִׁמּוּשֵׁי דְעַרְסָא,
הַכֹּל. קִבֵּל עָלָיו ר׳ ________ חֲתַן דְּנָן בְּמֵאָה זְקוּקִים כֶּסֶף צָרוּף. וְצָבִי
ר׳ ________ חֲתַן דְּנָן וְהוֹסִיף לָהּ מִן דִּילֵהּ עוֹד מֵאָה זְקוּקִים כֶּסֶף צָרוּף
אֲחֵרִים כְּנֶגְדָּן, סַךְ הַכֹּל מָאתַיִם זְקוּקִים כֶּסֶף צָרוּף. וְכַךְ אָמַר ר׳ ________
חֲתַן דְּנָן, אַחֲרָיוּת שְׁטַר כְּתוּבְּתָא דָא, נְדוּנְיָא דֵן וְתוֹסֶפְתָּא דָא קַבָּלִית עָלַי וְעַל
יָרְתַי בַּתְרָאִי לְהִתְפָּרַע מִכָּל שְׁפַר אֲרַג נִכְסִין וְקִנְיָנִין דְּאִית לִי תְּחוֹת כָּל שְׁמַיָּא,
דִּקְנָאִי וּדְעָתִיד אֲנָא לְמִקְנֵא, נִכְסִין דְּאִית לְהוֹן אַחֲרָיוּת וּדְלֵית לְהוֹן אַחֲרָיוּת,
כֻּלְּהוֹן יְהוֹן אַחֲרָאִין וְעַרְבָאִין לִפְרוֹעַ מִנְּהוֹן שְׁטַר כְּתוּבְּתָא דָא, נְדוּנְיָא דֵן
וְתוֹסֶפְתָּא דָא מִנָּאִי, וַאֲפִילוּ מִן גְּלִימָא דְעַל כַּתְפָּאִי, בְּחַיֵּי וּבָתַר חַיֵּי, מִן יוֹמָא

1. The form that is in general use is found in *Levush* 66:1; *Ezer LeYitzchak* 28; *Kitzur Nachalath Shiva* 10; *HaMadrikh* p. 17f. A slightly different version is found in *Nachalath Shiva* 12 from *Machzor Vitri,* p. 791; Maharil 65b. Other versions are found in Rabbi Yehudah Barceloni, *Sefer HaShetaroth* 36, p. 55; *Yad, Yibum* 4:33; *Teshuvoth Tashbatz* 3:301; *Kether Shem Tov* 42. An explanation of the kethubah is also found in *Teshuvoth Binyamin Ze'ev* 50, and it is obvious that he also had a somewhat different version.

דְנָן וּלְעָלַם. וְאַחֲרָיוּת שְׁטַר כְּתוּבְּתָא דָא, נְדוּנְיָא דֵין וְתוֹסֶפְתָּא דָא, קִבֵּל עָלָיו
ר׳ ______ חֲתַן דְּנָן כְּחוֹמֶר כָּל שְׁטָרֵי כְּתוּבוֹת וְתוֹסֶפְתּוֹת דְּנָהֲגִין בִּבְנוֹת
יִשְׂרָאֵל, הָעֲשׂוּיִן כְּתִקּוּן חֲכָמֵינוּ זִכְרָם לִבְרָכָה, דְּלָא כְּאַסְמַכְתָּא וּדְלָא כְּטוּפְסֵי
דִשְׁטָרֵי. וְקָנִינָא מִן ר׳ ______ בֶּן ______ (הַכֹּהֵן) חֲתַן דְּנָן
לְמָרַת ______ בַּת ר׳ ______ בְּתוּלְתָּא דָא עַל כָּל מַה דִּכְתוּב
וּמְפוֹרָשׁ לְעֵיל בְּמָאנָא דְּכָשֵׁר לְמִקְנֵא בֵיהּ,

וְהַכֹּל שָׁרִיר וְקַיָּם.

נְאוּם ______ בֶּן ______ עֵד.

וּנְאוּם ______ בֶּן ______ עֵד.

On the......day of the week, the......day of the [Hebrew] month of........, the year......after the creation of the world, according to the manner in which we count [dates] here in the community of.........., the bridegroom...........son of.........said to this virgin,..........daughter of..........., "Be my wife according to the law of Moses and Israel. I will work, honor, feed and support you in the custom of Jewish men, who work, honor, feed, and support their wives faithfully. I will give you the settlement (*mohar*) of virgins, two hundred silver zuzim, which is due you according to Torah law, as well as your food, clothing, necessities of life, and conjugal needs, according to the universal custom."

Miss..........agreed, and became his wife. This dowry that she brought from her father's house, whether in silver, gold, jewelry, clothing, home furnishings, or bedding, Mr..........., our bridegroom, accepts as being worth one hundred silver pieces (*zekukim*).

Our bridegroom, Mr..........agreed, and of his own accord, added an additional one hundred silver pieces (*zekukim*) paralleling the above. The entire amount is then two hundred silver pieces (*zekukim*).

Mr..........our bridegroom made this declaration: "The obligation of this marriage contract (*kethubah*), this dowry, and this additional amount, I accept upon myself and upon my heirs after me. It can be paid from the entire best part of the property and possessions that I own under all the heavens, whether I own [this property] already, or will own it in the future. [It includes] both mortgageable property and non-mortgageable property. All of it shall be mortgaged and bound as security to pay this marriage contract, this dowry, and this additional amount. [It can be taken] from me, even from the shirt on my back, during my lifetime, and after my lifetime, from this day and forever."

The obligation of this marriage contract, this dowry, and this additional amount was accepted by Mr.........., our bridegroom, according to all the strictest usage of all marriage contracts and additional amounts that are customary for daughters of Israel, according to the ordinances of our sages, of blessed memory. [It shall] not be a mere speculation or a sample document.

We have made a *kinyan* from Mr..........son of..........our bridegroom, to Miss .... daughter of ...., this virgin, regarding everything written and stated above, with an article that is fit for such a *kinyan*.

And everything is valid and confirmed.

.... son of .... Witness

.... son of .... Witness

The form of the *kethubah* is quite ancient. At least some of its elements date back to the time of Hillel, in the first century b.c.e.[2] Most of the *kethubah* in its present form is found as early as the eighth or ninth centuries c.e.[3] The *kethubah* is written in

2. See *Tosefta, Kethuboth* 4:1. See below, note 23.

3. Various wordings found in current kethuboth are found in Geonic writings;

Aramaic, which was the language used by most Jews around that time, since the main Jewish community was then in Babylon (which is now Iraq).[4]

The *kethubah* begins by stating the day of the week. It begins with the letter *beth* (ב). In this respect, it is just like the Torah itself, since the first word in the Torah is *Bereshith* (בְּרֵאשִׁית , "In the beginning"). This is because the Torah itself was like the *kethubah* between God and Israel.[5]

When the day of the week is mentioned, it is stated in terms of the Sabbath. Thus, Sunday is "the first day after the Sabbath," Monday is "the second day after the Sabbath," and so on. This is in keeping with the commandment, "Remember the Sabbath day to keep it holy" (Exodus 20:8). By counting all the days of the week from the Sabbath, the Sabbath is remembered every day.[6]

It is necessary to have the date on the *kethubah* because it is a legal document.[7] When a wife is widowed or divorced, in theory at least, she can collect her *kethubah* even from real estate that her husband has sold to another party, provided that it was sold *after* the *kethubah* was executed. In order to protect buyers of such real estate, as well as to provide the wife with proof of the *kethubah*'s date, this date must be included.[8]

see *Otzar HaGeonim* 500, p. 201. There are also wordings from the *nakdanim*, quoted in Rabbenu Chananel, *Otzer HaGeonim* 113, p. 54. It was a Geonic custom to write, "portable goods and real estate, during my lifetime and afterwards"; *Halakhoth Gedoloth* 65 end, quoted in *Otzar HaGeonim* 531, p. 210. The wording, "he agreed and added..." is found in *Teshuvoth HaGeonim, Shaarey Tzedek* 16, p. 56a; *Yam Shel Shlomo, Kethuboth* 1:39; *Teshuvoth Rashba* 7:452; *Otzar HaGeonim*, p. 53.

4. The custom of writing a bill of divorce (*get*) in Aramaic is found in *Teshuvoth HaGeonim* (Harkevey) 255, pp. 129, 130; *Otzar HaGeonim, Gittin*, p. 205; *Evven HaEzer* 126:1. See *Gittin* 87b.

5. *Tashbatz* 464. See above, Chapter 15, note 22.

6. *Mekhilta*, Ramban, on Exodus 20:8.

7. For details of how to write dates, see *Evven HaEzer* 126:2 ff.; *Nachalath Shiva* 4—7.

8. *Teshuvoth Tashbatz* 3:301; Binyamin Ze'ev 50.

The *kethubah* begins with the date, since this is the first thing that must be set when a wedding is planned.[9]

It is interesting to note that although the entire *kethubah* is written in Aramaic, the date is written in Hebrew. In particular, the Hebrew word for month, *chodesh* (חֹדֶשׁ), is used. The word *chodesh* is derived from the word *chadash* (חָדָשׁ), meaning "new," and it therefore denotes renewal. Every wedding is seen as the beginning of a new world.[10]

The years are counted from "the creation of the world." It has been the universal custom for at least one thousand years to date all legal documents in this manner.[11] The "creation of the world" here actually refers to the creation of Adam, which took place in 3761 b.c.e., as can be shown from a simple calculation based on the Biblical narrative.[12] Adam also married Eve that year, so in the *kethubah*, we are actually counting from the world's very first marriage.

As further means of identification, the place where the *kethubah* is signed must be included. If the *kethubah* is signed in one place, and the wedding held elsewhere, the place written in the *kethubah* must be the place where the *kethubah* is *signed.*[13]

The names of the bride and groom, as well as their parents, must be written with extreme care.[14] The rabbi must be

9. Other documents, aside from bills of divorce, usually have the date at the end. This is because they may be signed long after they are drawn up. The kethubah, on the other hand, is signed immediately; *Teshuvoth Tashbatz* 3:301. The kethubah may also begin with the date because the Talmudical tract of *Kethuboth* begins, "A virgin is married on the fourth day of the week (Wednesday)"; *Kethuboth* 2a; Original.

10. Cf. *Levush* 66:2.

11. See *Tosafoth, Gittin* 80b, s.v. *Zo, Avodah Zarah* 10a, s.v. *Safra*; Rosh, *Gittin* 8:9; Ran *Gittin*, Rif 42a; *Yad, Gittin* 1:27; *Evven HaEzer* 127:10; *Choshen Mishpat* 43:2.

12. See Ran, *Rosh HaShanah,* Rif 3a, s.v. *BeRosh*. Also see *Teshuvoth Tashbatz* 3:301.

13. See *Gittin* 80a; *Bava Bathra* 172a; *Evven HaEzer* 128:1, Binyamin Ze'ev 50. Also see *Choshen Mishpat* 43:20.

14. *Nachalath Shiva* 12:16.

thoroughly familiar with all the rules of writing Hebrew names.[15] If there is any question about a name, an expert in the field should be consulted.

The Torah specifically speaks of the "dowry of virgins" (Exodus 22:16); therefore, if the bride is a virgin, it is mentioned in the *kethubah*. Under normal circumstances, it is assumed that the bride is a virgin unless there is evidence to the contrary. If it is public knowledge that the bride is not a virgin, then the word "virgin" (*bethulta*, בְּתוּלְתָּא) is omitted.[16]

If the bride is a divorcee, the word *mathrakhta* (מַתְרַכְתָּא), Aramaic for divorcee, is substituted.[17] If she is a widow, the

15. See *Evven HaEzer* 129; *Nachalath Shiva* 46, 47; *Tiv Gittin; Ezer LeYitzchak*. If a person does not have a Jewish name, his English name may be used; *Evven HaEzer* 129:5; *Beth Shmuel* 129:10. The person's father's name must also be used; *Evven HaEzer* 129:9 in *Hagah*. If the father's name is forgotten, one should write, "the son (or daughter) of one whose name has been forgotten"; *Igroth Moshe, Evven HaEzer* 99. If one does not know the identity of one's father, "son of *ploni*" can be written; *Levush* 66:2. Alternatively, the father's name can be omitted completely; *Evven HaEzer* 129:9. If one's father is a gentile, one may use one's mother's name; *Degel Marvavah* 129:9; *Pith'chey Teshuvah* 129:23; *Beth David, Evven HaEzer* 40; *Yad Aaron* 66:39; *Igroth Moshe* 2:22. A convert writes his name, "son of Avraham Avinu, or Abraham our father"; (see note 19 below) *Evven HaEzer* 129:20.

If the person is a *cohen* or Levite, it is indicated after his name; *Evven HaEzer* 129:7 in *Hagah*; see 129:19.

16. *Nachalath Shiva* 12:15:3; *Ezer LeYitzchak* 28; *Kitzur Nachalath Shiva* 10. Some authorities say that the word *it'tha* (אִיתְתָא), meaning "woman," should be substituted for "virgin"; *Nachalath Shiva* 12:15:3. Others use the word *kaltha* (כַּלְתָא) meaning "bride"; *Teshuvoth Tashbatz* 3:301; *Chupath Chathanim*. Still others use the word *arusah* (אֲרוּסָה), meaning "betrothed"; *Beth Meir*. Others say that the word *beulta* (בְּעוּלְתָא), should be explicitly used; *Levush* 66:2; *Chelkath Mechokak* 66:41.

If a woman was taken captive, some say that this should be indicated in the kethubah, and that the word *shvuyata* (שְׁבוּיְתָא) should replace *bethulta; Yad, Yibum* 4:34; *Teshuvoth Maharam Mintz* 109; *Nachalath Shiva* 12:15:5.

17. *Yad, Yibum* 4:34; Binyamin Ze'ev 50; *Evven HaEzer* 66:11 in *Hagah; Nachalath Shiva* 12:15:1. Also see *Teshuvoth Tashbatz* 2:183; *Teshuvoth Chatham Sofer, Evven HaEzer* 130; *Pith'chey Teshuvah* 66:8.

The word *mathrakhta* is Aramaic for divorcee; see *Targum* on Leviticus

Aramaic word for widow, *armalta* (אַרְמַלְתָּא) is used.[18] If she is a convert to Judaism, the word *geyurta* (גִּיוֹרְתָּא), meaning proselyte, is used.[19]

The *kethubah* states that the groom said to the bride, "Be my wife...." along with all the particulars. It is to this statement that the witnesses attest.[20] In other legal documents, it is stated explicitly that the contract is the declaration of the witnesses signing it, but not in the *kethubah*.[21] Nevertheless, the *kethubah* is seen as the words of the witnesses, not those of the groom or the rabbi. The witnesses are the ones who make the *kethubah* a legally valid document.

The groom's declaration begins, "Be my wife[22] according to the law of Moses and Israel."[23] This is an ancient wording, dating at least back to the first century b.c.e.[24]

The "law of Moses" refers to laws actually derived from the Torah itself. The "law of Israel" refers to later legislation and custom.[25] This same wording is found in the formula that the

21:14, 22:13, Numbers 33:10. It is taken from the root *tarakh* (תָּרַךְ) meaning to banish; see *Targum* on Genesis 3:24, Exodus 11:1.

18. *Machzor Vitri*, p. 791; *Yad, Yibum* 4:34; Binyamin Ze'ev 50; *Nachalath Shiva* 12:5:1.

19. *Teshuvoth Radbaz* 1:180; *Pith'chey Teshuvah* 66:8. Her name is written, followed by, "daughter of Abraham our father"; *Evven HaEzer* 129:20.

20. One source has in the kethubah the explicit statement, "We bear witness that the groom said..." Binyamin Ze'ev 50.

21. Since it is understood; *Hagahoth Maimonioth* 4:33 #5; *Teshuvoth Tashbatz* 3:301; *Nachalath Shiva* 12:1. See *Sanhedrin* 32a.

22. See *Bava Metzia* 104a. The wording *havi li le-into* is found in *Targum* on Genesis 20:12; *Nachalath Shiva* 12:17. The kethubah does not use the wording *hithkadshi li* (marry me) because the witnesses are not testifying to the actual marriage; Binyamin Ze'ev 50. As discussed earlier, the witnesses to the kethubah are not the same as those to the marriage; above, Chapter 15, note 44.

23. *Tosefta, Kethuboth* 4:9. See *Yerushalmi, Kethuboth* 4:8, 29a; *Yerushalmi, Yevamoth* 15:3, 78a.

24. *Ibid.* Also see Tobit 7:14, especially in Kahanah.

25. *Sefer HaIttur*, quoted in *Nachalath Shiva* 12:18.

groom says when he places the ring on the bride's finger, "Behold, you are consecrated to me with this ring according to the law of Moses and Israel."[26]

The wording implies that the groom takes upon himself all the legal responsibilities of a Jewish husband, "according to the law of Moses and Israel."[27] At the same time, it also implies that, in order to be able to collect on her *ḳethubah*, the bride must follow all the laws applying to a married woman.[28] The groom is declaring that he is taking the bride as his legal wife, according to all usage and law, and not as a mere common law wife.[29]

The husband continues his declaration, "I will work, honor, feed and support you." This implies that, if necessary, the man will go to work to feed and support his wife.[30] It also implies that he will do the types of work around the house that it is customary for a man to do.[31] Some authorities state that "work" also includes the husband's conjugal responsibilities.[32]

He also promises to honor her. It is taught that a husband must honor his wife like his own body, and that this brings blessing to the home.[33]

He pledges to provide his wife with food. As we shall see, this is a requirement spelled out in the Torah itself.[34] The other

26. *Nachalath Shiva* 12:18.

27. *Teshuvoth Tashbatz* 3:301.

28. Binyamin Ze'ev 50; from *Kethuboth* 72a; *Teshuvoth Maharam Mintz* 109; *Nachalath Shiva* 12:18. Also see *Matteh Moshe* 3:1:7.

29. *Nachalath Shiva* 12:18. A common-law wife (*pilegesh*) does not have a kethubah; see above, Chapter 15, note 29.

30. *Tosafoth, Kethuboth* 63a, s.v. *BeOmer; Evven HaEzer* 70:3 in *Hagah; Chelkath Mechokak* 70:12; *Beth Shmuel* 70:8.

31. *Tosafoth Ibid.*, quoting Rabbenu Tam. See *Teshuvoth Tashbatz* 3:301.

32. *Nachalath Shiva* 12:19:2. See *Sotah* 36b; Rashi on Genesis 39:11.

33. *Yevamoth* 62a; Binyamin Ze'ev 50. It also implies that the husband will give his wife her food and other needs with honor; *Nachalath Shiva* 12:19:2.

34. Binjamin Ze'ev 50. A man must feed and support his wife; *Kethuboth* 63a.

"support" (*parnasah*) mentioned in the *kethubah* denotes clothing and other household needs.[35]

He promises that he will not fall short of the general custom in all these respects, stating that he will do all these things "in the custom of Jewish men."[36] He stresses that he will do so "faithfully" or "in truth" (*be-emeth*, בֶּאֱמֶת). What he does for his wife is meant to help set up the bond of faith and trust that is the hallmark of the Jewish marriage.[37]

He then states that he will give her the "settlement of virgins." This is the *mohar* mentioned in the Torah (Exodus 22:16), which consists of 200 zuzim. The term *mohar* applies only to a virgin. Therefore, if it is a second marriage for the bride, the term *mohar* is not used; the term "money" (*kesef*, כֶּסֶף) is substituted. Furthermore, the amount is then 100 zuzim rather than 200 zuzim.[38]

In the case of a divorcee, the term used here is, "the money of your divorced status, 100 zuzim that is due to you according to rabbinical law" (כֶּסֶף מְתָרְכוּתַיְכִי זוּזֵי מֵאָה דְחָזֵי לֵיכִי מִדְרַבָּנָן). For a widow, the term "your widowhood" (אַרְמְלוּתַיְכִי) is substituted. In other cases, such as for a proselyte, the wording is simply, "cash, 100 zuzim, that is due to you according to rabbinical law" (כֶּסֶף זוּזֵי מֵאָה דְחָזֵי לֵיכִי מִדְרַבָּנָן).[39]

35. This includes clothing; Binyamin Ze'ev 50; see Rashi, *Kethuboth* 48a, s.v. *Mefarnsin; Evven HaEzer* 114:12; *Choshen Mishpat* 60:3 in *Hagah*; HaGra, *Choshen Mishpat* 60:22; *Nachalath Shiva* 12:19:1. Some authorities say that it includes jewelry and cosmetics; see Rashi, *Kethuboth* 57a, s.v. *LeFarnes*. It also includes other needs; *Teshuvoth Tashbatz* 3:301; Cf. *Kethuboth* 64b; *Levush* 66:4.

The wording *yathikhi lekhi* (יָתִיכִי לִיכִי) is found in *Targum* on Genesis 30:20; *Teshuvoth Tashbatz* 3:301. Other authorities only write *lekhi; Nachalath Shiva* 12:22.

36. The wording is found in *Targum* on Exodus 21:9; Binjamin Ze'ev 50; *Teshuvoth Tashbatz* 3:301.

37. As it is written, "I will betroth you to Me in truth" (Hosea 2:21); Bienyamin Ze'ev 50; *Nachalath Shiva* 12:26.

38. *Levush* 66:6; *Nachalath Shiva* 12:29.

39. *Levush* 66:5; *Nachalath Shiva* 12:29.

The "settlement of virgins" is defined in the Torah as being 50 shekels (Deuteronomy 22:29).[40] Since there are four zuzim to a shekel, the shekels comes out to 200 zuzim.[41] A shekel is around 0.8 oz. of silver, or approximately the weight of a silver dollar. Therefore, when the United States was on the silver standard, the 200 zuzim was around $50.[42] With the current price of silver, it is closer to $300.

In the *kethubah*, the groom declares to the bride that this money "is due to you according to Torah law."[43] This seems to imply that the *kethubah* was a Torah law.[44] However, as we have seen, the majority of authorities maintain that the *kethubah* is not required by Torah law, but merely by rabbinical legislation. Some say that the expression here indicates that the coinage must be of unadulterated silver, as are all payments required by Torah law.[45] Others say that the wording indicates that the husband accepts his obligation to pay the *kethubah* as if it were Torah law.[46]

The *kethubah* also obligates the husband to provide his wife with food, clothing, other necessities,[47] and conjugal rights.[48]

40. See *Kethuboth* 29b; Rashi on Exodus 22:16.

41. *Midrash Sekhel Tov*, Hirsch, on Exodus 22:16. See *Targum* on 1 Samuel 9:8; *Bekhoroth* 50b.

42. *Eduth LeYisrael* (Henkin), p. 142. See *Nachalath Shiva* 12:31. Also see *Evven HaEzer* 66:6; *Chelkath Mechokak* 66:23; *Beth Shmuel* 66:14.

43. This was originally the custom primarily in the Holy Land; *Sefer HaMakhria* 42; *Otzar HaGeonim, Kethuboth*, p. 38.

44. *Ibid*.; Rabbenu Tam, *Tosafoth, Kethuboth* 10a, s.v. *Amar; Nachalath Shiva* 12:32; *Teshuvoth Tashbatz* 3:301. See above, Chapter 15, note 8.

45. Rosh, *Kethuboth* 1:19; *Evven HaEzer* 66:6; *Tosafoth Yom Tov, Kethuboth* 1:2. Cf. *Yerushalmi, Kethuboth* 1:2; HaGra, *Evven HaEzer* 66:17. Also see *Bekhoroth* 49b; *Bava Kama* 90b; Rashi, *Kethuboth* 65b. The common zuz was one-eighth of a Tyrrian zuz; *Evven HaEzer* 66:6 in *Hagah*. This was because the silver was alloyed with seven parts of copper; Rambam on *Bekhoroth* 8:7.

46. Meiri on *Kethuboth* 10a; *Sefer HaIttur*, p. 30a.

47. This includes such items as bedding; *Kethuboth* 64b; Binyamin Ze'ev 50;

These are obligations that the Torah itself imposes upon every Jewish husband, as it is written, "[The husband] may not diminish [his wife's] food, clothing, or conjugal rights" (Exodus 21:10).[49] Actually, it is not necessary to include these items in the *kethubah*, since even without a contract, the husband has this obligation. However, they are included in order to emphasize the husband's obligation.[50]

Having concluded the groom's initial declaration, the *kethubah* continues by saying that the bride has agreed to become his wife. The *kethubah* includes this, since no woman can marry without giving her consent.[51]

For the first time now, the bride is addressed as "Miss" (*marath* מָרַת). Since she has agreed to marry, she is addressed with a title of respect.[52] Similarly, now that the groom has agreed to his marital obligations, he is addressed as "Mr." (*mar,* מַר) and as "our bridegroom."[53]

The *kethubah* then goes on to speak about the dowry that

also, money for laundry; *Yad, Ishuth* 12:10; *Nachalath Shiva* 12:33; and all the other things a husband must give to his wife.

48. Literally, "coming to you," as in Genesis 38:18, see *Targum ad loc*; Binyamin Ze'ev 50. After this the words, "like the way of the world" are added; see *Targum* on Genesis 19:31; *Teshuvoth Tashbatz* 3:301; *Teshuvoth Maharam Mintz* 109; *Nachalath Shiva* 12:34.

49. *Yad, Ishuth* 12:2; *Kethuboth* 47b; *Evven HaEzer* 69:1. Other authorities, however, maintain that clothing is required only by rabbinical legislation; Ramban on Exodus 21:10; *Maggid Mishneh, Yad, Ishuth* 12:1. See *Chelkath Mechokak* 69:3; *Beth Shmuel* 69:1; *Nachalath Shiva* 12:19:2.

50. *Teshuvoth Tashbatz* 3:301; *Nachalath Shiva* 12:19:3.

51. See *Yevamoth* 110a; Binyamin Ze'ev 50; *Teshuvoth Tashbatz* 3:301. *Tzaviath* denotes agreement; see Daniel 4:14, 4:22, 4:29, 4:32, 5:19, 6:18, 7:19. Although the kethubah is written before the marriage ceremony, the expression "she became his wife" is not considered false, since the process has already begun by the time the kethubah is written; *Levush* 66:10.

52. *Teshuvoth Maharam Mintz* 109: *Levush* 66:3, 7; *Nachalath Shiva* 12:16, 12:35; *Yad Aaron* 66:34.

53. *Teshuvoth Maharam Mintz* 109, quoting Saadia Gaon; *Nachalath Shiva* 12:14.

the bride brings from her parents' house. This dowry consists of everything that the bride brings into the marriage. In Aramaic the dowry is known as the *nedunya* (נְדוּנְיָא)[54] while in Hebrew it is called *nadan* (נָדָן).[55]

According to Jewish law, although the husband has the right to use the dowry, he remains responsible to his wife for its full monetary value. Therefore, if the marriage is dissolved by death or divorce, the full original value of the dowry must revert to the woman, provided that the husband has accepted responsibility for it.[56]

The *kethubah* specifies that this dowry can consist of silver or gold articles. It can also consist of clothing, jewelry, household utensils and bedding. All these articles are mentioned explicitly to show that the bride is not coming into the marriage empty-handed.[57]

54. *Yad, Ishuth* 16:1; *Evven HaEzer* in *Hagah* 66:7, 66:11; *Tur* 66. See *Bava Metzia* 74b; *Kethuboth* 54a; *Taanith* 24a; Binyamin Ze'ev 50; *Teshuvoth Tashbatz* 3:301. This wording is found in *Geonica*, p. 77; *Otzar HaGeonim, Kethuboth* 500, p. 201.

55. See Ezekiel 16:33, Radak *ad loc; Midrash Sekhel Tov* on Genesis 16:14; *Teshuvoth Maharik* 73; *Terumath HaDeshen* 300; *Teshuvoth Rama* 89; *Teshuvoth Nodah BeYehudah, Evven HaEzer* 14; *Teshuvoth Chavath Yair* 197.

56. Rashi, *Yevamoth* 66a, s.v. *Hikhnisa*, 101a, s.v. *Nikhnesey; Yad, Ishuth* 16:1; *Maggid Mishneh, Lechem Mishneh, ad loc.*

If the husband accepts such responsibility for these items they become known as *tzon barzel* (צאן בַּרְזֶל), literally, "iron sheep." Then, even if these items are lost, the husband has full monetary responsibility for them. Like iron, the responsibility is never destroyed; Rashi, *Kethuboth* 101a, s.v. *Tzon; Teshuvoth Tashbatz* 3:301; Binyamin Ze'ev 50. The word *barzel* may be an acrostic for Bilhah, Rachel, Zilpah, Leah, the four wives of Jacob, whose dowry was demanded back by Laban (Genesis 31:43); original. See *Bava Metzia* 5:6; *Bekhoroth* 2:4.

If the husband does not accept such responsibility, his wife's possessions are known as *nikhsey melog* (נִכְסֵי מְלוֹג), literally, "pluckable possessions"; see *Arukh* s.v. *Malag; Yerushalmi, Yevamoth* 7:1; *Bereshith Rabbah* 45:1; *Teshuvoth Tashbatz* 3:301. Alternatively, the word *melog* is related to the Greek word *logos* meaning "word," and *nikhsey melog* denotes "verbal assets"; *Mussaf HaArukh*. If such property is lost, the loss is the wife's.

57. *Nachalath Shiva* 12:49:3, 12:52.

The *kethubah* assumes a usual situation where the bride is coming from her "father's house." If her father is deceased, then the expression *mi-bey nesha* (מִבֵּי נְשָׁא)[58] is substituted. This means "from her family's house,"[59] or "from the house that she is forgetting."[60] Some authorities maintain that if a girl has been on her own, she can write that she is bringing the dowry "from herself" (*mi-de-nafshey,* מִדְנַפְשֵׁה).[61]

No matter how much the dowry is worth, even if the girl does not have any dowry whatever, the groom accepts it for a fixed sum. There is a custom over a thousand years old for the groom to accept the dowry for a fixed amount, determined by custom, and usually more than the dowry is actually worth. A poorer girl is thus not embarrassed at her wedding.[62]

The standard amount set in the *kethubah* is one hundred silver pieces for a virgin, and fifty if it is a second marriage for the woman. The silver pieces are known as *zekukim* (זְקוּקִין).[63]

58. *Tosafoth, Shabbath* 23b, s.v. *DeBey; Evven HaEzer* 66:11 in *Hagah; Levush* 66:8; *Nachalath Shiva* 12:41. However, if "her father's house" is written in the kethubah, it is still valid; *Evven HaEzer loc. cit.*; see *Yoreh Deah* 216:4 in *Hagah.*

59. This also denotes her father's house; see *Yevamoth* 35b. Also see *Bava Bathra* 12b; *Shabbath* 23b, 156a; Binyamin Ze'ev 50.

60. Bachya on Genesis 42:51; *Mussaf HaArukh* s.v. *Nasha; Nachalath Shiva* 12:41.

61. *Teshuvoth Tashbatz* 3:301, *Chupath Chathanim* 5. In the case of a second marriage for the wife, some authorities omit the phrase "father's house" completely, and simply write, "that she brought". *Nachalath Shiva* 12:41. The same is true in the case of a foundling; *Ibid.; Levush* 66:8. If the bride is given away by someone other than her father, his name may be substituted for "father"; *Teshuvoth Tashbatz* 3:301; *Chupath Chathanim* 5.

62. See *Otzar HaGeonim, Kethuboth* 500, p. 211; *Tur, Evven HaEzer* 66; *Perishah* 66:26; *Sefer HaAgudah* 67. It was possibly a mere formality; *Evven HaEzer* 93:1 in *Hagah; Nachalath Shiva* 12:52; *Teshuvoth Ritzba* on *Maimoni* 6.

63. The *zakuk* was a pure silver coin used in medieval times; see Mordechai, *Kethuboth* 237, 306, *Bava Kama* 125; *Sefer Chassidim* 764, 765; *Sefer HaTerumoth* 46:5. It could be as much as a year's wage; Mordechai, *Bava Metzia* 305. In Poland, it was calculated as being four zuzim, or one shekel; see *Derishah* 66:4. In Lithuania, however, it was calculated as being 1.56 shekel; *Nachalath Shiva* 12:49:2. See *Beth Shmuel* 66:15. Also see next note.

The *zakuk* was a large coin weighing as much as five silver dollars. Therefore, the total of one hundred zekukim was around 500 silver dollars.[64] With the current price of silver (around $8 an ounce), this comes to around $4000. Thus, no matter how much a girl brings into the marriage, the groom obligates himself to pay her back this amount.

The bridegroom also adds to the *kethubah* an equal amount of one hundred zekukim on his own. This is in addition to the 200 zuzim that he is required to give by law. This additional amount is known as the *tosefta* (תּוֹסֶפְתָּא).[65] The groom gives it as a sign of his love and respect for his bride.[66] He also does so to show that he is generous to his bride, and is bringing into the marriage as much as she is.[67]

The *kethubah* thus consists of three elements. First, there is the *mohar*, which is required by law, consisting of 50 shekels or 200 zuzim (around $300). Then there is the dowry (*nedunya* or *nadan*) which the bride brings into the marriage, and which the groom accepts upon himself to pay her back. Third, there is the "additional amount" (*tosefta*), which the groom adds to his obligation on his own.[68] The last two are each 100 zekukim

64. *Eduth LeYisrael* (Henkin), p. 143, based on HaGra, *Evven HaEzer* 66:22. This is also discussed at length in HaGra, *Yoreh Deah* 305:4. There, he writes that a zakuk is 15 sela, which is 1.875 shekel. For further discussion, see *Teshuvoth Rivash* 66; *Teshuvoth Maharil* 76; *Chazon Ish, Evven HaEzer* 66.

65. *Kethuboth* 64b, *Tosafoth ad loc.* s.v. *Af Al Pi; Evven HaEzer* 66:7, 68:9. The kethubah must be in writing primarily because of the *tosefta*; otherwise, the legislation would be enough to guarantee that the woman would receive her basic kethubah; *Tosafoth, Bava Metzia* 17a, s.v. *HaTo'an*; Mordechai, *Bava Metzia* 253; *Teshuvoth Maharik* 114; *Nachalath Shiva* 12:65.

It is the custom to have the same amount for all marriages, no matter what the financial status of the couple; *Teshuvoth HaGeonim* (Harkevey) 210, p. 97; *Otzar HaGeonim, Kethuboth* 161, p. 51.

66. *Nachalath Shiva* 12:49:3.

67. *Nachalath Shiva* 12:52.

68. See *Tosafoth, Bava Bathra* 49b, s.v. *Hakhi Garsini; Derishah* 66:4; *Chelkath Mechokak* 66:31; *Nachalath Shiva* 12:49:3.

(around $3000), making the total *kethubah* around $6300.[69]

If it is the second marriage for the wife, all these amounts are halved.[70]

The bridegroom then makes a declaration accepting responsibility for these three obligations. This declaration is directed to the witnesses, so they can legally sign the *kethubah*.[71]

He then states that he accepts the obligation of the *kethubah*. This indicates that he accepts it as a debt in every manner.[72]

The wife collects the *kethubah* if the marriage is dissolved by divorce or by the death of the husband. The man therefore states that he accepts the obligation upon himself – if he divorces his wife – and upon his heirs – if he dies.[73]

The groom pledges the best[74] and most desirable[75] portions of his property to her. Actually, the Talmud teaches that it was legislated that a woman would only be able to collect her *kethubah* from the worst portion of her husband's real property. This was so that men would not refrain from marrying out of fear of losing their best land.[76]

69. However, some authorities maintain that the main kethubah is also included in the 200 zekukin; *Derishah* 77:4; *Beth Shmuel* 66:15.

70. *Nachalath Shiva* 12:47.

71. *Teshuvoth Tashbatz* 3:301. This would indicate that the groom must be the one to tell the witnesses to sign, not the rabbi. In general, witnesses may not sign a legal document until the maker tells them to; see *Bava Bathra* 40a; *Choshen Mishpat* 39:2. However, since the groom has made a kinyan in the presence of the witnesses, he need not tell them explicitly; *Choshen Mishpat* 39:3.

72. *Teshuvoth Tashbatz* 3:301; *Chupath Chathanim*.

73. *Yad, Ishuth* 16:3; *Evven HaEzer* 93:1. See below, note 88.

74. *Teshuvoth Tashbatz* 3:301; Binyamin Ze'ev 50.

75. The expression *shafar arag* is found in *Targum Yonathan* on Genesis 45:18, Psalms 45:14. The word *arag* (ארג) comes from the root *ragag* (רגג), meaning desirable. See *Targum* on Genesis 2:9, 3:6. The word *ethrog* comes from the same root; Ramban on Leviticus 23:40; *Nachalath Shiva* 12:55.

76. *Gittin* 48b; *Evven HaEzer* 100:2.

The clause in the *kethubah* pledging the man's best property is meant to override the Talmudic legislation, giving the wife the right to collect from her husband's best property. Although there is legislation to the contrary, in monetary matters, the two parties have the power to make an agreement to go beyond the letter of the law.[77] Furthermore, since he writes explicitly in the *kethubah* that this is binding on his heirs, they are also bound by this condition.[78]

The *kethubah* speaks of property already owned as well as that which will be owned in the future. Actually, there is a rule that a person cannot sell something that he does not yet have.[79] This rule, however, does not affect obligations: it is therefore possible for a person to obligate himself with regard to property that he does not yet own, but will own in the future.[80]

The *kethubah* speaks of mortgageable property and non-mortgageable property. According to Torah law, only real estate (*karka*) is mortgageable. Thus, if a person mortgages real estate as security for a debt, then even if he sells the property to a third party, the lender can seize the property from the third party (the buyer) if there are no other assets from which the debt can be collected. On the other hand, portable goods (*metaltelin*) are not mortgageable, and if they are sold, a creditor has no lien on them.[81]

There is also another reason that non-mortgageable property is mentioned in the *kethubah*. According to Talmudic law, when a man dies, his debts can only be collected from real

77. Mordechai, *Kethuboth* 312; *Teshuvoth Tashbatz* 3:301; *Bayith Chadash* 66 (98b); *Beth Shmuel 55:14, 100:11; Nachalath Shiva* 12:50:2.

78. See *Choshen Mishpat* 108:18; *Ba'er Hetiv, Evven HaEzer* 100:8.

79. *Bava Metzia* 33b; *Bava Bathra* 63a.

80. Binyamin Ze'ev 50. See *Kethuboth* 80b; *Nachalath Shiva* 12:57.

81. *Kiddushin* 1:5, 26a, Rashi *ad loc*; Binyamin Ze'ev 50; *Nachalath Shiva* 12:58; *Sefer Meirath Eynayim (Sema), Choshen Mishpat* 60:3, quoting *Arukh*, s.v. *Achar*. The word *acharayoth* (responsibility) denotes land; see *Targum* on Ezekiel 23:25. This wording in the kethubah comes from the *nakdanim*; see Rabbenu Chananel in *Otzar HaGeonim* 113, p. 54. Also see *Halakhoth Gedoloth*, quoted in *Otzar HaGeonim, Kethuboth* 531, p. 210.

estate that he left to his heirs, not from portable property.[82] In 784 c.e., however, the Geonim (post-Talmudic leaders) decreed that debts should be collectable even from portable property left to the heirs.[83] This same decree also enables a widow to collect her *kethubah* even from portable property that her husband left to his heirs.[84] Nevertheless, it is customary to state this explicitly in the *kethubah*, so as to give her claim legal weight, even without the Geonic decree.[85]

The groom pledges to pay the *kethubah*, "even from the shirt on my back." This is a formula that was often used in Talmudic times.[86] Of course, this does not mean that he may literally be stripped naked to pay the *kethubah*, but that, if he has extra clothing, it may be taken to pay the debt.[87]

He pledges that he will be obligated for the *kethubah* both during his lifetime and after. As before, he is obligating himself during his lifetime if the marriage is terminated by divorce, and later, if it is terminated by his death.[88]

The declaration ends with the words, "from this day and forever." This is a Talmudic expression, indicating that the

82. *Kethuboth* 95b; *Yad, Malveh VeLoveh* 11:9; *Choshen Mishpat* 107:1. See *Kethuboth* 51a, 69b.

83. This decree was made by Rav Hunah mar HaLevi, son of Rav Yitzchak in the year 1096 of *Shetaroth*, which is 4544 after creation, or 784 c.e.; *Iggereth Rav Sherira Gaon*, p. 105; *Otzar HaGeonim*, p. 210; Rif, *Kethuboth* 30b; Mordechai 313; *Tosafoth, Kethuboth* 51a, s.v. *MiMikarkai, Yad, Malveh VeLoveh* 11:11; *Choshen Mishpat* 107:5. This decree was sealed by the head of the academy and the *Rosh Galutha*; Rosh, *Kiddushin* 3:14.

84. *Ibid.; Yad, Ishuth* 16:8, *Malveh VeLoveh* 11:11.

85. See *Yad, Ishuth* 16:8; *Malveh VeLoveh* 11:11.

86. See *Bava Kama* 11b; *Bava Bathra* 157a. Also see *Choshen Mishpat* 111:1.

87. *Choshen Mishpat* 97:28. See *Bava Metzia* 113b; *Tosafoth, Bava Metzia* 114a, s.v. *Mahu*. Some authorities, however, take this expression literally; see *Teshuvoth Tashbatz* 3:301; Rabbenu Tam, *Sefer HaYashar* 602.

88. See above, note 73. Also see Binjamin Ze'ev 50; *Nachalath Shiva* 12:63. This wording is found in *Halakhoth Gedoloth*, quoted in *Otzar HaGeonim, Kethuboth* 531, p. 210.

obligation begins from the time the document is signed. Although it is not necessary, it is the custom to include this wording.[89]

The *kethubah* then states that the bridegroom accepts the contract according to the "strictest usage." This indicates that the bridegroom accepts upon himself all the special rules through which the *kethubah* can be collected, no matter how strict they will be toward him.[90]

The *kethubah* states explicitly that it is not a speculation nor a sample document. This is a Talmudic formula.[91]

It is important the he declare that the *kethubah* is not a mere speculation. The world for speculation here is *asmakhta* (אסמכתא), which is like a gamble and would not obligate him. He cannot say that he consented to the *kethubah* thinking that it would never be collected, and therefore, it was merely a speculation. Rather, he must accept it as a full obligation.[92]

He also declares that this *kethubah* was not written as a sample document (*tofsey di-shtarey*, טופסי דשטרי). Then he cannot argue that he only allowed his name to be placed on the *kethubah* so that it could be used as a sample to show others.[93]

The *kethubah* states that a kinyan has been made. This has been discussed at length in the previous chapter. The scribe may write this in even before the kinyan is made.[94] In printed *kethuboth*, however, it is best not to fill it in until after the kinyan.[95]

The kinyan is a type of barter (*chalipin*, חליפין). Therefore, as the *kethubah* states explicitly, it must be made with an article

89. See *Gittin* 85b, Rashi *ad loc.* s.v. *De Mashma*; Binyamin Ze'ev 50.

90. *Teshuvoth Tashbatz* 3:301; *Chupath Chathanim.*

91. *Bava Bathra* 44b.

92. *Teshuvoth Tashbatz* 3:301; Binjamin Ze'ev 50; *Nachalath Shiva* 12:68. See *Choshen Mishpat* 112:1.

93. *Teshuvoth Tashbatz* 3:301; Binyamin Ze'ev 50.

94. *Teshuvoth Tashbatz* 3:301; *Chupath Chathanim.*

95. *Taamey HaMinhagim*, p. 410. See above, note 51.

that can be used for such a transaction. Specifically, the article used for a kinyan cannot consist of coinage or food.[96] Rather, an article of clothing, a handkerchief, a napkin, a scarf, or the like are ordinarily used.

The *kethubah* ends with the expression, "And everything is valid and confirmed" (*ve'ha-kol sharir ve'kayam*, והכל שריר וקים). This is a Talmudic formula that is usually put at the end of all legal documents.[97] These words indicate that it is the end of the document, so that nothing can be added after the document is signed.[98]

The witnesses sign after the kinyan is made. When they sign the *kethubah*, it becomes like their testimony, and the document is then valid.

96. *Teshuvoth Tashbatz* 3:301; Binyamin Ze'ev 50; *Sefer HaAgudah, Bava Metzia* 63.

97. *Bava Bathra* 160b; *Teshuvoth Tashbatz* 3:301.

98. *Choshen Mishpat* 44:5,9. See Rashbam, *Bava Bathra* 162a, s.v. *Amar; Tosafoth, Ibid.* s.v. *LePhi.*

Chapter 17

PREPARING FOR THE CEREMONY

After the *kethubah* has been executed and signed, it is a custom to recite the Afternoon (Mincha) Service.[1] In many circles, the Service is said before the bride is veiled, so that there will not be any interruption between the veiling and the wedding ceremony.[2] In some circles, however, it is customary not to recite the Mincha Service until after the bride is veiled.[3]

In any case, unless the wedding is in the morning, the Mincha Service should be recited before the ceremony.[4] It is a custom to hold the Mincha Service in the same place as the wedding, usually in the room where the groom's reception is being held.[5]

One reason for this custom may be that Adam was created in the afternoon, during the time of the Afternoon Service. Indeed, it is taught that the first prayer ever uttered was the Mincha Service.[6] Since Eve was brought to Adam just after he was created, it comes out that he recited the Mincha Service before he was married. This custom exists to this very day.[7]

As discussed earlier, it is customary for the bride and groom to recite the Yom Kippur confession at this Service.[8]

1. *Chupath Chathanim; Eduth LeYisrael* 8:3.

2. Rabbi Yaakov Jofen, private communication. The veiling is considered to be chupah, and therefore should be held before the ceremony with minimal interruption.

3. *Shulchan HaEzer* 7:1:9; *Minhagey Mattersdorf* 110. The original custom was to have the veiling in the morning, when it would automatically be before Mincha; Maharil 64b; *Teshuvoth Maharam Mintz* 109.

4. *Orach Chaim* 232:2.

5. Abudarham, p. 361: *Shulchan HaEzer* 7:1:8.

6. Rabbi Chaim Yosef David Azzulai (Chida), *Midbar Kademuth, Tav* 4.

7. Original.

8. See above, Chapter 12, note 27. According to most authorities, Tachanun is

One of the important preparations for the ceremony is the veiling of the bride. In Yiddish, this is known as *bedekung*.[9] This custom is found in sources at least six hundred years old.[10] It may also have roots in the Talmud.[11]

The band strikes up a lively tune. In many circles, it is the song *VaYehi BiYeshurun*:[12]

וַיְהִי בִישֻׁרוּן מֶלֶךְ בְּהִתְאַסֵּף רָאשֵׁי עָם יַחַד שִׁבְטֵי יִשְׂרָאֵל:
עוֹד יִשָּׁמַע בְּעָרֵי יְהוּדָה וּבְחוּצוֹת יְרוּשָׁלַיִם קוֹל שָׂשׂוֹן וְקוֹל שִׂמְחָה קוֹל חָתָן וְקוֹל כַּלָּה:

And it was when there was a King in Jeshurun that all the people were gathered together – all the tribes of Israel together (Deuteronomy 33:5). There shall once again be heard in the cities of Judah and the outskirts of Jerusalem, a sound of joy, a sound of gladness, a sound of the bridegroom, a sound of the bride.

The bridegroom is accompanied by his parents, the rabbi, the other dignitaries, and the guests to the place where the bride is sitting. In many circles, the groom's friends dance before him in a lively manner as he is led to the bride's hall.

Some authorities maintain that bringing the groom to meet the bride at this time is the main concept of "bringing in the

not said at this service; *Ba'er Hetiv, Orach Chaim* 131:14; *Shaarey Teshuvah* 131:14; *Birkey Yosef* 131:5; *Mishneh Berurah* 131:26.

9. *Likutey Maharich* 3:130a; *Eduth LeYisrael* 8:4. Others call it *badekunish; Sefer HaMinhagim* (Lubatvitch), p. 76.

10. Maharil 64b; *Tashbatz* 463.

11. See below, notes 15, 21.

12. *Betrothed Forever*, p. 13. The Lubavitcher custom is to sing the Alter Rebbe's Niggun; *Sefer HaMinhagim*, p. 76.

bride" (*hakhnasath kallah*, הכנסת כלה). This is considered an important mitzvah.[13]

The groom approaches the bride, and places the veil over her face. In some circles, he is assisted by the rabbi and the parents.[14]

The custom of veiling the bride at the wedding appears to be mentioned in the Talmud.[15] Some say that it is a sign of modesty. The bride is the center of attention at the ceremony; she covers her face so that no one other than her husband will gaze at her beauty. On this day, her beauty is for her husband alone.[16]

Some say that another reason the groom covers the bride's face is to indicate that he is not primarily interested in her physical beauty. Beauty is something that will fade in time, but if the groom is also attracted to the girl's spiritual qualities, he is attached to something that she will never lose.[17]

The custom that the bride covers her face when she approaches her groom has biblical antecedents. Just before Rebecca met Isaac, the Torah says, "She took a veil and covered herself" (Genesis 24:65).[18] This is a sign of modesty that brides keep to this very day.[19] Moreover, Isaac's marriage to Rebecca marked the beginning of the Jewish people. The bride emulates Rebecca in the hope that she will be equally worthy in her marriage.

13. *Derishah* 65:1. See *Turey Zahav, Yoreh Deah* 342.

14. *Eduth LeYisrael* 8:4. See *Kitzur Shulchan Arukh* 147:3. Also see *Arukh HaShulchan, Evven HaEzer* 55:24, 64:17.

15. *Kethuboth* 17b, Rashi *ad loc.* s.v. *K'ritha*. Some say that the Talmudic word *hinuma* comes from the Greek *ynem*, denoting a veil; *Mussaf HaArukh*. See *Mataamim* 51. It is also taught that the curtain hung in front of the Tabernacle (*Mishkan*) like a bride's veil; Rashi on Exodus 26:9.

16. *Likutey Maharich; VaYaged Moshe* p. 17, from *Sukkah* 49b. See *Sichoth HaRan* 86; *Mataamim* 53. Also see below, note 19.

17. *Mataamim* 55.

18. Maharil 64b; *Teshuvoth Maharam Mintz* 109; *Tashbatz* 463.

19. Ralbag, *Chizzkuni, ad loc.*

Some authorities maintain that the veiling also has legal ramifications. There are two parts to the wedding ceremony, the betrothal (*erusin*), and the actual marriage (*nesu'in*). *Nesu'in* consists of the bride and groom setting up house together. The process through which *nesu'in* takes place is known as *chupah*.[20]

According to these authorities, *chupah* consists of the groom placing the veil on the bride.[21] The Talmud thus speaks of the husband "placing his garment" on the bride as an integral part of the marriage process.[22] Similarly, when Ruth wanted Boaz to marry her, she asked him to place his garment over her (Ruth 3:9).[23]

This is because one of the things that a husband must provide for his wife is clothing.[24] In placing the veil over her face, the groom is symbolically doing one of the things that he must do as a husband. This, in itself, is an act of setting up a household together. Hence, according to this opinion, it constitutes *chupah*.[25]

According to this opinion, the one to place the veil over the bride must be the bridegroom himself.[26] However, in many

20. See below, Chapter 18.

21. *Tosafoth, Yoma* 13b s.v. *LeChada; Evven HaEzer* 55:1 in *Hagah; Chelkath Mechokak* 55:9; *Tashbatz* 463; Abudarham p. 357; *Mataamim* 50. Although the veiling is done before the kiddushin, it is the beginning of nesuin; *Arukh HaShulchan, Evven HaEzer* 55:10. Furthermore, some authorities maintain that chupah need not be after kiddushin; see below, Chapter 18, note 47.

22. *Kiddushin* 18b; see Rashash *ad loc* According to this, it would appear that the veil should belong to the groom.

23. See Rashi, Ibn Ezra, *Dena Pishra, ad loc.* Also see Ezekiel 16:8, Radak, *Metzudoth, ad loc*; Abudarham, p. 357.

24. Exodus 21:10. See above, Chapter 16, note 49. Of the three things mentioned in the Torah, only clothing is explicit; the other two are merely alluded to.

25. Original. See *Choter Yishai* on Ruth 9:3; Malbim *Ibid.*

26. *Bayith Chadash* 61, s.v. *HaIsh.* Some say that if someone other than the groom veils the bride, the groom should make him his agent; *Degel*

circles, the custom is that the rabbi or the parents veil the bride.[27]

Some circles have the custom of covering the bride's face with a totally opaque veil, so that she can neither see nor be seen. This is, particularly, a Chassidic custom.[28]

Some authorities maintain that this is so that the bride cannot see the ring. When she is married, she accepts anything that her husband gives her on faith.[29]

There is also a Kabbalistic reason for this. The bride represents the nation of Israel, which is described as "the beautiful girl who has no eyes."[30] Israel follows God with utter, blind faith, not questioning anything. So does the bride show that she has such utter faith in her husband that she is willing to walk blindly into the marriage.[31]

Nevertheless, other authorities maintain that the groom and witnesses should be able to see the bride at the time of the ceremony. They therefore recommend that the veil either be somewhat transparent, or be lifted so that the bride can be seen briefly.[32]

After the veiling, it is customary to bless the bride with the blessing that was first given to Rebecca:

אֲחֹתֵנוּ, אַתְּ הֲיִי לְאַלְפֵי רְבָבָה. וַיִּירַשׁ זַרְעֵךְ אֶת שַׁעַר שׂוֹנְאָיו יְשִׂימֵךְ אֱלֹהִים כְּשָׂרָה, רִבְקָה, רָחֵל וְלֵאָה.

Marvavah, Yoreh Deah 342. It would also appear that witnesses are required; see below, Chapter 18, note.

27. See *Turey Zahav* 65:2; *Shulchan HaEzer* 9:1:3. Other sources also do not mention the groom; *Kitzur Shulchan Arukh* 147:3.

28. See *Betrothed Forever,* p. 17.

29. *Teshuvoth Rashba* 1186, quoted in *Evven HaEzer* 31:2 in *Hagah; Derishah* 31:1; *Beth Yosef* 31, p. 57b; *Eduth LeYisrael* 9:7.

30. *Sichoth HaRan* 86; *Zohar* 2:95a; *Netzutzey Oroth ad loc; Pri Etz Chaim, Shaar K'riath Sh'ma,* end of Chapter 24. See *Likutey Moharan* 62:5.

31. *Mataamim* 54.

32. *Otzar Kol Minhagey Yeshurun* 16:7; *Kether Shem Tov* 30; *Shulchan HaEzer* 8:1.

> Our sister, may you become thousands of myriads. May your descendants inherit the gates of your foes (Genesis 24:60). May God make you like Sarah, Rebecca, Rachel and Leah.

The blessing given to the first Jewish bride is repeated for all her descendants.[33]

It is a custom from Talmudic times for a groom to wear white. In modern times, in most circles, the groom wears a white robe known as a *kittel*.[35] The *kittel* is a simple white robe, without pockets, made of linen or cotton. In some circles, it is customary for the groom to wear a light coat over the *kittel*.[36]

The most obvious reason for the white garment is that white symbolizes purity. As we have discussed, on their wedding day, the bride and groom are forgiven all their sins. As a sign of this spiritual purity, it is customary for them both to wear white. White is a symbol of purity, as it is written, "If your sins are like scarlet, they shall be as white as snow" (Isaiah 1:18).[37]

When a person is immersed in sin, he is like a slave. The only truly free being is God. A person's sins separate him from God. Now, when the bride and groom are forgiven their sins, they are truly free. They therefore wear white garments, which are a sign of freedom.[38]

33. *Kitzur Shulchan Arukh* 147:3; *Likutey Maharich* 3:130a; *Shulchan HaEzer* 7:1:6.

34. *Shabbath* 114a. See Maharsha *ad loc*; HaGra, *Yoreh Deah* 352:1. From the above sources, however, it also appears that shrouds were white to remind the corpse of the bridegroom.

35. *Kitzur Shulchan Arukh* 147:4; *Sichoth HaRan* 86; *Shulchan HaEzer* 7:1:10; *Eduth LeYisrael* 8:5; *Likutey Maharich* 3:131b, *Sefer HaMinhagim* (Lubavitch), p. 76. See *Moed Katan* 27b. *Kittel* is German for a robe or long shirt.

36. Possibly because there was a self-imposed decree that Jews not wear white garments on the outside; see *Takanoth Vaad Arba HaAratzoth* 179, 188; quoted in *Otzar Yisrael*, s.v. *Beged* (2:301).

37. *Matteh Moshe* 3; *Taamey HaMinhagim* 957; *Mataamim* 86. See above, Chapter 12, note 11.

38. *Shulchan HaEzer* 7:1:10, quoting *Mataamim*. See *Magen Avraham* 472:5.

Beyond that, now that the bride and groom are free of sin, they must be even more careful to keep themselves pure. It is written, "At all times let your clothes be white" (Ecclesiastes 9:8), which means that a person must keep himself free of sin at all times. On this day of their wedding, when the bride and groom are making a new commitment to each other, they also make a new commitment to God. This commitment is symbolized by the white garments that they wear.[39]

The white kittel that the groom wears is also meant to remind him of the white shrouds that he will wear when he dies.[40] On the simplest level, even on this happiest day of his life, he must remember that he is mortal.[41] When a person recalls his own mortality, it keeps him from sin.[42] Thus, although the bridegroom is rejoicing, he should not forget his reverence and awe of God, as it is written, "Serve God in awe; rejoice with trembling" (Psalms 2:11).[43]

The idea of remembering one's day of death is not merely negative. It also has the connotation that marriage is meant to last until the day of death.[44] The bride and groom wear white on the day of their wedding, and they will once again wear white when they are buried. Between that time, their bond of love will always remain strong. Regarding such love, it is written, "Love is as strong as death" (Song of Songs 8:6).

There is also another important relationship between death and marriage. We see this juxtaposition in the Torah. After commanding Adam not to eat from the Tree of Knowledge, God told him, "On the day you eat it, you will have to die" (Genesis

39. *Kol Bo* 75, p. 44c; *Mataamim* 85; *Taamey HaMinhagim* 957.

40. *Sichoth HaRan* 86; *Siddur Rabbi Yaakov Emden, Beth Yaakov*, p. 124b. See *Orach Chaim* 610:4 in *Hagah*.

41. Thus, when Rav Hamnuna was asked to say something at a wedding he said, "Woe to us, for we are mortal", *Berakhoth* 31a.

42. See *Berakhoth* 5a.

43. *Teshuvoth Radbaz* 1:693. See *Berakhoth* 30b. White is also worn in memory of the Temple; Maharil; *Teshuvoth Maharam Mintz* 109.

44. *Teshuvoth Maharam Shick, Evven HaEzer* 88; *Ezer LeYitzchak* 17:6.

2:17). Immediately afterward, God said, "It is not good for man to be alone, I will make him a helper who is his counterpart" (Genesis 2:18). Once death came to the world, marriage also had to exist to perpetuate the species. As soon as there was the possibility that man would die, he had to have a mate. Therefore, the joy of a wedding is tempered by the realization that the need for marriage came about as a result of man's mortality.[45]

This also explains the custom that the groom does not put on the kittel himself, but has it put on by his attendants or parents. Just as the dead do not dress themselves, so the groom does not dress himself.[46]

The groom also wears white because white is the color of royalty, and the groom is like a king.[47] And, just as a king is dressed by his attendants, so is the groom.[48]

The Talmud mentions the custom of placing ashes on the groom's head in memory of the destruction of the Jerusalem Temple (*Beth HaMikdash*).[49] In many circles, this custom is kept to this day.[50] Some have the custom to wipe the ashes off immediately,[51] while others leave them on during the ceremony.[52] In some circles, however, the custom of placing ashes on the groom's head is no longer kept.[53]

45. *Likutey Maharich* 3:131a, from *Berakhoth* 31a; *Shnei Luchoth HaBrith, Pinchas; Derekh HaChaim.*

46. *Mataamim* 137; *Taamey HaMinhagim* 958, quoting Yaavatz.

47. *Yalkut Yitzchak* 552:19. See *Pirkey Rabbi Eliezer* 16 end.

48. *Mataamim* 136; *Yalkut Yitzchak* 552:18.

49. *Bava Bathra* 60b. Some sources also indicate that it was placed on the bride's head; *Midrash Tehillim* 121:3.

50. *Yad, Taanith* 5:13; *Orach Chaim* 560:2; *Evven HaEzer* 65:3; *Shulchan HaEzer* 7:1:11; *Eduth LeYisrael* 8:5; *Siddur Rabbi Yaakov Emden.*

51. *Arukh HaShulchan* 65:5.

52. *Shulchan HaEzer* 7:1.11.

53. Some say that the ashes are to be placed in the place of tefillin; therefore, if people are not careful with regard to tefillin, the ashes should not be used;

It is a custom for the groom's father to bless him before the wedding ceremony.[54] The bride is blessed in a similar manner by her parents.[55] We learn this from God Himself. Before God married Adam and Eve, the Torah states, "God blessed them saying: Be fruitful and multiply..." (Genesis 1:28). Just as the first bride and groom were blessed, so are every bride and groom today.[56]

The custom is for the father to place his hand on the groom's head while blessing him.[57] He then says:[58]

יְשִׂמְךָ אֱלֹהִים כְּאֶפְרַיִם וְכִמְנַשֶּׁה:

May God make you like Ephraim and Manasseh (Genesis 48:20).

This is the traditional blessing to children.[59] He then recites the priestly blessing:

יְבָרֶכְךָ יְיָ וְיִשְׁמְרֶךָ: יָאֵר יְיָ פָּנָיו אֵלֶיךָ וִיחֻנֶּךָּ: יִשָּׂא יְיָ פָּנָיו אֵלֶיךָ וְיָשֵׂם לְךָ שָׁלוֹם:

May God bless you and keep you. May God make His face

Kol Bo, quoted in *Beth Yosef* 65; *Perishah* 65:7. Some Sephardim had the custom of placing olive leaves, which are bitter, on the groom's head as a crown; *Tur, Evven HaEzer* 65.

54. *Kitzur Shulchan Arukh* 147:4; *Siddur Beth Yaakov* 124b; *Shulchan HaEzer* 7:1:12; *Eduth LeYisrael* 8:6.

55. *Shulchan HaEzer* 7:1:12.

56. *Tanya Rabathai* 91; *Taamey HaMinhagim* 956. See below, Chapter 21, note 42; Chapter 22, note 55.

57. Most sources indicate that only one hand is used; *Maaver Yaavak* 3:43; quoted in *Ketzeh HaMatteh* on *Matteh Ephraim* 619:7; *Devash LePhi, Beth* 9; *Peleh Yo'etz*, s.v. *Berakhoth* (Tel Aviv, no date), p. 30. Other sources, however, indicate that both hands are used, just as they are when the *cohen*-priests recite their blessing; *Siddur Beth Yaakov* 150a #7.

58. *Maaver Yaavak* 3:43; *Siddur Beth Yaakov* 150a #7.

59. Rashi *ad loc.* See *Tanya Rabathai* 95.

shine on you and be gracious to you. May God lift His countenance upon you and grant you peace (Numbers 6:24 — 26).

Some also add the verse:[60]

וְנָחָה עָלָיו רוּחַ יְיָ רוּחַ חָכְמָה וּבִינָה רוּחַ עֵצָה וּגְבוּרָה רוּחַ דַּעַת וְיִרְאַת יְיָ׃

May God's spirit rest on him, a spirit of wisdom and understanding, a spirit of counsel and might, a spirit of knowledge and the fear of God (Isaiah 11:2).

Beyond this, the parents may add any blessing or prayer that they desire.[61] The parents should pray that the marriage be a happy one.[62]

60. *Maaver Yaavak* 3:43.

61. *Matteh Ephraim* 619:2.

62. *Kitzur Shulchan Arukh* 147:4; *Siddur Beth Yaakov* 124b.

Chapter 18

THE MARRIAGE CANOPY

After the preliminaries, the groom and bride are led to the marriage canopy for the ceremony. In Hebrew, the marriage canopy is known as the *chupah* (חֻפָּה).[1] Usually, the chupah consists of a cloth held up by four poles. In order to understand its significance, however, one must understand the structure of a wedding.

The Jewish wedding ceremony actually consists of two parts. First there is betrothal, or *erusin* (אֵרוּסִין), and then there is marriage, or *nesuin* (נְשׂוּאִין). These two ceremonies were originally held as much as a year apart, but it later became the custom to hold them together.

Although *erusin* is usually translated as betrothal, there is actually no English equivalent for the word.[2] Erusin is like an engagement, in that it does not permit the couple to live together or to share marital intimacy. On the other hand, as soon as erusin is completed, the woman has the full status of a married woman,[3] and the man also has the status of a married

1. Some maintain that the word chupah is derived from the root *chafah* (חפה), meaning to cover or hide; see 2 Samuel 15:30, Jeremiah 14:3, Esther 6:12, 2 Chronicles 3:5; *Tashbatz* 463; *Sefer HaKaneh* 91a.

   Other authorities maintain that it comes from the root *chafaf* (חפף), meaning to protect, as in Deuteronomy 33:12; Rashi on Isaiah 4:5; Radak, *Sherashim*; Ibn Janach; *Kol Bo* 75, 44c; Abudarham, p. 357; *Sefer HaTishbi; Arukh HaShulchan* 55:15.

   The word chupah itself denotes a canopy; see *Bava Bathra* 75a. The Targum on Joel 2:16, Psalms 19:6, renders it as *genuna* (גְנוּנָא) from the root *ganan* (גנן) meaning to protect. In Ladino, it is known as *talamo*, which denotes a bridal canopy in Spanish; see *Kether Shem Tov* note 733; Cf. *Sefer HaIttur* 2:2, 63a.

2. See Hirsch on Exodus 22:15. Neither erusin nor chupah exists for a gentile; *Sanhedrin* 57a; *Yad, Ishuth* 1:1, *Melakhim* 9:7; Abudarham, pp. 358, 369; Ritva, *Kethuboth* 7b, s.v. *BeBirkath*. See *Yerushalmi, Kiddushin* 1:1, *Sanhedrin* 1:1; *Bereshith Rabbah* 18:5, from Genesis 20:3.

3. *Yad, Ishuth* 1:3; *Arukh HaShulchan* 55:1. Once a woman is an arusah, she

man.[4] If the couple wish to break the union after erusin, a Jewish bill of divorce (*get,* גֵט) is required.[5] If anything, the penalties for adultery with a woman after erusin are more serious than for adultery with a married woman.[6]

The rite of erusin is completed when the groom places the ring on the bride's finger. As we have discussed, it can be accomplished by his giving her anything of value and declaring her to be his bride, and her accepting it. This rite is also known as *kiddushin* (קִדּוּשִׁין), which means sanctification.[7]

The word erusin is a Biblical term.[8] The Torah speaks of a man, "who has completed erusin with a woman, but has not taken her as a wife" (Deuteronomy 20:7). From this, it is obvious that erusin and marriage are two different processes.

The word erusin comes from the verb *aras* (אָרַס). This is closely related to the word *asar* (אָסַר), meaning to bind. Erusin thus has the power to bind a couple to each other, even though they are not considered completely married.[9] The word *aras* also means "to speak," indicating that the woman is already spoken for.[10]

may no longer contract a marriage with another man, and any such marriage would be null and void; *Kiddushin* 10a.

4. Thus, under the *cherem* of Rabbenu Gershom, after erusin, the man cannot take a second wife; *Teshuvoth Maharik* 63; *Ba'er Hetiv, Evven HaEzer* 1:21; *Teshuvoth Chakham Tzvi* 124; *Teshuvoth Maimonioth* 34; *Teshuvoth Maharil* 101. Other authorities, however, maintain that it is permitted; *Evven HaEzer* 10:1; Cf. *Teshuvoth Maharik* 101:3; *Shevuth Yaakov* 2:112; *Ibid., Choshen Mishpat* 52; *Teshuvoth Mabit* 2:209; *Teshuvoth Rashdam* 78. See below, note 11.

5. *Yad, Ishuth* 1:3.

6. See Deuteronomy 22:23. The penalty for adultery with an arusah is *sekilah,* while for a nesuah it is *chenek.*

7. See above, Chapter 6.

8. See Exodus 22:15, Deuteronomy 20:7, 22:28, 28:30, 2 Samuel 3:14, Hosea 2:21, 22. Also see *Kethuboth* 48b, *Sanhedrin* 66b, from Deuteronomy 22:23; Rashba on *Kethuboth* 7b.

9. See Shlomo Mandelkern, *Concordance.* It was like a covenant (*brith*); Ezekiel 16:8, Malachi 2:14, Proverbs 2:17.

10. See Psalms 21:3. "Speaking for" denotes marriage; see Song of Songs 8:8;

Individually, erusin has the power to give the bride the status of a married woman and the groom the status of a married man.[11] Nevertheless, as a pair, they do not have the status of a married couple. At this time, they are forbidden to each other physically, like any other unmarried couple.[12]

Mandelkern, *Concordance*. The root *aras* also has the connotation of a monetary transaction, as in the word *aris* (אריס), a tenant farmer; Mandelkern, *Concordance*; Yosef (Julio) Fuerst, *Concordance* (Leipzig, 1840). It also has the connotation of inheritance and possession; see Deuteronomy 33:4; *Pesachim* 49b.

11. Under some conditions, such as when she has no other family, he must even support her; *Yad, Ishuth* 19:15; *Evven HaEzer* 55:4. See above, note 4.

12. It was forbidden by rabbinical legislation; *Yad, Ishuth* 10:1; *Evven HaEzer* 55:1. The penalty for cohabitation was *makkoth marduth; Yerushalmi, Pesachim* 10:1, 68b; *Yad, Ishuth* 10:1; Riv, *Pesachim* 16a; Rosh, *Pesachim* 3:7; *Tanya Rabathai* 89. It would also render a person unfit to be a witness; *Sefer Meirath Eynayim (Sema)* 34:4; *Shoshanah HaAmakim* 5a.

Some say that this prohibition was part of the legislation forbidding seclusion (yichud) with an unmarried woman; Rashi, *Kethuboth* 7b, s.v. *VeAsar; Evven HaEzer* 55:1. She is also forbidden because the blessings have not yet been pronounced; Rashi, *Kethuboth* 7b, s.v. *VeAsar; Or Zarua, K'riath Sh'ma* 25; *Kesef Mishneh, Ishuth* 10:1; *Kol Bo* 75. See below, note 26. The Prenuptial Blessing also states explicitly, "who has forbidden arusoth to us"; *Kethuboth* 7b; *Kesef Mishneh, Ishuth* 10:1.

Even those authorities who maintain that premarital intercourse is forbidden by Torah law, hold that an arusah is forbidden to her betrothed only by rabbinical law; Rashba, *Kethuboth* 7b.

Some authorities maintain that a child born to an arusah is a mamzer; *Yevamoth* 69b, *Kiddushin* 75a; see *Yad, Issurey Biyah* 15:17; *Evven HaEzer* 4:27; Hai Gaon, quoted in *Shitah Yeshanah, Shitah Mekubetzeth, Kethuboth* 7b; *Otzar HaGeonim, Kethuboth*, p. 24.

Some derive tne prohibition for an arusah with her betrothed from the verse, "a virgin arusah" (Deuteronomy 22:23). This would indicate that as long as a girl is an arusah, she must remain a virgin, and not have the marriage consummated; Abudarham, p. 357, quoting Rabbi Avraham ben Yitzchak Av Beth Din, author of the *Sefer HaEshkol.*

Other sources derive the prohibition from the verse, "He shall join to his wife" (Genesis 2:24) — "to his wife," and not to his arusah; *Midrash Lekach Tov ad loc; Siddur Rabbi Shlomo of Garmiza* (Jerusalem, 1972), p. 249; Raavan, *Kethuboth* 7b; *Sefer HaIttur* 2:1, 62b.

Similarly, they are still two separate economic units; he does not have any obligation to support her,[13] and he does not have any claim to her property.[14]

The Torah actually spells this out in a way. It says that when a man marries a woman, "he may not diminish her food, clothing or conjugal rights" (Exodus 21:10). This teaches that as long as the husband does not have any obligations regarding conjugal relations, he also does not have any obligations regarding food or clothing.[15]

The second stage in contracting a marriage is known as *nesuin* (נִשׂוּאִין).[16] This is derived from the verb *nasa* (נָשָׂא), meaning to lift or take.[17] *Nasa* is also a Biblical term for marriage, indicating that the man is taking the woman as a wife.[18]

Until nesuin, the bride's allegiance is primarily toward her own family. After nesuin, it is primarily toward her husband.[19] Although husband and wife are bound to each other with erusin, they do not become related to each other as family until the nesuin.[20]

13. *Evven HaEzer* 55:2.

14. *Evven HaEzer* 55:5; *Kiddushin* 10a; *Yevamoth* 29b, 43b; *Kethuboth* 53a, 89b; *Bava Metzia* 18a; *Sanhedrin* 28a; *Yerushalmi, Kethuboth* 7:4, 28b.

15. *Levush* 54:4; *Perishah* 55:2. See Chapter 16, note 49.

16. *Levush* 54:1; *Arukh HaShulchan* 55:12.

17. See Genesis 27:3, 45:19.

18. Judges 21:23, Ruth 1:3,4, Ezra 9:1,2, Nehemiah 23:25.

19. Thus, when a woman is an arusah, her father must also annul her vows, but as a nesuah, only her husband can do so; *Kiddushin* 10a; *Nedarim* 73b; *Yad, Nedarim* 11:8; *Yoreh Deah* 234:2; Ritva, *Kethuboth* 7b.

20. Thus, if the husband is a *cohen*-priest, he may defile himself for her after nesuin, but not after erusin; see *Kiddushin* 10a; *Yoreh Deah* 373:4; Cf. Rashi, *Bava Metzia* 18a, s.v. *VeLo*, and s.v. *Methah*. Ordinarily, a *cohen* may only defile himself for a relative; see Leviticus 21:2; *Yevamoth* 22b; Rashbam, *Bava Bathra* 109b, s.v. *Sh'ero; Tosafoth Yom Tov, Bava Bathra* 8:1, s.v. *VeHaIsh; Torah Temimah*, Leviticus 21:10.

There are two basic ways of accomplishing nesuin. First, it can be done by consummating the marriage.[21] Second, it can be accomplished by chupah.[22] There is, however, a major dispute among the authorities as to precisely what constitutes chupah.[23]

Although theoretically the nesuin could be sealed by consummation, in practice, this was frowned upon.[24] Nesuin was seen as a holy rite, where people would be invited and the Seven Blessings recited.[25] Without such a ceremony, the marriage would not be complete. The sages thus legislated that "a bride without the blessings is forbidden."[26] According to

21. *Yad, Ishuth* 10:1; *Maggid Mishneh ad loc; Yevamoth* 55b; Rif 18b; Rabbenu Nissim Gaon, quoted in *Tosafoth, Kiddushin* 10a, s.v. *Kol; Or Zarua* 1:650, 90b. See Rabbenu Yerocham 23:2, p. 184b; *Levush* 54:1; *Chelkath Mechokak* 55:5; *Arukh HaShulchan* 55:5. Also see *Evven HaEzer* 33:1 in *Hagah*; HaGra 33:5.

    The *biyah*, however, must be specifically for the sake of nesuin; *Chelkath Mechokak* 55:4; *Beth Shmuel* 55:1,2; HaGra 55:6.

    Although premarital *biyah* is forbidden, for the sake of nesuin it is permitted; Ran, *Kiddushin*, Rif 5b; *Chelkath Mechokak* 55:5; *Beth Shmuel* 55:3.

22. *Yad, Ishuth* 10:1; *Evven HaEzer* 61:1; see *Shitah Yeshanah*, in *Shitah Mekubetzeth, Kethuboth* 7b, from *Kethuboth* 48b.

23. For discussion, see *Evven HaEzer* 55:1 in *Hagah*; *Arukh HaShulchan* 55:4 ff; *Eduth LeYisrael* 4:2; *Nachalath Shiva* 12:8; *Yam Shel Shlomo, Kethuboth* 1:17; *Tosafoth Yom Tov, Kethuboth* 5:3; *Levush* 54:1; *Likutey Maharich* 3:131a.

24. See *Arukh HaShulchan* 55:14. Furthermore, nesuin needs witnesses; see *Tosafoth Ri HaZaken, Kiddushin* 10a; *Arukh HaShulchan* 55:5, 55:14; *Or Same'ach, Ishuth* 10:2; *Beth Mishteh* 5; *Yad Ramah* 52; *Yaalath Chen* 12; *Shulchan HaEzer* 8:8:2, 8:1:20 end. See below, Chapter 23, note 13. There is also a question as to whether nesuin can be conditional; *Or Same'ach, Ishuth* 10:2.

25. *Kethuboth* 7b. See Chapter 22.

26. *Mesekhta Kallah* 1:1; Rashi, *Kethuboth* 7b, s.v. *VeAsar; Beth Yosef* 55; *Kesef Mishneh, Ishuth* 10:1; *Perishah* 55:1; Ritva, *Kethuboth* 7b; *Tosafoth, Kethuboth* 7b, s.v. *Rabbi;* Mordechai, *Kethuboth* 131. Some sources indicate that this is to be taken literally, to mean the blessings; *Gemara, Kallah Rabathai* 1:1. See *Zohar* 2:168b. Some say that the nesuin is not

many authorities, the legislation did not actually involve the blessings themselves; rather, the ceremony of chupah which would generally be accompanied by the blessings.[27]

The word chupah is a Biblical term.[28] We thus find, "Let the bridegroom go forth from his chamber, and the bride from her chupah" (Joel 2:16). The scripture also speaks of a "bridegroom coming out of his chupah" (Psalms 19:6). From these references, it is clear that chupah is associated with marriage.

In general, chupah is an act through which the couple demonstrates clearly and unambiguously that they are husband and wife.[29] Torah law recognizes it as an act that binds the couple together.[30] There is, however, a dispute among

complete without the blessings; *Arukh HaShulchan* 55:19,20. For the reason that the Talmud says that she is forbidden like a niddah, see *Perush HaTefilloth* of Rabbi Yehudah ben Yakar, p. 37.

It is only after nesuin that a woman is forbidden without the blessings; *Teshuvoth Ramban* 284; Abudarham, p. 358.

27. *Terumath HaDeshen, Pesakim* 140; *Teshuvoth HaRosh* 37:1; *Beth Shmuel* 55:1; *Arukh HaShulchan* 55:4.

28. *Sefer HaTishbi*; Rabbi Yitzhak Isaac of Kamarna, *Meirath Eynayim*. See Isaiah 4:5.

29. It is preparation for *biyah; Arukh HaShulchan* 55:17; Cf. *Tosafoth, Yevamoth* 57b, s.v. *Rav*. It is thus taught, "Everyone knows why a bride goes into the chupah"; *Shabbath* 33a; *Arukh HaShulchan* 55:15.

30. Chupah is a *kinyan* (acquisition); *Kiddushin* 5a; *Sefer HaIttur* 2:2, 63a; *Tanya Rabathai* 90; Abudarham, p. 357.

Most authorities maintain that chupah is derived from Torah law; Rashba, Ritva, *Kethuboth* 7b; *Shaar HaMelekh, Ishuth* 10, in *Chupath Chathanim* 5 (Bryn, 1803), p. 53a; *Pith'chey Teshuvah* 61:2. It is derived from the verse, "I have given my daughter to this man" (Deuteronomy 22:16); Rashi, *Kethuboth* 47a, s.v. *Hah; Shaar HaMelekh Ibid.; Sefer HaManhig*, p. 540.

Other authorities maintain that it is rabbinical in origin; *Teshuvoth Mohara ibn Sason* 173, quoted in *Shaar HaMelekh loc. cit.; Kavod Chupah* on *Shaar HaMelekh Ibid.*, p. 54a. One source indicates that the main point of chupah is to publicize the wedding; *Perush HaTefilloth* of Rabbi Yehudah ben Yakar, p. 38. Some say that it is rabbinical legislation from the time of Moses; *Arukh HaShulchan* 55:14.

the early authorities exactly as to how they must demonstrate their status. There are three main opinions.

The first opinion is that chupah alludes to the couple being alone together.[31] In a number of places, the Torah recognizes that for a couple, being alone together is a prelude to intimacy.[32] This is why an unmarried couple is forbidden to be alone together in a place where they would have enough privacy to be intimate.[33] However, once the couple is married, the very fact that the two are together indicates that they are ready for intimacy. This symbolic act is enough to complete the nesuin.

The second opinion is that chupah consists of the husband performing any of his husbandly duties toward his bride. The three basic husbandly obligations spelled out in the Torah are "food, clothing, and conjugal rights" (Exodus 21:10). Therefore, by feeding or clothing the bride, the man attains the status of her husband. As we have seen, this is one reason for veiling the bride, since it is a symbolic act of "clothing" her.[34]

Actually, the husband need not actually provide the bride with a garment. Any garment that brings the two together is sufficient. Therefore, according to this opinion, it was the custom to drape a veil or tapestry over the couple,[35] or hold it

31. That is, yichud; *Tosafoth Ri HaZaken, Kiddushin* 5a, 10a; Ran, *Kethuboth*, Rif 1a s.v. *ShePirsa*, first opinion. See *Rokeach* 363; Rashba, *Kethuboth* 4a; *Tur, Evven HaEzer* 61; *Shaar HaMelekh, Chupath Chathanim* 57c. Some say that it is the main concept of chupah; *Ezer Mekudash* 55.

The Rambam also maintains that chupah is the groom bringing the bride into his house plus yichud; *Yad, Ishuth* 10:1. Without yichud, there is no nesuin; *Yad, Ishuth* 10:6.

One source, however, states that no one holds that chupah is yichud; *Chelkath Mechokak* 55:6.

32. See *Kiddushin* 80a; *Sanhedrin* 21b; *Avodah Zarah* 36b. Cf. *Sotah* 2a. Some say that this is a Torah law; *Tosafoth, Shabbath* 13a, s.v. *Mah; Sefer Mitzvoth Gadol*, Negative Commandment 126; *Beth Shmuel* 22:1.

33. *Avodah Zarah* 36b; *Yad, Issurey Biyah* 22:3.

34. See above, Chapter 17, notes 21 — 25. Also see *Tosafoth Rid, Kiddushin* 3a; *Shiltey Gibborim, Kethuboth* Rif 2b, *Lashon Riaz* s.v. *Ketzad; Kol Bo* 75, 44c. See *Sefer HaIttur* 2:2, 63a.

35. The chupah is therefore seen as a sheet; *Yerushalmi, Sotah* 9:15, 46a;

over their heads.[36] In some communities, it was the custom to drape a tallith over the couple.[37] In any case, it had the connotation of the bride and groom being under a single garment, and thus being part of a single household.

Eating together would also have this connotation. Therefore, some authorities held that eating together also constituted chupah.[38]

The third opinion is that chupah consists of the husband and wife setting up house together.[39] Since as man and wife

Rashi, *Sotah* 49a, s.v. *Zehorith; Tosafoth, Gittin* 7a, s.v. *Ataroth*; HaGra, *Evven HaEzer* 55:9; see *Tosefta, Sotah* 15:19; *Midrash Tehillim* 79:3.

Therefore, some say that chupah is a tapestry draped over the couple; *Teshuvoth HaGeonim* (Assaf) 34 end, quoted in *Otzar HaGeonim, Kethuboth* 66, p. 21; *Sefer HaManhig,* p. 540; *Evven HaEzer* 55:1 in *Hagah; Chelkath Mechokak* 55:7; Abudarham, p. 357; *Arukh HaShulchan* 55:9. In some localities, the *parokheth* was used; *Magen Avraham* 154:13; *Otzar Kol Minhagey Yeshurun* 16:2; see *Pirkey Rabbi Eliezer* 41 (97b).

36. See *Tashbatz* 461; *Rokeach* 353; Maharil; *Kenesseth HaGedolah, Evven HaEzer* 61. This is the Sephardic custom; *Kether Shem Tov* 37.

37. *Otzar HaGeonim, Kethuboth* 66, p. 21; *Sefer HaManhig*, p. 540; *Sefer HaKaneh* 91a; Abudarham, p. 357; *Kol Bo* 75, 44c; *Matteh Moshe* 1; *Taamey HaMinhagim* 963; *Shulchan HaEzer* 7:3:1.

This was a German custom; *Nachalath Shiva* 12:8. It is also a custom in some Sephardic communities; *Ben Ish Chai, Shoftim* 12.

Some say that the groom must say a blessing over the tallith if it is daytime; *Sheyarey Kenesseth HaGedolah, Hagahoth Beth Yosef, Orach Chaim* 8:8; *Halakhoth Ketanoth* 1:22; *Shomer Emeth, Orach Chaim* 19. Others maintain that no blessing is said; *Ginath Veradim, Orach Chaim* 1:25. For discussion see *Shulchan HaEzer* 7:3:1; *Kether Shem Tov* 37, note 733.

38. *Arukh HaShulchan* 55:16. It can also consist of the couple merely being together; *Arukh HaShulchan* 55:15. Sitting together is also sufficient; Cf. *Chelkath Mechokak* 55:7. See *Tosafoth, Sukkah* 25b, s.v. *Ain;* Rosh, *Sukkah* 2:8 *Tur, Evven HaEzer* 62; *Arukh HaShulchan* 55:8.

39. Some say that it must be the groom's house; Ran, *Kethuboth,* Rif la, s.v. *O ShePirsa; Evven HaEzer* 55:1 in *Hagah*; HaGra 55:9; see *Kethuboth* 48b; HaGra 55:6.

Others say that it can be his domain in any sense; Rabbenu Yerocham 23:2, p. 184b; Bertenoro, *Kethuboth* 3:5.

they will be living together, any manner in which they do so symbolically constitutes chupah. As soon as the two are in a single domain, the nesuin is complete, and they are man and wife.[40]

This third opinion is also alluded to in the Torah. The Torah speaks of a wife as being "in the house of her husband" (Numbers 30:11). This indicates that coming together in one house makes the couple man and wife.[41]

The prevalent custom is to follow all three opinions.[42] Therefore, the couple are secluded together; they are under a cloth; and they are placed in a symbolic house. The seclusion (*yichud*) takes place after the ceremony, as we shall discuss in Chapter 23.

Other authorities maintain that it is bringing her into his house, plus yichud; *Yad, Ishuth* 10:1, 10:6; *Teshuvoth HaRosh* 37:1, from *Bava Bathra* 146b; *Beth Sh'muel* 55:4; *Shaar HaMelekh, Ishuth* 10, *Chupath Chathanim* 8, p. 57c; *Arukh HaShulchan* 55:4. Others, however, state that it does not require yichud, but merely the two of them being together; *Arukh HaShulchan* 55:15.

Some authorities maintain that chupah is the bride's father giving her over to the groom's authority; Mordechai, *Kethuboth* 132; *Hagahoth Asheri, Kethuboth* 1:12; *Tanya Rabathai* 90; Rabbi Yisrael Isserlein, *Leket Yosher* on *Orach Chaim* (Berlin, 1903), p. 28; *Arukh HaShulchan* 55:10.

40. Some maintain that any house can be used; *Derishah, Evven HaEzer* 61:1; *Perishah* 61:2. Cf. *Kethuboth* 48b; *Evven HaEzer* 57:1; *Rishon*, quoted in *Shaar Hamelekh, Chupath Chathanim* 8, 57d; *Arukh HaShulchan* 55:12. See *Yerushalmi, Kethuboth* 7:4, 28b; Rashi, *Kiddushin* 10b, s.v. *Zu*. It is seen as a chamber; *Bereshith Rabbah* 28:6. Also see Tobias 7:16, where it is called a bridal chamber.

According to this opinion, even the bride's father's house can be used if he allows the groom to use it; *Turey Zahav, Evven HaEzer* 57:4, 64:1; *Pith'chey Teshuvah* 55:2.

Other authorities maintain that chupah is a house with a special feature or addition specifically for the wedding; *Sefer HaIttur* 2:2, 63a; *Tanya Rabathai* 90; Abudarham, p. 357; *Arukh HaShulchan* 55:7. See *Megillah* 5b; *Taanith* 14b, Rashi *ad loc.* s.v. *Bayith*.

41. Ran, *Kethuboth*, Rif 1a, s.v. *O ShePirsa*.

42. *Bayith Chadash* 61; *Beth Shmuel* 55:5.

The last two opinions involve the marriage canopy that is customarily used at all weddings today. The canopy usually consists of a square piece of velvet or other cloth, held up by four poles. The poles may be held up by four men, or they may be on a frame so that they are self-supporting.

In one sense, the canopy, or chupah, is a symbolic house. It is a single domain into which the groom welcomes the bride.[43] Although other people may be under the chupah, it is still a domain where bride and groom are together, and this completes the nesuin.[44]

The chupah, which consists of a piece of cloth, is also the symbolic garment held over the couple.[45] Although there are many authorities who maintain that the placing of the garment is fulfilled by the veiling of the bride,[46] others hold that chupah must take place after the ring is given.[47] When the bride and groom stand under the cloth chupah, it is equivalent to the groom placing a "garment" over the bride.

Thus, the chupah held up by poles fulfills both functions: It is symbolic both as a house and as a garment.

The practice of using such a chupah is explicitly mentioned

43. *Levush* 54:1; HaGra 55:9; *Ezer Mekudash* 55; *Arukh HaShulchan* 55:18; *Ben Ish Chai, Shoftim* 12.

44. *Rokeach* 353; *Sefer HaManhig*, p. 540.

45. Cf. *Nachalath Shiva* 12:8.

46. See *Chelkath Mechokak* 55:9.

47. Rabbenu Yerocham 22:2, 184b; *Sefer HaMakneh, Kuntres Acharon* 26; *Massah Binyamin* 90; *Pith'chey Teshuvah* 61:1. Cf. *Tosafoth, Yevamoth* 57b, s.v. *Rav*; Rashba *Ibid.*; *Yam Shel Shlomo, Kethuboth* 1:17. Also see *Halakhoth Gedoloth* (Warsaw, 1875), p. 66d; *Or Zarua, K'riath Sh'ma* 25; Meiri, *Kiddushin* 5a.

Other authorities, however, maintain that chupah can take place before kiddushin; Mordechai, *Kethuboth* 132; Ritva, *Kiddushin* 10a, according to *Mishneh LaMelekh* 10:2; *Teshuvoth Radbaz* 1:372; *Chelkath Mechokak* 55:9. The chupah then remains in effect until after the kiddushin; *Shaar HaMelekh, Chupath Chathanim* 8; *Shaar Ephraim* 115; *Tosafoth, Yevamoth* 89b, s.v. *MiSheTigdal*. Also see *Nachalath Shiva* 12:8. See *Perush HaTefilloth* of Rabbi Yehudah ben Yakar, p. 38.

for the first time in the sixteenth century.[48] There are, however, some Talmudic allusions to a chupah being held up with poles.[49]

The chupah is like a house that is open on all four sides. In this sense, it is like Abraham's house, which, according to tradition, had entrances on all four sides.[50] This was a reflection of Abraham's great trait of hospitality, that he would always take in guests and wayfarers. So important was this to Abraham, that on one occasion, he even interrupted a divine theophany to greet possible guests (Genesis 18:2).[51] He had entrances on all four sides of his house, so that a stranger coming from any direction would not have to search for the door.

48. See *Evven HaEzer* 55:1 in *Hagah* (which was first published in 1578). Also see *Levush* 54:1; *Bayith Chadash* 61; *Matteh Moshe* 1; *Turey Zahav, Yoreh Deah* 342:1 s.v. *Acher* (who states that it is not the veiling of the bride); *Turey Zahav, Evven HaEzer* 66:1; *Kitzur Shulchan Arukh* 147:5.
The custom is to use wooden poles; Rabbi Avraham (ben Yosef) Levensohn, *Mekorey Minhagim* 73 (Berlin, 1847); *Arukh HaShulchan* 55:9, 18; *Chokhmath Adam* 129:1.

Originally, only Ashkenazim used poles, not Sephardim; but now many Sephardim also do; *Eduth LeYisrael* 4:10; see *Kether Shem Tov* 37. The Sephardim began using poles in the late nineteenth century; *Ben Ish Chai, Shoftim* 12.

German Jews did not begin using poles until after the seventeenth century; before that it was a custom only in Poland, but not in Germany; *Nachalath Shiva* 12:8.

It is said that the unmarried men holding the poles would be married within the year; *Betrothed Forever*, p. 16. The four poles are said to represent the four corners of the world; *Ibid.* p. 15.

49. It is thus taught that in Betar there was a custom to plant trees when children were born, and then to use them for the chupah poles; *Gittin* 57a, Rashi *ad loc.* s.v. *Ganna*. Also see Rashi, *Sotah* 49b, s.v. *Avel*. Cf. *Bereshith Rabbah* 28:6; *Eikhah Rabbah* 4:14, *Matnath Kehunah ad loc.*

50. *Midrash Tehillim* (Constantinople, 1512) 110; Rabbenu Yonah, Bertenoro, HaGra on *Avoth* 1:5. However other sources indicate that it was Job who had his house open on all sides; *Avoth DeRabbi Nathan* 7:1; Rashi on *Avoth* 1:5.

51. See *Shabbath* 127a, from Genesis 18:3; Cf. Rashi *ad loc.*

In coming under the chupah, the couple begins their life in a "house" resembling that of Abraham, the first Jew. They make a statement that their house will be open to guests and hospitality, just like Abraham's.[52]

The chupah is also reminiscent of the first wedding in the Garden of Eden. It is taught that before God married Adam and Eve, He erected ten canopies for them in the Garden.[53] God then blessed them under the canopies and said, "Be fruitful and multiply" (Genesis 1:28). Today, the cantor blesses the couple under the chupah just as God blessed Adam and Eve.[54]

The chupah also recalls the revelation at Mount Sinai. The revelation at Sinai is seen as the marriage between God and Israel, and many marriage laws and customs are derived from the Sinai experience.[55] It is taught that before giving the Torah to the Israelites God held the mountain over their heads.[56] The mountain over their heads was like the chupah under which the bridal couple stands.[57]

This also explains why the kiddushin (giving the ring) is performed under the wedding canopy, even though by law, kiddushin precedes chupah. The giving of the Torah was like the kiddushin between God and Israel.[58] Just as the Israelites stood under the mountain when they were betrothed to God, the bride stands under the canopy at the time of her kiddushin.[59]

52. *Ezer Mekudash, Evven HaEzer* 55:1.

53. *Bava Bathra* 75a; *Pirkey Rabbi Eliezer* 12, 31a; *Bereshith Rabbah* 18; *VaYikra Rabbah* 20; *Koheleth Rabbah* 8; *Avodath HaKodesh, Chelek HaAvodah* 43 end. See *Zohar* 2:145a.

54. *Pirkey Rabbi Eliezer* 12, 31a; Radal *ad loc.* 12:60. Cf. *Zohar* 3:44b.

55. *Tashbatz* 467; *Sichoth HaRan* 86. See *Sukkah* 49b.

56. *Shabbath* 88a.

57. Rokeach 353; *Matteh Moshe* 1; *Shulchan HaEzer* 7:3:3. Some say that the chupah represents the Clouds of Glory; *Perush HaTefilloth* of Rabbi Yehudah ben Yakar, p. 38.

58. *Taanith* 26b. This was erusin, from Deuteronomy 33:4, *Pesachim* 49b. See Maharsha, *Aggadoth, Kethuboth* 7b on *Birkath Erusin.* See above, Chapter 6, note 16.

59. *Hafla'ah, Kethuvoth* 7b, s.v. *Mekadesh*; *Mataamim HaChadash* 57; *Divrey Yosef.*

There is also another reason that the kiddushin is performed under the canopy. The custom is to have many people at the wedding. The kiddushin, however, is a private ceremony that should be done only in the presence of two witnesses. It was considered in extremely bad taste to perform the kiddushin in public.[60] The kiddushin is therefore held under the canopy, which is like a small private domain where the bridal couple and the witnesses are set apart from the other guests.[61]

There was also another canopy for the wedding between God and Israel. This was the Tabernacle (*Mishkan*) that the Israelites built in the Sinai desert. Like the chupah, it was the "house" where the bride and Groom began their life together. Just as the Tabernacle was made of tapestries on top of poles and beams, so the chupah is made of a tapestry on poles. Since it represents the Tabernacle, the chupah should be as beautiful as possible.[62]

On a deeper level, the chupah represents the divine light that surrounds all creation. Just as the chupah covers the bridal couple, this light surrounds all of God's creation.[63] This is the light of Wisdom which is the root of all existence.[64]

60. See *Yevamoth* 52a; *Kiddushin* 12b.

61. *Sefer HaManhig*, p. 540; *Mataamim* 59. See *Beth Shmuel* 62:1; *Arukh HaShulchan* 62:10. In some places there was a decree that the kiddushin should only be under the chupah; *Teshuvoth Tashbatz* 1:133, quoted in *Pith'chey Teshuvah* 45:3 end; see HaGra 65:11.

Some authorities, however, maintain that the kiddushin should not be under the chupah; *Bayith Chadash* 61, s.v. *HaIsh*. However, this opinion is discounted in practice; *Arukh HaShulchan* 55:20.

62. *Zohar* 2:169a. Also see *Shnei Luchoth HaBrith, Shaar HaOthioth* 1:62b; *Taamey HaMinhagim* 963. Some maintained that according to Kabbalah, a second chupah should be erected for the Shekhinah; *Siddur HaAri* of Rav Asher, p. 149a; *Or HaChaim* in *Or HaLevanah* (of Rabbi Shalom Sharabi, Jerusalem, 1925), p. 100. However, others say that it is not necessary; *Ibid.* in note.

63. Siddur of Rabbi Shneur Zalman of Liadi, p. 131d.

64. This is Chokhmah, the covering of the Merkava; *Sefer HaKaneh* 91a; *Metzudoth David* 125.

Some say that the chupah is Kether, the walls, Chokhmah, and the

Since the chupah is considered a special domain, some say that the cloth should be at the very top of the poles. Two poles and a cloth or string on top legally constitute a doorway (*tzurath ha-pethach*), and a doorway has the same status as a wall.[65] Thus, if the chupah is constructed with the cloth at the very top of the poles, it actually has the legal status of a small private room.[66]

Since the chupah is meant to represent a house, it should preferably be erected outdoors.[67] A house inside another building is not very much of a house. In many communities, it was customary to have the wedding ceremony outdoors in the synagogue courtyard.[68]

There is evidence that even in Biblical times there may have been a custom of holding weddings outdoors. The prophet thus speaks of "the sound of the bridegroom and the sound of the bride" in "the cities of Judah and the *streets* of Jerusalem" (Jeremiah 7:34). This may indicate that the original custom was to have weddings outdoors in the streets.[69]

opening, Binah; *Pardes Rimonim* 23:8. This would indicate that the chupah must have walls. I have seen Rabbi Yekuthiel Yehudah Halberstam, the Klausenberger Rebbe, make sure that the chupah has short "walls" coming down from the top.

Some sources indicate that the four poles of the chupah are Chesed, Gevurah, Netzach and Hod; *Kehilath Yaakov*. It is also taught that the chupah is Binah; *Siddur HaAri* of Rabbi Yaakov Kopel, p. 121b; *Kehilath Yaakov*.

The Ari taught that the chupah is the chamber of Abba (Chokhmah) and Imma (Binah); *Etz Chaim, Shaar MaN U'MaD* 1, p. 224. This seems to reconcile both opinions above. See *Shaarey Gan Eden* 81c. Significantly, the chupah was traditionally erected by the groom's father; *Berakhoth* 25b; *Sanhedrin* 108a; *Bereshith Rabbah* 28:6.

65. *Orach Chaim* 362:11.

66. Rabbi Tzvi Hirsch (ben Yaakov) Kava of Buchach, *Neta Shaashu'im, Azharoth* 2 (Zolkiev, 1829); *Shulchan HaEzer* 7:3:4. See above, note 43.

67. HaGra, *Evven HaEzer* 55:9; *Arukh HaShulchan* 55:18; *Shulchan HaEzer* 7:2:6. The chupah was used instead of a house, so as not to embarrass a groom who did not own property; *Ezer Mekudash* 55.

68. HaGra *loc. cit.*

69. Original. See Radak, *Sherashim*, s.v. *Chutz*. It is possible that people

Another reason that the chupah is erected outdoors is so that the wedding will be under the stars. When God chose Abraham, He promised that his children would be like "the stars of heaven" (Genesis 15:5). Since every Jewish marriage continues this process it is fitting that the marriage be conducted under the stars.[70]

In many circles, there was strong opposition to holding wedding ceremonies in the synagogue sanctuary,[71] but there are many authorities who permit it.[72] In many wedding halls, there is a window or skylight over the place where the chupah stands, so that it is technically "outdoors."[73]

In many Sephardic communities, however, it is customary to hold the wedding ceremony indoors.[74] The Sephardim maintain that the primary purpose of the chupah is to be a garment spread over the couple.[75]

In the case of a second marriage, it is the custom to have the ceremony indoors.[76] Our sages teach that the first Tablets were given to Moses publicly, while the second were given privately.[77] Just as the second Tablets were given privately, so

stopped having weddings outdoors during times of religious persecution; see below, Chapter 19, note 30.

70. *Teshuvoth Maharam Mintz* 109; *Evven HaEzer* 61:1 in *Hagah*, end; *Kitzur Shulchan Arukh* 147:1; *Shulchan HaEzer* 7:2:1; *Otzar Kol Minhagey Yeshurun* 16:6; *Eduth LeYisrael*, p. 26f. It was an ancient custom to have the chupah outdoors; see *Tosafoth, Sukkah* 25b, s.v. *Ain; Darkey Moshe, Yoreh Deah* 391:2.

71. See above, Chapter 5, note 8.

72. *Ibid.* note 9.

73. See *Teshuvoth Pri HaSadeh* 4:97; *Shulchan HaEzer* 7:2:1.

74. *Kenesseth HaGedolah, Hagahoth Beth Yosef* 61:2; *Sedey Chemed, Chathan VeKallah* 2; *Eduth LeYisrael* (Henkin) 45, p. 141.

75. See *Ben Ish Chai, Shoftim* 12; *Kether Shem Tov* 37.

76. *Pith'chey Teshuvah* 62:1; *Sedey Chemed, Chathan VeKallah* 2; *Shulchan HaEzer* 7:2:9.

77. *Tanchuma, Ki Thisa* 31; Rashi on Exodus 34:3.

is a second marriage held privately, indoors.[78]

Any cloth or drape on poles can be used as a chupah. However, the general practice is for all synagogues and wedding halls to have a special chupah that is used.[79] In recent times, it has become the practice of some brides to make their own. I know of one family where a homemade chupah has been used for three generations.

78. *Likutey Maharich* 3:131a.

79. *Shulchan HaEzer* 7:3:1.

Chapter 19

THE PROCESSIONAL

After the bride is veiled, the couple is led to the chupah for the actual ceremony.[1]

It is customary that the groom be led to the chupah first.[2] There are several reasons for this.

The first reason is legalistic. The chupah is seen as the domain of the groom; he must therefore be the first one there to make it his domain. Only then does he welcome his bride into the chupah.[3] It is very much like buying or building a house, and then bringing one's bride into it.[4]

This custom is also rooted in the very first wedding. After Adam and Eve were created, the Torah says that God took Eve, "and brought her to Adam" (Genesis 2:22).

Adam was the first of the two created. Looking at the creation, each subsequent creature involved a higher form of life. Since Eve would have to be able to hold new life (the fetus) in her body, her essence was considered more refined than that

1. *Kitzur Shulchan Arukh* 147:5.

2. Maharil 64b, 65a; *Matteh Moshe* 1. Cf. *Rokeach* 353; *Shulchan HaEzer* 7:4:3; *Eduth LeYisrael* 8:9.

   Some derive this custom from the verse, "I have given my daughter to this man" (Deuteronomy 22:16), which indicates that the bride is brought into the groom's domain; *Zohar* 2:235a.

   Others say that it is because a marriage cannot take place without the woman's consent; she goes to the groom to show that she desires the marriage; *Likutey Maharich* 3:131b.

   In many circles it is the custom for the rabbi, or the rabbi and cantor, to march up the aisle before the groom. There does not, however, appear to be any classical Jewish source for this.

3. See HaGra, *Evven HaEzer* 55:9. See Chapter 18, note 43.

4. It is thus taught that a man should "plant a field, build a house, and then marry"; *Sotah* 44a.

of Adam, and she was created later.[5]

Thus, Adam was the first human in the world; only later did he have Eve brought to him. Adam was thus the first one under the chupah that God had made in the Garden of Eden, and Eve was brought into this chupah. Similarly, today, the groom is the first one under the chupah, and the bride is brought to him.[6]

This was reflected in the wedding between God and Israel. The Torah says, "Moses led the people out of the camp to greet God" (Exodus 19:17). The Midrash teaches that Moses led the Israelites to God, just as a bride is led to the groom. Just as God was the first one at Sinai, so the groom is the first one at the chupah.[7]

In many circles, it is a custom for the groom to undo all the knots in his clothing.[8] The groom is about to be bound to his bride, and at this time, he should not be bound in any other way.[9]

5. See *Berakhoth* 61a; Rashi on Genesis 2:22.

6. *Zohar* 1:49a; *Agra DeParka* 67; *Mataamim* 76; *Mataamim HaChadash* 48; *Shulchan HaEzer* 7:4:3.

7. *Pirkey Rabbi Eliezer* 41; see *Mekhilta* on Exodus 19:17; *Tanchuma, Nasso* 20. *Cf.* Rashi on Deuteronomy 33:4; *Mataamim* 75; *Yalkut Yitzchak* 552:27; *Otzar Kol Minhagey Yeshurun* 16:5.

8. Rabbi Yisrael, the Koznitzer Maggid, *Avodath Yisrael,* on Yom Kippur (Lemberg, 1858), p. 89b; *Otzar Yisrael,* s.v. *Nesuin.* It is also a Lubavitcher custom; *Sefer HaMinhagim,* p. 76.

   It is also a custom in many circles to undo the bride's hair; Maharil 64a; *Taamey HaMinhagim* 948, 949; *Likutey Maharich* 3:130b; *Otzar Kol Minhagey Yeshurun* 16:5; *Shulchan HaEzer* 7:1. This was because God fixed Eve's hair before bringing her to Adam; *Berakhoth* 61b.

9. Original. This is also a sign that the groom will not be "bound" and rendered impotent on his wedding night; *Mataamim* 78; *Shulchan HaEzer* 7:4:2; *Otzar Kol Minhagey Yeshurun* 16:6. See *Targum Yonathan* on Deuteronomy 24:6; *Perush Yonathan ad loc*; *Charedim,* Negative Commandment 5:42; Rabbi Menasheh ben Yisrael, *Nishmath Chaim* 3:18; *Margolioth HaYam, Sanhedrin* 13b, 13 end.

   It is similarly a custom not to have any knots in shrouds; *Rokeach* 316, p. 194; *Maaver Yaavak* 2:6; *Gesher HaChaim* 10:1:5; *Kol Bo al Aveluth,* p. 91.

It is also a custom in many circles for the groom not to have anything in his pockets.[10]

One reason for this is so that the bride will take him as he is — even with empty pockets. This indicates that she accepts him for what he is, and not for his possessions.[11] For much the same reason, it is a custom for a bride not to wear any jewelry under the chupah.[12]

Furthermore, the groom is in the place of Adam when he was first created. Just as Adam did not have any private possessions, neither does the groom.[13]

As we have discussed, one of the reasons that the groom wears a kittel on his wedding day is to recall the day of his death. The kittel is a garment without pockets, indicating that a person takes nothing with him when he leaves this world.[14] Similarly, the groom has nothing in his pockets during the wedding ceremony, to remind him that he will leave the world empty-handed.[15]

It is also taught that, on his wedding day, a bridegroom is like the High Priest (*Cohen Gadol*) going into the Holy of Holies. The Holy of Holies is like the wedding chamber (chupah), and the High Priest is drawing himself into an intimate relationship with God, just as a bridegroom is preparing for an intimate relationship with his bride. Just as the garments of the High Priest do not have any pockets, so the groom goes into the chupah with nothing in his pockets. Just as on Yom Kippur, the High Priest went in with plain white vestments (Leviticus 16:4), so the groom goes in wearing a plain white kittel. Just as the High Priest wore no gold on this day,

10. *Sefer HaMinhagim* (Lubavitch), p. 76; *Betrothed Forever*, p. 18.

11. Original.

12. *Avodath Yisrael* on Yom Kippur, p. 89b; *Taamey HaMinhagim* 951.

13. Original.

14. Psalms 49:18. Shrouds similarly have no pockets; *Gesher HaChaim* 10:1:4.

15. Rabbi Aaron Levin, *Birkath Aaron* (Drovovitz, 1913); quoted in *Eduth LeYisrael* 8:5.

the groom wears no jewelry when he enters the chupah.[16]

It is a custom to instruct the groom to begin the march with his right foot first. In this way, he will start out his marriage "on the right foot." This also indicates that his marriage will be "right."[17]

It is a custom to play music as the bridegroom is led to the chupah. In the Holy Temple in Jerusalem, the Levites would play music as the *cohen*-priests marched to their divine service; in a similar fashion, music is played for the bride and groom when they are led to the chupah.[18]

It is customary for two people to lead the groom to the chupah.[19]

This also has its antecedents in the first wedding in Eden. The Midrash teaches that when Adam married Eve, the two archangels, Michael and Gabriel, accompanied him to the chupah.[20] In a similar manner, today, the groom is accompanied by two attendants.[21]

16. *Avodath Yisrael,* on Yom Kippur, p. 89b; *Taamey HaMinhagim* 951.

17. *Mataamim* 141; *Shulchan HaEzer* 7:4:2; *Otzar Kol Minhagey Yeshurun* 16:2. See *Yoma* 11b; *Menachoth* 34a.

18. Rabbi Chaim Yosef David Azzulai (Chida), *Chomath Anakh, Tzav* 8; *Mataamim HaChadash* 11. The Lubavitch custom is to play the Alter Rebbe's Niggun; *Sefer HaMinhagim*, p. 76. See *Sefer HaOrah* 15; above, Chapter 5, notes 32 — 34.

19. *Yoreh Deah* 391:3 in *Hagah*. See above, Chapter 9, notes 13 — 16. Other sources indicate that many people should accompany the groom, just as a king is accompanied by a large retinue; *Tashbatz* 467; *Mataamim* 140; *Likutey Maharich* 3:131a. God was similarly accompanied by many angels at Sinai; *Mataamim* 139.

    Many sources indicate that both the bride and the groom should be accompanied by a man and a woman. In such a case, the man and woman should be husband and wife, father and daughter, or mother and son, but not two unrelated people; *Chothem Kodesh* 10. The custom also is not to use a childless couple, or one where either party has been married a second time; *Shulchan HaEzer* 7:4:1; *Shaarim Metzuyanim BeHalakhah* 147:9.

20. *Bereshith Rabbah* 8:13.

21. *Matteh Moshe* 2; *Likutey Maharich* 3:131a; *Yalkut Yitzchak* 552:25. See above, Chapter 9, note 18.

Also, when God came to Sinai for His great marriage to Israel, He was accompanied by two attendants. In this case, the two "attendants" were the two Tablets upon which the Ten Commandments were written.[22]

There are varied customs as to who accompanies the groom. In many circles, the groom's father and mother accompany him. Similarly, when the bride walks down the aisle, she is accompanied by her father and mother.[23] The Zohar states explicitly that "the father and mother of the bride bring her to the domain of the groom."[24]

In other circles, however, the groom is accompanied by his father and his future father-in-law. Similarly, the bride is accompanied by her mother and the groom's mother. This is the custom in Chassidic circles, as well as among some German Jews.[25]

None of this, however, is a hard and fast rule; where it is impossible for a parent to accompany the bride or groom, any other close friend or relative may be substituted.[26]

It is a custom for the ones leading the groom and bride to the chupah to carry candles in their hands.[27] In many circles, they

22. *Tanchuma, Ekev* 10. See above, Chapter 9, note 22.

23. See Rabbi Mordechai Leib (ben Naftali) Winkler, *Levushey Mordechai* 4:22:2 (Budapest, 1924). It was also the custom in England among the Sephardim; *Kether Shem Tov* 35. This is also the prevailing custom in most American communities; *Shaarim Metzuyanim BeHalakhah* 174:9.

24. *Zohar* 1:49a; cited in *Etz Chaim, Shaar MaN U'MaD* 1, p. 224. See *Shulchan HaEzer* 7:4:1. Cf. *Zohar* 1:48b.

25. See *Eduth LeYisrael* 8:7. This is the Lubavitcher custom; *Sefer HaMinhagim*, p. 76. Some say that it is indicated by *Yoreh Deah* 391:3 in *Hagah*, which states that the groom is accompanied by two *men*; *Mishneh Halakhoth* 7:247. It may also be based on the Midrash which states that Adam was accompanied by Michael and Gabriel, who are seen as masculine; see above, note 20. See *Kether Shem Tov* 5.

26. See above, Chapter 9, notes 13 — 15.

27. Maharil 64b; *Shulchan HaEzer* 7:4:4. In some places, it was the custom for everyone present to carry candles. Also, where weddings were outdoors, the candles were thrown; *Matteh Moshe* 3. See *Zohar* 1:48b.

use braided havdalah candles.[28]

It is possible that this custom dates back to Biblical times. The prophet speaks of, "the sound of a bridegroom, the sound of a bride... the light of a lamp" (Jeremiah 25:10).[29] In Talmudic times, candles or lamps were always associated with weddings.[30]

On the simplest level, the reason for this custom is that candles and light are always associated with joy.[31] It is thus written, "The Jews had light, gladness, joy and honor" (Esther 8:16). The candles indicate that the couple's life together will be one of light and joy.

This same light and joy was also present at Mount Sinai, at the great wedding between Israel and God, when the Torah was given. The Torah describes Mount Sinai as surrounded by lightning flashes and fire. The Israelites were accompanied by lightning (Exodus 19:16), and God was accompanied by fire (Exodus 19:18). The bride and groom today are similarly accompanied by fire.[32]

Some authorities say that this is the reason that braided havdalah candles are used. Such candles are like torches, and the Talmud teaches that the light of a torch flickers and jumps.[33] The braided candles have a light that resembles the

28. *Eduth LeYisrael* 8:8. See below, note 34.

29. See *Megillath Taanith* 6; *Tosafoth, Sanhedrin* 32b, s.v. *Kol.* Also see *Chidushey HaRan; Chamra VeChaya; Margolioth HaYam* 13; on *Sanhedrin* 32b.

30. *Gittin* 89a; *Arukh* s.v. *Or* (אור). Under the Romans, there was a time of persecution where there was special danger of new brides being ravished, so weddings were not publicized. The only sign of a wedding was that lamps remained lit even by day. Even after the period of persecution, this custom remained in force; *Megillath Taanith* 6; *Yerushalmi, Kethuboth* 1:5, 5b; *Teshuvoth HaGeonim, Zekher LeRishonim* 361; Rabbenu Chananel, *Sanhedrin* 32b.

31. *Teshuvoth Maharam Mintz* 109.

32. *Rokeach* 353; *Tashbatz* 467; *Taamey HaMinhagim* 960; *Mataamim* 88, 89; *Likutey Maharich* 3:131b.

33. *Pesachim* 8a.

flickering lightning at Sinai.[34]

Another reason for the fire is based on an important analysis of man and woman. In Hebrew, the word for man is *ish* (איש), while the word for woman is *ishah* (אִשָׁה). Both these words are the same, except that *ish* is written with a *yod* (י), while *ishah* is written with a *heh* (ה). However, one of God's names is Yah (יה),[35] and the Talmud teaches that the *Yod* of this name is in the word *ish*, meaning man, while the *heh is in the word ishah*, meaning woman. This indicates that when there is love and harmony between man and woman, God's name is with them.

However, in both *ish* and *ishah*, if the letters of God's name are removed, what remains is the word *esh* (אֵשׁ), meaning fire. This teaches that when God is not with a man and woman, their relationship can be disharmonious and as painful as fire.[36]

Some sources note that the bride and groom are accompanied by torches to remind them that their relationship can be joyous, but if God is removed, it can be as painful as fire. It is to remind them that they must always maintain peace and harmony in their relationship.[37]

Another interesting reason given for the candles is based on the fact that every Hebrew letter has a numerical value. The Hebrew word for candle or lamp is *ner* (נֵר), which has a numerical value of 250. Since each of the individuals accompanying the groom (or bride) carries a candle, there are two candles, having a combined numerical value of 500.

It is also taught that a man has 248 limbs,[38] while a woman

34. *Likutey Maharich* 3:131b.

35. See HaGra, *Yoreh Deah* 276:19; *Midrash Tehillim* 114:3. In any case, the two letters are the first two of the Tetragrammaton.

36. *Sotah* 17a.

37. *Mataamim HaChadash* 16; *Otzar Kol Minhagey Yeshurun* 16:4; *Shulchan HaEzer* 7:4:4. This might have also been the reason for the fire at Sinai; see *Mekhilta* on Exodus 19:18.

38. *Oholoth* 1:8.

has 252.[39] Adding up these two numbers, one has a sum of 500. This is the sum of the two candles. Therefore, the two candles allude to the man and woman coming together.[40]

The blessing to have children in the Torah is, "Be fruitful and multiply" (Genesis 1:28), *peru u'revu* (פְּרוּ וּרְבוּ) in Hebrew. *Peru* (פְּרוּ) has a numerical value of 286, while *u'revu* (וּרְבוּ) has a value of 214. Added together, the two also add up to 500. The two candles with this numerical value thus allude to the hope that the couple will have a fruitful, abundant marriage.[41]

When the groom approaches the chupah, the cantor chants:

בָּרוּךְ הַבָּא:

Blessed is he who comes.

This is an idiomatic expression meaning "welcome." The groom is greeted like a king under the chupah.[42]

Then, while the groom is standing under the chupah, the cantor chants:[43]

מִי אַדִּיר עַל הַכֹּל, מִי בָּרוּךְ עַל הַכֹּל, מִי גָּדוֹל עַל הַכֹּל [מִי דָגוּל עַל הַכֹּל] הוּא יְבָרֵךְ אֶת הֶחָתָן וְאֶת הַכַּלָּה:

He who is mighty over all, He who is blessed over all,
He who is great over all, [He who is supreme over all],
may He bless the bridegroom and the bride.

39. *Bekhoroth* 45a.

40. *Matteh Moshe* 2; *Mataamim* 90, 91; *Taamey HaMinhagim* 959; *Yalkut Yitzchak* 552:26; *Likutey Maharich* 3:131b.

41. *Ibid.*

42. *Shulchan HaEzer* 7:4:5; *Eduth LeYisrael* 8:10.

43. *Shulchan HaEzer* 7:4:6; see *Taamey HaMinhagim*, p. 408. Other sources, however, indicate that it is chanted while the bride walks around the groom; *Eduth LeYisrael* 9:2. The poem is in alphabetical order, containing the first four letters of the Hebrew alphabet.

The earliest printed source of this chant is in *Birkath HaMazon*, Dyherenfurth, 1791. Some say that it was written by the same author as the Seder chant, *Adir Hu*, in the late 15th century; *Otzar Kol Minhagey Yeshurun* 16:3.

This poem is chanted as a praise to God. It is taught that before blessing a human being, one should first bless God.[44] Since the bride and groom will be blessed under the chupah, a chant is first sung that praises God.[45]

In some circles, it is customary to have a regular procession, including brothers and sisters of the bride and groom, grandparents, ushers, bridesmaids, and flower girls. While there is no objection to this practice, it is of very recent origin, and apparently has no source in Jewish tradition.[46] In some circles, the only ones marching to the chupah are the bride and the groom.

In any case, the last one to come under the chupah is the bride.[47] It is taught, "last is most precious."[48] Since the star of the wedding is the bride, she is led to the chupah last. The music played while the bride comes to the chupah is considered very important, and should be chosen with the greatest care. In some circles, there are special melodies that are played for the bride.[49]

44. See *Nedarim* 32b, from Genesis 14:18.

45. *Shulchan HaEzer* 7:4:6. See *Devash LePhi, Beth* 9.

46. The original custom was to bring the bride right after the groom; Maharil 64b; *Shulchan HaEzer* 7:4; *Eduth LeYisrael* 8:10; *Mishneh Halakhoth* 5:229. However, even in the most observant circles, the custom is to have others be part of the processional; see *Betrothed Forever*, p. 16. Some sources, however, object to bridesmaids marching down the aisle; *Mishneh Halakhoth* 5:229.

47. It was once customary for the rabbi and other dignitaries to accompany her to the groom; Maharil 64b. Ancient sources appear to indicate that she was accompanied by girls; Psalms 45:15; I Samuel 25:42. See above, Chapter 9, note 8.

Some say that this is part of the mitzvah of "bringing in the bride" (*hakhnasath kallah*); for general discussion, see *Sedey Chemed, Chathan VeKallah* 22; *Mataamim HaChadash* 24. In some circles, because of this mitzvah, it was the custom for those under the chupah to greet the bride, and then lead her back to the chupah; *Turey Zahav* 65:2; *Kitzur Shulchan Arukh* 147:5; *Shulchan HaEzer* 7:4:7.

48. *Bereshith Rabbah* 78:11; Rashi on Genesis 33:2. See *Bava Kama* 36a.

49. *Betrothed Forever*, p. 17. The Lubavitcher custom is to play the Alter Rebbe's Niggun continuously for both the groom and the bride; *Sefer HaMinhagim*, p. 76.

In many circles,[50] it is the custom for the bride to be led around the groom.[51] In some places, the custom is that she is led around the groom three times.[52]

This custom is based on the Biblical verse, "God has created a new thing on earth: a woman shall go around a man" (Jeremiah 31:21).[53]

The Talmud derives an important lesson from this verse, teaching, "Whoever lives without a wife, lives without a wall."[54] The commentaries state that a wife is like a wall for her husband, protecting him from external temptation.[55] The bride marches around the groom, indicating that, in their married life, she will protect him from untoward desires.[56]

The Biblical verse is primarily a Messianic prophecy.[57] Hence, the woman marching around the man indicates our hope for the coming of the Messianic age.[58]

As we discussed earlier, one of the symbolisms of the wedding ring is that of the aura of protection that the husband gives the wife.[59] However, in the Messianic era, man and

50. It is not, however, a custom among Sephardic Jews; *Shulchan HaEzer* 7:4:8; *Shaarim Metzuyanim BeHalakhah* 147:10.

51. *Shulchan HaEzer* 4:7:8. The earliest reference seems to be Rabbi Dov Baer of Lubavitch, notes on *Torath Chaim* of Rabbi Shneur Zalman of Liadi, *VaYeshev* 15, on Genesis 37:7 (Kapust, 1826). However, also see Rabbi Yaakov Emden, *Siddur Beth Yaakov* (Lemberg, 1904), p. 124b.

52. *Shulchan HaEzer* 7:4:8; *Mataamim* 79; *Taamey HaMinhagim* 961; *Mekor HaMinhagim* 74; *Siddur Beth Yaakov*, p. 124b.

53. In some Hebrew editions, it is 31:21. The translation is based on the Talmudic interpretation in *Yevamoth* 62b. Others translate the verse, "a woman shall go around after a man"; Rashi, Radak; or, "a woman shall be transformed into a man"; Rashi, Abravanel, *Metzudoth*.

54. *Yevamoth* 62b. A woman is likened to a wall; Song of Songs 8:9, 10.

55. Maharsha *ad loc* See Sforno on Song of Songs 8:9.

56. Original.

57. Rashi, Radak, *ad loc.*, and from context. See *Midrash Tehillim* 73:4.

58. *Mataamim* 79; *Yalkut Yitzchak* 552:35.

59. See above, Chapter 6, note 28.

woman will be equal, and the wife will also be able to protect her husband.[60] The woman walks around the man to indicate their hope that the Messianic era will become a full reality.[61]

Another reason for this custom is that the groom is like a king. The bride and her attendants walk around the groom, just as troops parade around a king.[62] Thus, in some circles, the entire wedding party accompanies the bride around the groom.[63]

The bride walking around the groom also indicates that she is binding him with certain obligations. As we have seen, a groom has three Torah obligations to his bride: food, clothing, and conjugal relations. In places where the bride walks around the groom three times, the circuits represent these three obligations.[64] The custom of her making seven circuits may indicate the seven additional obligations that were legislated by the rabbis.[65]

The most ancient sources state that it was a custom for the bride to be "given to the groom three times." The reason stated is that the expression, "when a man takes a wife" occurs three times in the Torah (Deuteronomy 22:13, 24:1, 24:5).[66] Later, this

60. See *Bereshith Rabbah* 20:20; *Tanchuma, VaYigash* 8. See Genesis 3:16; *Gur Aryeh* on Genesis 1:28.

61. Original. See Meiri, *Yevamoth* 62b.

62. *Taamey HaMinhagim* 961.

63. This is a Lubavitcher custom; *Sefer HaMinhagim*, p. 76.

64. *Otzar Kol Minhagey Yeshurun* 16:7; *Ezer LeYitzchak* 28, p. 55. See above, Chapter 16, note 49. It also relates to the groom being blessed three times; *Siddur Rashban; Rokeach* 355; *Eduth LeYisrael* 9:1. It also relates to the three methods of contracting kiddushin.

65. Original. The seven additional obligations are: [1] the kethubah, [2] to pay her medical expenses, [3] to ransom her if she is taken captive or kidnapped, [4] to pay her burial expenses, [5] to support her with his estate after his death, [6] to support her other children, [7] to have her sons inherit her kethubah; *Yad, Ishuth* 12:2; *Evven HaEzer* 69:2; HaGra 69:1.

66. *Tashbatz* 467.

developed into the bride walking around the groom three times.[67]

The three times also indicate that the husband is bound to his bride by three moral obligations. These are spelled out in God's promise to Israel: "I will betroth you to Me forever. I will betroth you to Me with fairness, justice, love and compassion. I will betroth you to Me with faith — and you shall know God" (Hosea 2:21, 22). In His relationship to Israel, God was accepting upon Himself the highest obligations that a husband accepts when he marries.[68]

The prevalent custom of the bride walking around the groom seven times is of Kabbalistic origin.[69] On the simplest level, the seven circuits represent the seven revolutions that the earth made during the seven days of creation.[70] The earth is

67. See *Likutey Maharich* 3:131b. Also see *Taamey HaMinhagim* 961; *Otzar Kol Minhagey Yeshurun* 16:7; *Mataamim* 80; *Yalkut Yitzchak* 552:36.

Other reasons for the three circuits include: because of the three camps that surrounded the Tabernacle: the camp of the Divine, the camp of the Levites, and the camp of Israel; *Shulchan HaEzer* 7:4:8. Also because a man is matched with his wife three times: before birth, in this physical life, and in the World to Come; *Ezer LeYitzchak* 28, p. 55.

68. *Ezer LeYitzchak* 28, p. 55; *Otzar Kol Minhagey Yeshurun* 16:7. It also parallels the three windings of the tefillin strap around the finger; Rabbi Nathan Shapiro, *Matzah Shemurah*; quoted in *Mekorey HaMinhagim* 75. Also see *Or HaChamah* on *Zohar* 3:230b, p. 91a, s.v. *VeTalath*. The verses from Hosea are said when these three windings are made. See above, Chapter 6, note 31.

69. This is assumed in a number of sources, but no primary source is cited. However, the verse, "a woman shall go around a man" (Jeremiah 31:22) is clearly associated with seven circuits in *Tikkuney Zohar* 6, 23a.

It is also noted that in this verse, the word for man is *gever* (גֶּבֶר), while the word for woman is *nekevah* (נְקֵבָה). The initial letters of the two words spell out *gan* (גַן), Hebrew for garden. The word *gan* also has a numerical value of 53, the number of portions in the Torah; *Tikkuney Zohar* 13, 29b. Thus, the woman going around the man indicates that she is giving him the power to gain a deeper understanding of Torah now that he will be married; *Likutey Maharich* 3:131b, from *Yevamoth* 62b.

70. A similar idea is discussed regarding the seven circuits of Hoshanah Rabbah; see *Shaar HaKavanoth, Inyan Sukkah, Drush* 8, p. 320. Also see *Etz Chaim, Shaar HaKelalim* 1, p. 2.

represented by the woman ("mother earth"). Since every marriage is a re-enactment of the creative process, she walks around the groom to indicate that these seven cycles are now being repeated.[71]

The seven circuits also indicate that she is binding him in another manner. As soon as he marries her, seven of her relatives become forbidden to him.[72]

The seven circuits also indicate that the bride is praying that the merit of the seven prophetesses[73] and the seven shepherds of Israel[74] protect her marriage and ensure its success.[75]

While the bride is walking around the groom, the cantor chants:[76]

מִי בֶּן שִׂיחַ שׁוֹשַׁן חוֹחִים אַהֲבַת רֵעִים מְשׂוֹשׂ דוֹדִים
הוּא יְבָרֵךְ אֶת הֶחָתָן וְאֶת הַכַּלָּה

71. Original.

72. Original. See *Mesekhta Derekh Eretz Rabbah* 1. The seven relatives are her mother, her daughter, her sister, her mother's mother, her father's mother, her son's daughter, and her daughter's daughter; *Yevamoth* 40b.

73. The seven prophetesses were Sarah, Miriam, Deborah, Hannah, Abigail, Huldah, and Esther; *Megillah* 14a.

74. See *Shaar HaKavanoth, Inyan Sukkah, Drush* 8, p. 320. The seven shepherds here are Abraham, Isaac, Jacob, Moses, Aaron, Joseph, and David.

75. Original.

76. This version is found in *Ezer LeYitzchak* 28:4; *Shulchan HaEzer* 7:4:9. The earliest mention of this chant appears to be Rabbi Moshe Theumim, *Devar Moshe* B 109 (Lvov, 1864).

Other sources have *mi ben sichi shoshan chochi* (מִי בֶּן שִׂיחִי שׁוֹשָׁן חוֹחִי); *Shulchan HaEzer Ibid.*; *Likutey Maharich* 3:131b. Others have *mi ben suach* (מִי בֶּן שׂוּחַ); *Eduth LeYisrael*. Some sources leave out the words *ahavath dodim, mesos reyim* (אַהֲבַת דוֹדִים מְשׂוֹשׂ רֵעִים); *Taamey HaMinhagim* p. 407, quoting *Siddur HaRav, Shaar HaKolel*.

Other sources, such as *HaMadrikh*, have an entirely different chant:

בְּרוּכָה הַבָּאָה. חָתָן בָּרוּךְ הוּא.
אַדִּיר אֱלֹהֵינוּ. כַּלָּה בְּרוּכָה וְנָאָה.
סִימָן טוֹב וּמַזָּל טוֹב.

> May the One[77] who speaks of the rose of thorns, the affection of lovers, the joy of the beloved, may He bless the bridegroom and the bride.

The "rose of thorns" refers to the modest, chaste brides of Israel, regarding whom it is written, "Like a rose among the thorns, so is my beloved among the maidens" (Song of Songs 2:2).[78] This is chanted in honor of the bride, who is like the "rose among thorns" to her groom. Furthermore, the Bible speaks of a "hedge of roses" (Song of Songs 7:3). This is the spiritual protection from external temptation that the bride gives the groom.[79]

After the circuits are completed, the bride stands to the right of the groom, and remains there for the entire ceremony. This symbolizes that she will always be at his right side to help him.

The custom is alluded to in the verse, "a queen shall stand at your right side" (Psalms 45:10). In Hebrew this is *nitzvah shegal le-yemin-kha* (נִצְּבָה שֵׁגַל לִימִינְךָ), which has as its final letters

In some places, it is the custom to chant *Mi Adir* when the bride walks around the groom; *Eduth LeYisrael* 9:2. The general custom, though, is to chant *Mi Adir* for the groom, and *Mi Ben Siach* for the bride; *Shulchan HaEzer* 7:4; *Avney Shoham.*

In Jerusalem it is the custom to chant, but without words.

77. It is thus speaking of God. *Ben siach* (בֶּן שִׂיחַ) is a strange expression, apparently found nowhere else. Others would translate the poem, "May the One spoken of as the rose among thorns (the cantor)...;" *Devar Moshe* B 109, quoted in *Likutey Maharich* 3:131b; see *VaYikra Rabbah* 23:4; *Shir HaShirim Rabbah* 2:2:4.

78. Rabbi Tzvi Yechezkel Michelson, *Tirash VeYitz'har* (Belgorei, 1937), quoted in *Ezer LeYitzchak* 28:4. Cf. *Sanhedrin* 37a; *Zohar* 3:37b; *Netzutzey Oroth ad loc.*

Some sources indicate that the "rose among thorns" refers to Rebecca, the bride of Isaac, who went to meditate (*su'ach*) in the fields (Genesis 24:63); *VaYikra Rabbah* 23:4; *Shir HaShirim Rabbah* 2:2:4.

79. See *Matteh Yehudah,* quoted in *Ezer LeYitzchak* 28:4. It is also possible that the rose here alludes to psalm 45, which is a Psalm "on roses, a song of love" (Psalms 45:1). It was once a custom to chant this entire psalm at the wedding ceremony; *Chesed LeAvraham* 4:48.

Heh Lamed Kaf (הלך). When these letters are re-arranged, they spell out *kallah* (כלה), meaning bride.[80]

The bride stands to the groom's right only under the chupah. At all other times, the groom is to the right of the bride.[81]

In most circles, the bride and groom face the assembled guests during the ceremony.[82] When performing the wedding ceremony, the rabbi then faces them, and has his back to the guests.[83] Some set up the chupah so that the rabbi is facing east when he recites the blessings.[84]

However, in communities where it is the custom to have the wedding in the synagogue, it is more proper for the bride and groom to face the ark.[85] The rabbi should not have his back to

80. *Rokeach* 353; Maharil 64b; *Teshuvoth Maharam Mintz* 109; *Kenesseth HaGedolah, Hagahoth Beth Yosef* 61:3; *Ba'er Hetiv* 61:7; *Likutey Maharich* 3:131b; Rabbi Shlomo (ben Yeshia Yosef) Vilf, *Im'roth Shlomo, Anaf* 5 (Lvov, 1884); *Taamey HaMinhagim* 963; *Mataamim* 77; *Yalkut Yitzchak* 552:37; *Kether Shem Tov* 24; *Kitzur Shulchan Arukh* 147:5; *Shulchan HaEzer* 7:5:10; *Eduth LeYisrael* 9:3.

An early source (from the 16th century) states that the bride stands to the right of the groom, so that he can place his right foot on her left foot during the ceremony, symbolizing that he will dominate her; *Chesed LeAvraham* 4:48; *Midbar Kademuth, Kaf* 17; *Midrash Talpioth,* s.v. *Chathan; Yalkut Yitzchak* 552:47, 48; *Kether Shem Tov* 38.

81. *Chesed LeAvraham* 4:48; *Midbar Kademuth, Kaf* 17. Also see *Zohar* 3:230b; Rabbi Yitzchak DeMin Acco, *Meirath Eynayim* (Jerusalem, 1975), p. 317, *Yeffey Eynayim ad loc.* 18.

Some Kabbalists maintain that since the Temple was destroyed, the groom should be to the bride's right, since it is written, "He has drawn back His right hand" (Lamentations 2:2); Ari, quoted in Rabbi Aaron (ben Moshe) Alfandari, *Yad Aaron* 61:4 (Izmir, 1757); quoted in Rabbi Shmuel Yehudah Ashkenazi, *Beth Oved* (Livorno, 1843); *Chupath Chathanim* 6:6, 33a, quoting Chida; *Sedey Chemed, Chathan VeKallah* 30.

82. See note 84.

83. Just as the *cohen*-priests face the people when they recite the Priestly Blessing; *Arukh HaShulchan* 62:9. One source states that the bride and groom should face south, and the rabbi should face east; Maharil 64b.

84. This is the most ancient custom; *Machzor Vitri* 475, p. 592; Maharil 64b; Rabbi Yaakov Emden, *Siddur Beth Yaakov*, p. 124; *VaYaged Moshe*, p. 18. See *Kitzur Shulchan Arukh* 147:5; *Kerem Shlomo, Evven HaEzer* 62.

85. *Ba'er Hetiv* 61:7. Some sources say that, in general, the bride and groom

the ark, but should stand somewhat to the side.[86] There is a custom cited where the couple and the rabbi stand to the sides of the chupah, so that neither the couple nor the rabbi has their back to the guests.[87] Since there are a variety of customs, in the absence of a definite local practice, the couple can follow their personal preference.[88]

In some circles it is a custom for the rabbi to give a sermon before the ceremony.[89]

If any of the parents of the bride or groom are deceased, it is a custom to recite the prayer *El Maley Rachamim* (אֵל מָלֵא רַחֲמִים) for the parent before the ceremony.[90]

It is customary for the parents of the bride and groom to stand with them under the chupah during the ceremony.[91] Other members of the wedding party may also be present under the chupah.[92]

In many circles, it is customary for everyone present to stand during the entire ceremony. This is out of respect for the bride and groom, since they are standing, and they are like a king and queen.[93] Furthermore, at the revelation at Sinai,

should face east; *Shulchan HaEzer* 4:7:11; *Arukh HaShulchan* 62:9. This is the custom in Jerusalem; *Shulchan HaEzer loc. cit.*

86. *Ba'er Hetiv* 61:7. Cf. *Kitzur Shulchan Arukh* 147:5.

87. In such cases the bride and groom face south; see Maharil 64b; *Teshuvoth Maharam Mintz* 109; *Ba'er Hetiv* 61:7. There are also Kabbalistic reasons for this; *Shoshan Sodoth,* p. 60b.

88. Some say that there is no fixed rule; *Kenesseth HaGedolah* 62:9; *Im'roth Sh'lomo, Anaf* 5.

89. *Kether Shem Tov* 1, 6, note 697.

90. *Eduth LeYisrael* 9:5, *Netzutzey Zohar* 3:219b —6.

91. Maharil 64b.

92. See above, Chapter 18, note 44.

93. *Kenesseth HaGedolah, Hagahoth HaTur* 62:2; *Ba'er Hetiv* 62:1. Also see *Sheyarey Kenesseth HaGedolah, Hagahoth Beth Yosef, Orach Chaim* 282:11; *Elef Lekha Shlomo, Evven HaEzer* 3,4; *Shulchan HaEzer* 7:5:1; *Eduth LeYisrael* 9:4.

Another reason for this is that the guests are also included in the blessing "It shall be heard in the cities of Judah...," and when people are which was the great wedding between God and Israel, it is written, "the people *stood* at a distance" (Exodus 20:15).[94] There are also Kabbalistic reasons for this.[95] Nevertheless, in many circles it is the practice for the guests to sit during the ceremony.

Everyone present should be respectful during the ceremony. They should be very careful to avoid talking, smoking, or levity.[96]

A minyan, a quorum of ten adult (over 13 years of age), male Jews, should be present for the entire ceremony.[97]

blessed, they must stand; Rabbi Yaakov de Castro, *Lechem Rav* 61, from *Sotah* 38a.

94. Original. This may also be alluded to in the verse, "They *stood* under the mountain" (Exodus 19:17). It is from this verse that we learn that the bride and groom are married under the chupah, above, Chapter 18, note 57.

95. *Tikkuney Zohar* 10, 26a; but see *Netzutzey Zohar ad loc.* #9. Also see *Sefer HaPeliyah,* quoted in *Kenesseth HaGedolah* 62:2.

96. There is considerable discussion regarding the prohibition against smoking; *Sedey Chemed, Chathan VeKallah* 3; *Shulchan HaEzer* 7:5:2; *Teshuvoth China VeChisda,* part 1, *Hashmatoth* 16, p. 38; *Zekher LeAvraham,* part 1, *Orach Chaim,* s.v. *Yom Tov; Im'roth Shlomo* 5:5; *Avodath HaKodesh, Moreh BeEtzba* 7:212.

97. See below, Chapter 20, note 12. Also see Chapter 22, note 76.

Chapter 20

THE PRENUPTIAL BLESSING

As discussed earlier, the wedding ceremony originally consisted of two parts. The first part was the erusin or kiddushin (betrothal), which today consists of the groom giving the bride the ring. The second part was the nesuin or marriage, where the bride and groom symbolically began their life together as husband and wife.[1]

However, around the time of Rashi (Rabbi Shlomo Yitzchaki; 1040 — 1105), it became the custom to hold both ceremonies together.[2] One reason was that wedding parties had become more lavish, while people were becoming poorer. When the kiddushin and nesuin were held separately, each required a separate feast. To save expenses, it became customary to have both ceremonies together, so that one feast would suffice for both.[3]

Another reason was that, once the couple was betrothed, they felt "married" and the temptation was much greater than before. In order to minimize this temptation, it became the custom that the nesuin be held immediately after the kiddushin.[4] By the fifteenth century, there were places where community enactments required that kiddushin and nesuin be held at the same time.[5]

The ceremony begins with the Prenuptial Blessing (*Birkath*

1. See Chapter 18. Also see *Kethuboth* 7b.

2. Rashi, *Sefer HaOrah* 2:7, 2:11; *Pardes,* p. 100; *Machzor Vitri* 469, p. 587. Also see *Tur Evven HaEzer* 62; *Hagahoth Maimonioth, Ishuth* 10:3 #60; *Rokeach* 351; *Sefer HaManhig,* p. 537; *Shiltey Gibborim, Kethuboth,* Rif 2a #4; *Evven HaEzer* 55:1 in *Hagah.*

3. *Sefer HaOrah* 2:10; *Pardes,* p. 100; *Machzor Vitri* 469, p. 587; *Maaseh HaGeonim,* p. 73; *Mataamim HaChadash* 6.

4. *Mataamim HaChadash* 7. See HaGra, *Evven HaEzer* 55:11.

5. *Teshuvoth Tashbatz* 1:133, quoted in *Pith'chey Teshuvah* 45:3; *Shulchan HaEzer* 4:1:3.

Erusin, בִּרְכַּת אֵרוּסִין). As in all such cases, the blessing precedes the act.[6] Actually, it is not a blessing for the commandment to marry and have children,[7] even though it has a similar form.[8] Rather, it is a blessing of thanks, praising God for giving us the holiness of marriage.[9]

In reciting this blessing, we bring God's blessing to the marriage.[10] There are thus three essential elements to the

6. *Evven HaEzer* 34:1; see *Pesachim* 7a. It is the opinion of the majority of authorities that the blessing comes before the kiddushin; *Teshuvoth Rif* 293; *Yad, Ishuth* 3:23; *Teshuvoth P'er HaDor* 8; Rabbi Yitzchak Gayoth, quoted in *Sefer HaEshkol, Hilkhoth Milah,* part 2, p. 129; *Teshuvoth HaRosh* 26:1; *Tanya Rabathai* 89; *Sefer HaIttur* 2:1, 62b; *Piskey Recanti* 235; Maharsha, *Pesachim* 7a; *Beth Shmuel* 34:4. Also see *Siddur Rav Saadia Gaon,* p. 97. See note 10. For other opinions, see note 9.

   However, if the blessing is not said first, it can be said later; *Beth Shmuel* 34:4; *Chelkath Mechokak* 34:3. If it is not said before the kethubah is read, see *Mishneh Halakhoth* 7:245.

7. However, it does exempt the groom from such a blessing; *Sefer Mitzvoth Katan* 183. Some say that it is like a blessing over physical enjoyment; *Levush* 34:1.

8. Rosh, *Kethuboth* 1:12; Ran, *Kethuboth,* Rif 2a, s.v. *VeAsar;* Mordechai, *Kethuboth* 133; Ritva, *Kethuboth* 7b, s.v. *U'Man; Tosafoth Rid, Kethuboth* 7b; *Sefer HaIttur* 2:1, 62b.

   Because of this, and also because a second person is involved, who might back out after the blessing, many authorities maintain that the blessing is said after the kiddushin; *Halakhoth Gedoloth,* quoted in *Or Zarua* 1:25; *Sheiltoth, Chayay Sarah* 16 (with *HaAmak Sh'elah,* Vilna, 1861), p. 95a; Raavad, *Ishuth* 3:23; *Teshuvoth Rashba* 4:206; *Teshuvoth Rashbash* 186; *Teshuvoth Tashbatz* 2:218; *Tashbatz (katan)* 461; *Sefer HaManhig,* p. 540. See *Yerushalmi, Berakhoth* 9:3, 66a.

   For discussion, see *Hagahoth Maimonioth, Ishuth* 3:23 #60; *Tur, Evven HaEzer* 34; Rosh, *Kethuboth* 1:12; *Teshuvoth Maharshal* B. *Yoreh Deah* 58; Rabbenu Yerocham 23:2, p. 186a; *Eduth LeYisrael* 11:4.

9. In all Ashkenazic communities, and in most Sephardic communities, the custom is to say the blessing first. However, among the Sephardim in Amsterdam and Algiers, there was a custom to say the blessing after the kiddushin; *Kether Shem Tov* 8, note 704; *Siddur Tefillah Kol Peh.* However, in *Siddur Ati Ya'esh* (*minhag* Amsterdam), the blessing is first.

   If the bride's family has one custom, and the groom's another, the custom of the groom's family is always followed; *Teshuvoth Makor Barukh* 22; Rabbi Akiva Eiger, *Evven HaEzer* 34:1.

10. *Sefer HaKaneh* 95a; Radbaz, *Metzudoth David* 125, 26b.

wedding ceremony: the kiddushin, the chupah, and the blessing.[11]

There should be a minyan, a quorum of ten adult Jewish males (over thirteen years of age) at the ceremony. Although a minyan is required primarily for the Seven Blessings, as we shall see, it is also preferable for this blessing.[12]

The Prenuptial Blessing is:

בָּרוּךְ אַתָּה יְיָ, אֱלֹהֵינוּ מֶלֶךְ הָעוֹלָם, בּוֹרֵא פְּרִי הַגָּפֶן.

> Blessed are You, O God our Lord, King of the Universe, Creator of the fruit of the grapevine.

בָּרוּךְ אַתָּה יְיָ, אֱלֹהֵינוּ מֶלֶךְ הָעוֹלָם, אֲשֶׁר קִדְּשָׁנוּ בְּמִצְוֹתָיו וְצִוָּנוּ עַל הָעֲרָיוֹת, וְאָסַר לָנוּ אֶת הָאֲרוּסוֹת, וְהִתִּיר לָנוּ אֶת הַנְּשׂוּאוֹת לָנוּ עַל יְדֵי חֻפָּה וְקִדּוּשִׁין. בָּרוּךְ אַתָּה יְיָ, מְקַדֵּשׁ עַמּוֹ יִשְׂרָאֵל עַל יְדֵי חֻפָּה וְקִדּוּשִׁין.

> Blessed are You, O God our Lord, King of the Universe, who sanctified us with His commandments, and commanded us regarding sexual prohibitions, forbidding to us [women] who are merely betrothed, but permitting to us [women] who are married to us through chupah and kiddushin. Blessed are You, O God, who sanctifies Israel through chupah and kiddushin.

The blessing itself is Talmudic in origin.[13] Like most such blessings, it was probably ordained some 2300 years ago by Ezra and his academy, known as the "Great Assembly" (*Kenesseth HaGedolah*), in the early days of the second Jerusalem Temple.[14]

11.. Ramban, *Derush LeChathunah* (in Chavel, *Kithvey HaRamban*) 1:138.

12. According to most authorities, this blessing does not require a minyan, but it is preferable that ten men be present; *Evven HaEzer* 34:4; *Chelkath Mechokak* 34:8; *Beth Shmuel* 34:7; *Ba'er Hetiv* 34:10; *Shulchan HaEzer* 8:6:4. For various opinions, see *Tur* 34.

13. *Kethuboth* 7b.

14. See *Berakhoth* 33a.

It is a custom to begin the Prenuptial Blessing with the blessing over wine.[15] The cup should be washed out before the ceremony, and should be filled to the brim.[16] The rabbi holds the cup of wine in his right hand, and begins with the usual blessing over wine, "Creator of the fruit of the grapevine" (*Borey p'ri ha-gafen*).

Although the blessing over wine is not mentioned explicitly in the Talmud, it appears that it was a custom in the Holy Land even in Talmudical times.[17] In those times, however, it was not a universal custom.[18] It did not become a universal custom until around the tenth century.[19]

15. *Yad, Ishuth* 3:24; *Evven HaEzer* 34:2. See Rosh, *Kethuboth* 1:16, Rabbenu Yerocham 23:2, p. 168a; Abudarham, p. 357; *Shulchan HaEzer* 8:1:5; *Eduth LeYisrael* 5.

    There is an earlier mention of wine for the Seven Blessings; see *Mesekhta Kallah* 1:1; *Zohar* 2:169a; *Sheiltoth, Chayay Sarah* 16, p. 102; see below, Chapter 22, notes 29—31. However, even for the Seven Blessings it was not a universal custom until the time of Rav Yehudai Gaon (757 c.e.). See note 19.

    If there is no wine, or not enough for two cups, it can be omitted here, or another beverage may be substituted; *Evven HaEzer* 34:2; Rosh, *Kethuboth* 1:16; Rabbenu Yerocham 23:2, 186a; *Nachalath Shiva* 12:5:1,2; *Arukh HaShulchan* 62:7.

16. See below, Chapter 25, notes 5, 7.

17. See *Yerushalmi, Sotah* 8:5, 37b; *Peney Moshe, Korban HaEdah, ad loc; Rokeach* 351. In Babylonia, it was also the custom to drink wine at a wedding; *Berakhoth* 9a. It was also the custom to pass wine before the bride; *Kethuboth* 16b. Some say that the custom of reciting the blessing over wine before the nuptial blessings is derived from this custom; see Rabbi Avraham ben Yehudah Elimelekh, *Lekutey Shikcha U'Peah* (Ferara, 1556), p. 14b. The custom, however, is not mentioned in the Babylonian Talmud; *Teshuvoth Tashbatz* 3:65.

18. See Abudarham, p. 357.

19. It is not mentioned in *Sheiltoth* 16. It is also not mentioned in *Siddur Rav Amram Gaon* (p. 181), which was written around 858 c.e. However, in *Siddur Rav Saadia Gaon* (p. 96), which was written around 928 c.e., it is mentioned. A century later, Rabbenu Nissim states that it is a fairly accepted custom; Rosh, *Kethuboth* 1:16; see *Otzar HaGeonim, Kethuboth* 76, p. 25.

    Around 757 c.e. Rav Yehudai Gaon ordained that a cup of wine be used for the Seven Blessings; Rabbenu Tam, *Sefer HaYashar* 627, quoted in *Eduth LeYisrael*, p. 31. See *Halakhoth Pesukoth* 13; *Machzor Vitri* 475, p. 592; *Kol Bo* 75, 44a. See below, Chapter 22, note 30.

A cup of wine is used because this blessing is a prayer of sanctification, very much like the Kiddush recited on the Sabbath and festivals.[20] Before invoking God's name, it is customary to recite the blessing over wine, as it is written, "I lift a cup of salvation and call in God's name" (Psalms 116:13).[21]

Wine is also a symbol of joy, as it is written, "Wine cheers God and man" (Judges 9:13). Whenever people have joy in performing one of God's commandments, there is joy for "God and man." There is joy for man, and there is also joy for God, because His commandments are being kept. In such a situation, a cup of wine is indicated. It is thus taught, "Songs of praise are only said over wine."[22]

It is also taught that when God married Adam and Eve, He "took," as it were, a cup of wine and blessed them.[23] Wine can bring drunkenness and pain, but it can also bring relaxation and a desirable closeness between husband and wife.[24]

The earliest sources actually indicate that the groom should be the one to recite the Prenuptial Blessing.[25] The custom today, however, is to have someone other than the groom recite it.[26] This is so as not to embarrass a groom who does not know the blessing.[27] Furthermore, even if he knows the blessing, the

20. Ritva, *Kethuboth* 7b. See *Sefer HaManhig*, p. 537.

21. Cf. *Zohar* 2:169a.

22. *Berakhoth* 35a. Although this rule is not applied to the wedding blessings, it is applied to the blessing over circumcision; see Mordechai, *Yoma* 727; *Beth Yosef, Yoreh Deah* 265: *Turey Zahav, Yoreh Deah* 265:4. See *Shnei Luchoth HaBrith, Shaar HaOthioth* 1:162b; *Arukh HaShulchan* 34:9.

23. *Bereshith Rabbah* 8:13. This, however, may relate to the Seven Blessings; see Rashash *ad loc* #7. See below, Chapter 22, note 46.

24. Cf. *Daath Zekenim* (*Baaley Tosafoth*) on Leviticus 10:9.

25. *Yad, Ishuth* 3:24; *Evven HaEzer* 34:1.

26. *Evven HaEzer* 34:1 in *Hagah*; *Hagahoth Maimonioth* 3:23 #60; *Darkey Moshe* 34:1; *Sefer Mitzvoth Gadol,* Positive Commandment 48, p. 125a; *Nachalath Shiva* 12:6; *Arukh HaShulchan* 34:8.

27. *Orachoth Chaim* 2:64; *Hagahoth Sefer Mitzvoth Katan* 183:19; *Teshuvoth Rama* 125; *Derishah* 34:1; *Beth Shmuel* 34:2; *Ba'er Hetiv* 34:2. See *Bikkurim*. 3:7.

Some authorities, however, dispute this reason, and state that the main reason is that, if the groom says it, it may seem as if he is showing off;

groom may be too nervous and confused to recite it.[28]

When the rabbi recites the blessing, both he and the groom should have in mind that the blessing is being said to fulfill the groom's obligation. It is a general rule that one person can say a blessing for the sake of another.[29] When the groom responds Amen, it is as if he himself recited the blessing.[30]

Some say that the rabbi recites the blessing very much as God recited the blessing for Adam and Eve. The rabbi or cantor of today stands in God's place to recite the blessing.[31]

Since a blessing was said over the wine, someone must at least take a sip of it.[32] Since the blessing was said for the bride and groom, the custom is to give them some of the wine to sip.[33] This custom is over one thousand years old.[34]

The cup is first given to the groom to sip, and then to the

Mordechai, *Kethuboth* 131, quoting Rav Sar Shalom Gaon; *Otzar HaGeonim, Kethuboth* 53, p. 14; Maharshal on *Sefer Mitzvoth Gadol*, Positive Commandment 48; *Yam Shel Shlomo, Kethuboth* 1:17; *Teshuvoth Be'er Sheva* 49. These blessings were not universally known; *VaYikra Rabbah* 23:4. They were among the things that a scholar was supposed to know; *Chullin* 9a.

28. *Sefer HaManhig*, p. 540; *Mataamim* 65.

29. *Teshuvoth HaGeonim, Shaarey Tzedek* 45, p. 7a; *Otzar HaGeonim, Kethuboth* 54, p. 14. See *Ezer LeYitzchak* 43.
Other authorities, however, maintain that the responsibility to recite this blessing is not necessarily that of the groom; *Turey Zahav, Yoreh Deah* 1:17; *Teshuvoth Be'er Sheva* 49; *Pachad Yitzchak*, s.v. *Birkath Chathanim*, p. 60d; *Otzar Kol Minhagey Yeshurun* 16:14.

30. *Kol Bo* 75, p. 44c; *Ben Ish Chai, Shoftim* 2.

31. *Pirkey Rabbi Eliezer* 12, 31a; Radal *ad loc.* 12:60; *Zohar* 3:44b. Cf. *Bereshith Rabbah* 8:13.

32. *Teshuvoth Tashbath* 3:65. See *Teshuvoth HaGeonim, Meah Shaarim* (Porta, 1861), p. 8, quoting Rav Matithyahu; *Pardes*, p. 100.

33. *Yad Aaron* 34:2; *Otzer Kol Minhagey Yeshurun* 16:11.

34. The earliest reference is from the time of Rav Shalom Gaon (904 c.e.); *Teshuvoth HaGeonim* (Assaf) 40; *Otzar HaGeonim, Kethuboth* 88, p. 27. Also see *Teshuvoth HaGeonim, Chemdah Genuzah* 118, quoting Rav Tzemach Gaon; *Teshuvoth Geoney Mizrach U'Maarev* 123.

bride.[35] In some circles, the rabbi takes a sip of wine first, since it was he who said the blessing.[36]

The wine is given to the groom for one particular reason — because the first time he tasted wine was at his circumcision ceremony. At the circumcision, it is customary to give the child a drop of wine. The circumcision defined the groom's procreative powers along Torah lines. Now that he is being married, these powers are being fulfilled. Therefore, he is again given a cup of wine to sip.[37]

When a child is circumcised, the people bless the infant and say, "Just as he entered the covenant [of circumcision], so may he enter Torah, the marriage canopy, and good deeds."[38] Just as, when the groom entered the covenant, he was given a cup of wine, so he is given one now.[39] What was originally only a promise is now a reality.

35. *Sefer HaOrah* 2:14; *Machzor Vitri* 476, p. 592; *Teshuvoth Rabbenu Nissim* 52; *Rokeach* 351, p. 239; Maharil, p. 64b.
The bride and groom need only take a small sip; *Kenesseth HaGedolah*, quoted in *Ba'er Hetiv* 34:6; *Chupath Chathanim*, p. 34; *Sedey Chemed, Berakhoth* 3:5; *Shulchan HaEzer* 8:1:9.
They need not recite a blessing over the wine; *Shulchan HaEzer* 8:1:10; *Ezer LeYitzchak* 43, note 3. See *Peney Yehoshua* on *Kethuboth, Kuntres Acharon* 21; *Pith'chey Teshuvah, Evven HaEzer* 34:5; *Shenoth Chaim, Orach Chaim* 1:2:36.

36. See *Eduth LeYisrael* (Henkin) 45, p. 141; *Ik'rey HaDat, Orach Chaim* 10:53; *Kether Shem Tov* 40, note 736.
However, it is not necessary for the rabbi to drink from the cup; *Teshuvoth Tashbatz* 3:65; *Yad Aaron* 34:2; *Arukh HaShulchan* 34:9, 62:8; *Taamey HaMinhagim*, p. 411; *Shulchan HaEzer* 8:1:9. It is the custom in Egypt for the rabbi not to drink; *Nahar Mitzraim*, p. 123; *Neveh Shalom* 23; *Kether Shem Tov*, note 736.

37. *Otzar Kol Minhagey Yeshurun* 16:11; *Shulchan HaEzer* 8:1:9.

38. *Shabbath* 137b.

39. Original.

Chapter 21

THE KIDDUSHIN

Immediately after the Prenuptial Blessing, the kiddushin takes place. This is actually the erusin or "betrothal," which is the first part of the ceremony. It is called kiddushin (קִדּוּשִׁין), which literally means sanctification or consecration. As soon as the kiddushin is completed, the bride and groom are consecrated to each other, and each is considered a married person.

Most important to the kiddushin are two witnesses. The witnesses are not there merely to be able to testify later that a marriage took place. Rather, the function of the witnesses is to create the marriage. A marriage can be valid if there is no rabbi present, but if two proper witnesses are not present, the marriage simply does not exist.[1]

The Torah thus says, "By the power of two witnesses, or by the power of three witnesses, shall a matter be established" (Deuteronomy 19:15). The "matter" here specifically includes such things as marriage and divorce. Thus, in order for a marriage to be "established," it must be done in the presence of two proper witnesses.[2]

There is a major body of Jewish law with regard to witnesses.

First, they must be Jewish males over thirteen years of age.

Second, they may not be in any way related to the bride or

1. *Kiddushin* 65a; *Yad, Ishuth* 4:6; *Evven HaEzer* 42:2; see Ruth 4:11. Some authorities maintain that if one of the witnesses is valid, then there is a question that the kiddushin may be valid, and that a Jewish divorce (*get*) is required if the marriage is to be dissolved; *Sefer Mitzvoth Gadol,* Positive Commandment 48. This, however, is a minority opinion; *Teshuvoth Rashba* 8956; *Teshuvoth Rivash* 266; *Teshuvoth Tashbatz* 1:130; *Teshuvoth Moharit* 1:15; *Chakham Tzvi* 135; *Evven HaEzer* 42:2 in *Hagah*.
   The two witnesses represent Netzach and Hod (*Metzudoth David* 125, 25d), as well as Yakhin and Boaz; *Ibid.* 26b.

2. *Sotah* 3b; Rashi, *Gittin* 2b, s.v. *VeAin, Kiddushin* 65a, s.v. *Mahu.*

groom, either by blood or by marriage.[3] Similarly, the two witnesses may not be related in any way to each other.[4]

Third, the witnesses must be "virtuous" men. For all practical purposes, this means that they must be religious Jews, who keep the Sabbath, kashruth, morality, and all the other laws of Judaism.[5] If even one of the witnesses is a relative, or is non-religious, the marriage is invalid.

If the rabbi and cantor are traditionally religious Jews, they may serve as the witnesses.[6]

The Torah says, "By the power of two witnesses, or by the power of three witnesses, shall a matter be established." Since the Torah states that two witnesses are sufficient, the statement regarding three witnesses appears to be redundant. This extra clause teaches an important lesson. If there are two witnesses, and one of them is invalid as a witness, because he is a relative, then the pair itself is invalid. Since "three witnesses" are likened to two, the same is true of a group of three or more witnesses. Thus, if three or more witnesses come to court as a group to testify, and one of them is unfit as a witness, the entire group becomes invalid. The fact that there remain two valid witnesses is of no avail; their testimony cannot be accepted.[7]

There are some authorities who extend this rule to a marriage ceremony. Thus, if all the guests at a wedding are considered a single group of witnesses, the presence of relatives or other invalid witnesses would invalidate the entire group.[8]

3. *Choshen Mishpat* 33:2. The rabbi may be a relative, as long as he is not also acting as a witness.

4. *Choshen Mishpat* 33:17.

5. *Choshen Mishpat* 34:2. However, if the witnesses are invalid only because of rabbinical legislation, then the marriage is questionable; *Evven HaEzer* 42:5.

6. *Teshuvoth Rivash* 82; Rabbi Yitzchak Aaron Eitinger, *Teshuvoth Maharya, Evven HaEzer* 40 (Lvov, 1893); *Arukh HaShulchan* 42:40; *Shaarim Metzuyanim BeHalakhah* 147:7.

7. *Makkoth* 5b.

8. Thus, if one of the relatives has in mind to be a witness, it can invalidate the entire marrige; see *Choshen Mishpat* 36:1.

These authorities therefore require that the witnesses to the wedding be separated from the rest of the guests. The two witnesses to the kiddushin must be specifically designated to the exclusion of all others.[9]

The prevailing custom is therefore that, through the rabbi, the groom designates two witnesses to be witnesses to the kiddushin, to the exclusion of everyone else present. These two witnesses will be the ones to "establish" the marriage. The rabbi must make certain that they are traditionally religious Jews, and not related to the bride or groom, or to each other. Of course, even if the witnesses are not designated, most authorities maintain that the marriage is valid, and this is the accepted view.[10]

As discussed earlier, some authorities hold that the witnesses to the kiddushin should not be the same as those for the kethubah.[11]

The rabbi (or other officiant) takes the ring from the groom,[12] and asks him if it is his.[13] The groom should respond yes.

The rabbi then shows the ring to the witnesses, and asks them if the ring is worth a perutah.[14] [The perutah was the

9. *Hagahoth Sefer Mitzvoth Katan* 183:7; *Sifethey Cohen, Choshen Mishpat* 36:8; *Ketzoth HaChoshen* 36:1; *Teshuvoth Radbaz* 2:707; *Siddur Derekh Chaim; Siddur Beth Yaakov*, p. 124b; *Shulchan HaEzer* 8:1:20; *Eduth LeYisrael* 6:6. See *Pith'chey Teshuvah* 42:11; *Arukh HaShulchan* 27:2; *Teshuvoth Panim Meiroth* 3:25; *Teshuvoth Maharam Shick, Choshen Mishpat* 57. Also see *Tosafoth, Makkoth* 6a, s.v. *Shmuel.*

10. *Evven HaEzer* 42:4. See *Teshuvoth Chatham Sofer, Evven HaEzer* 100. Also see *Metzudoth David* 125, 26a; *Derekh Pekudekha,* note in Introduction, p. 3; *Shaarim Metzuyanim BeHalakhah* 147:7.

11. See above, Chapter 15, notes 44, 45.

12. *Chupath Chathanim* 6, p. 34; *Shulchan HaEzer* 8:1:14.

13. *Ba'er Hetiv* 28:36; *Shulchan HaEzer* 8:1:14. See above, Chapter 6, note 5.

14. *Evven HaEzer* 31:2 in *Hagah*; Maharil 64b; *Teshuvoth Maharam Mintz* 109; *Matteh Moshe* 7; *Chupath Chathanim* 6, p. 34; *Ba'er Hetiv* 27:1; *Shulchan HaEzer* 8:1:22; *Eduth LeYisrael* 6:6.

In some areas, however, this was not done; *Arukh HaShulchan* 27:4.

smallest coin in ancient times.][15] The witnesses examine the ring and respond yes.[16]

The witnesses should position themselves so that they can actually see the ring placed on the bride's finger.[17] They are eyewitnesses to the kiddushin, and the act of kiddushin consists of the groom placing the ring on the bride's finger.

According to many authorities, the witnesses should also see the faces of the bride and groom.[18] If the bride is heavily veiled, some say that the veil should be lifted for the witnesses to see her face.[19] However, it is sufficient that the witnesses be positively aware of the identity of the bride and groom.[20]

The bride and groom should also be able to see the witnesses, and thus realize that the kiddushin is being witnessed.[21] Both of them must be aware that they are performing a valid transaction.[22]

15. The ring must be worth a perutah; *Kiddushin* 2a. A *perutah* is about 1/40 gram (25 milligrams) of pure silver. Some say that it is 1/46 gram (21.7 milligrams); *Shulchan HaEzer* 8:1:23 end. In monetary terms, this is around 0.8c.

16. Maharil 64b; *Eduth LeYisrael* 6:6, p. 41.

17. *Evven HaEzer* 42:4 in *Hagah*, from *Teshuvoth Rashba* 780; *Shulchan HaEzer* 8:1:25. However, if the witness is certain that the ring was placed on the finger, then the marriage is valid, even if he did not actually see it; *Chavath Yair* 19; *Pith'chey Teshuvah* 42:12. Cf. Mordechai, *Kiddushin* 531.

18. *Shulchan HaEzer* 8:1:26; *Ba'er Hetiv* 42:12; *Teshuvoth Maharival* 2:105; *Teshuvoth Rashakh* 2:134; Maharil 64b; *Pith'chey Teshuvah* 31:5; *Teshuvoth Mabit* 226.

19. *Matteh Moshe* 3; *Kether Shem Tov* 30, note 726. The bride and groom should also be able to see each other; *Ben Ish Chai, Shoftim* 5.

20. See *Teshuvoth Radbaz* 1:126; *Pith'chey Teshuvah* 31:5.

21. *Evven HaEzer* 42:3; *Shulchan HaEzer* 8:1:27; from Rashba, *Gittin* 81b, s.v. *Eleh*; Ran, *Gittin,* Rif 35b s.v. *VeKathav; Maggid Mishneh, Ishuth* 3:8; *Teshuvoth Rivash* 266. If the couple is aware the witnesses are present, then the marriage is valid even if they do not see the witnesses; *Teshuvoth Radbaz* 1:4, 1:275; *Ba'er Hetiv* 42:9; *Pith'chey Teshuvah* 143:9. At a wedding, it is assumed that the bride and groom will be aware that witnesses are present; *Teshuvoth Pri HaSadeh* 1:90.

22. See *Beth Shmuel* 42:9,10; *Arukh HaShulchan* 42:25.

Some sources indicate that the groom should say a short silent prayer before placing the ring on the bride's finger.[23]

It is a custom that the bride not wear gloves when the ring is placed on her finger.[24] The ring must be placed on her finger, and not on a glove. However, if the bride strongly feels that gloves are an integral part of her accessories, the finger of the glove can be slit open, so that the ring is placed directly on her finger. [The glove can later be repaired.]

The groom takes the ring in his right hand, and places it on the bride's finger.[25] The giving of the ring is likened to God's giving of the Torah. The Torah was given, as it were, with God's "right hand," as it is written, "From His right hand a fiery law was given to them" (Deuteronomy 33:2). The groom similarly gives the ring with his right hand.[26]

The custom is for the groom to place the ring on the bride's right forefinger. This custom is at least one thousand years old.[27]

23. This is a prayer, or statement, "I am about to keep the commandment of kiddushin"; *Shnei Luchoth HaBrith, Shaar HaOthioth* 1:62b; *Or HaChaim* (in *Or HaLevanah*), p. 109; *Siddur Korban Mincha* (Vilna, 1882), p. 176; *Shulchan HaEzer* 8:2:7.

24. This is most probably for Kabbalistic reasons, see below, note 32. See *Kerem Shlomo, Teshuvah* 86; *Pith'chey Teshuvah* 27:1; *Ezer LeYitzchak* 18:3; *Sh'elath Shalom* 60; *Pri HaSadeh* 1:93; *Simchah LaIsh, Orach Chaim* 4; *VaYitzbor Yosef* 60; *Teshuvoth Divrey Malkiel* 5:206; *Shaarim Metzuyanim BeHalakhah* 147:7.

This was primarily an Ashkenazic custom, whereas Sephardim were not particularly concerned about it; *Sedey Chemed, Chathan VeKallah* 26, s.v. *Zoth.* If a woman was married with a coin, the Sephardic custom in some places was to cover her hand with a cloth so that she not appear to be taking charity; *Ben Ish Chai, Shoftim* 7.

25. *Ba'er Hetiv* 27:1; *Teshuvoth Maharam Mintz* 109; *Shulchan HaEzer* 8:2:2. A lefty, however, might take the ring in his left hand.

26. Original. See above, Chapter 6, note 16. Also see *Berakhoth* 6a, 62a; *Mesekhta Sofrim* 3:10.

27. The custom is first mentioned by Rabbi Eliezer of Worms (1162-1232), *Rokeach* 351, p. 238. Also see Maharil 64b; *Ba'er Hetiv* 27:1; *Shulchan HaEzer* 8:2:2; *Eduth LeYisrael* 6:7, p. 41; *Kether Shem Tov* 19.

The simplest reason is that women used to wear rings on this finger; even though this is no longer the practice, the custom was retained at

The ring is placed on the right hand, because the right hand represents love. It is taught that the right hand is love and the left hand is strength.[28]

There are a number of reasons why the ring is placed on the forefinger. Some say that the right hand of the groom is directly opposite the left hand of the bride. Therefore, counting the five fingers of the bride's left hand, and then the thumb and forefinger of the right, the forefinger comes out to be the seventh finger. Since everything associated with the wedding is associated with the number seven, this finger is used.[29] As mentioned earlier, every wedding is a re-enactment of creation, which took place in seven days.

weddings; *Teshuvoth Maharam Mintz* 109, quoted in *Kenesseth HaGedolah, Hagahoth* on *Tur* 27:1; *Chupath Chathanim* 6, p. 34.

Another reason for this custom is that the forefinger is the most prominent finger, and the one most often used; *Nachalath Shiva* 12:2; *Ezer LeYitzchak* 18:1; *Otzar Kol Minhagey Yeshurun* 16:9, p. 46.

In some circles, however, it was the custom to place the ring on the left middle finger, the same finger upon which the tefillin strap is wound; Rabbi Yaakov Kopel, *Siddur Kol Yaakov,* p. 121b. This was once the custom of the Sephardim in Jerusalem; *Kether Shem Tov* 19. Also see note on *Tikkuney Zohar* 10, 25b; *Ben Ish Chai, Shoftim* 9. See above, Chapter 6, note 31.

All of this, of course, is merely custom, and the marriage is valid regardless how he gives her the ring; *Arukh HaShulchan* 27:4; *Eduth LeYisrael* (Henkin) 45, p. 141.

28. Original. See *Tikkuney Zohar* 21, 55b. There are also other Kabbalistic reasons for placing the ring on the finger. For one, the finger represents the Yesod of the female; HaGra on *Tikkuney Zohar* 47b, s.v. *Tul; Nitzutzey Zohar* on *Tikkuney Zohar* 44b #14.

29. *Likutey Maharich* 3:133a. It is also taught that the finger is like a *vav*, which has a numerical value of six. The ring is an extra unit, making a total of seven; *Tikkuney Zohar* 10, 25b.

The five fingers are also associated with the five senses; the pinky with hearing, the ring finger with sight, the middle finger with touch, the forefinger with smell, and the thumb with taste; Bachya on Leviticus 8:23; *Sheviley Emunah* 4; Cf. *Nachalath Shiva* 12:2. The sense of smell is associated with sexuality; see *Berakhoth* 53b; *Parparoth LeChokhmah ad loc; Eruvin* 21b; *Yevamoth* 60b. Hence, this finger is used for marriage.

There is also an allusion to using this finger from Psalm 19; see *Chupath Chathanim* 6, p. 34; Rabbi Yehudah ben Moshe Eli, *Kemach Soleth* (Salonika, 1798), quoted in *Ben Ish Chai, Shoftim* 9; *Otzar Kol Minhagey Yeshurun* 16:9, p. 46; *Taamey HaMinhagim* 975; *Mataamim* 34; *Yalkut Yitzchak* 552:41.

The marriage is also seen as a unification of God's holiest, unutterable name, YHVH (יהוה).

The ring represents the concealed Wisdom of creation, which is closed just as a ring is. This is the *yod* (י), the first letter of creation. The numerical value of *yod* is ten, denoting the ten sayings of creation.[30]

The first *heh* (ה) is the groom's hand. The numerical value of *heh* is five, denoting the five fingers of the hand.[31]

The *vav* (ו) is the bride's finger, which has the shape of a *vav*.

The final *heh* (ה) is the bride's hand.

The giving of the ring thus completes the Divine Name. In a mystical sense, this Name represents the marriage of the masculine and feminine elements of creation, as well as the masculine and feminine elements of divine providence.[32]

It is very important that the groom give the bride the ring, and that the couple not exchange rings. The kiddushin consists of the groom giving the bride something of value, as noted earlier. If the bride also gives the groom a ring at this time, the ring that he gives her is part of an exchange, rather than a gift. This would raise questions regarding the validity of the entire marriage.[33]

The custom is that at the time of the kiddushin, the bride extends her right forefinger, and the groom places the ring on it.[34]

Before placing the ring on the bride's finger,[35] the groom

30. *Avoth* 5:1.

31. Other sources state that the two letters *heh* represent the two witnesses; *Tikkuney Zohar* 10, 25b; Rabbi Yehudah Chait, *Minchath Yehudah* on *Maarekheth Elokuth* 7 (Mantua, 1558), p. 75b; *Shnei Luchoth HaBrith, Shaar HaOthioth* 1:162b. Otherwise, the teaching is the same as that of the sources cited in note 32.

32. Rabbi Shalom Sharabi, *Or HaChaim* (in *Or HaLevanah*), p. 108; *Siddur HaAri* of Rav Asher, p. 149b; *Im'roth Shlomo* 4:20; *Ben Ish Chai, Shoftim* 9.

33. *Igroth Moshe, Evven HaEzer* 3:18.

34. *Shulchan HaEzer* 8:2:2.

35. Many authorities require that the formula be said before the ring is placed

recites the traditional formula:[36]

הֲרֵי אַתְּ מְקֻדֶּשֶׁת לִי בְּטַבַּעַת זוּ כְּדַת מֹשֶׁה וְיִשְׂרָאֵל

> *Harey at mekudesheth li betaba'ath zu, ke-dath Moshe veYisrael.*
> Behold, you are consecrated to me with this ring according to the law of Moses and Israel.

The word *mekudesheth*, which means "consecrated," refers to the kiddushin. As noted earlier, kiddushin means consecration.[37]

The formula, *Harey at..*, contains 32 letters. These represent

on the bride's finger; *Chupath Chathanim* 6; *Sefer HaMakneh, Kuntres Acharon* 26; *Shulchan HaEzer* 8:2:5.

From the Talmud, however, it appears that it was said afterward, and some authorities maintain that this is the correct procedure; Rabbi Shlomo Yehudah (ben Pesach Tzvi) Tabak, *Erekhy Shai, Evven HaEzer* 27:1 (Sighet, 1909); quoted in *Shulchan HaEzer* 8:2:5.

36. The earliest use of the expression "with this ring," appears to be in Rashi, *Issur VeHeter* 309 (manuscript), quoted in *Sefer HaOrah* 2:3, p. 177 in note. The full wording that we use is found in *Sefer HaManhig* 104, p. 536; *Orachoth Chaim* 2:57; *Tanya Rabathai* 89, 97b; *Teshuvoth Rashba* 1:1186; *Matteh Moshe* 7; *Kol Bo* 75, 44b. Also see *Evven HaEzer* 27:1 in *Hagah; Ba'er Hetiv* 27:3; *Shulchan HaEzer* 8:2:7; *Eduth LeYisrael* p. 73; *Kether Shem Tov* 14.

The Talmudic formula was simply, *Harey at mekudesheth li; Kiddushin* 5b; *Yad, Ishuth* 3:1.

The additional wording, "According to the law of Moses and Israel," is first found in the context of the kethubah; see *Tosefta, Kethuboth* 4:9; *Likutey Maharich* 3:133a; above, Chapter 16, note 24. It is closely associated with all aspects of the marriage; see *Tosafoth, Kethuboth* 3a, s.v. *A-Data; Gittin* 33a, s.v. *Kol*; also see *Machzor Vitri* p. 586; *Sefer HaOrah* 2:3, p. 177. In a pre-Talmudic source, the expression, "take her according to the law of Moses," is found; Tobit 7:13.

Other ancient sources have the wording, *tehey mekudesheth li betabaath zu* (תהא מְקוּדֶשֶׁת לִי בְּטַבַּעַת זוּ...); *Tikkuney Zohar* 5, 19a; 21, 55b; *Tikkuney Zohar Chadash* 100b; *Machzor Vitri, p. 586, Sefer HaOrah* 2:3, p. 177; *Rokeach* 351; Abuderham p. 359. See *Kether Shem Tov*, note 710. A completely different formula is found in *Siddur Rav Saadia Gaon*, p. 97.

37. *Tosafoth, Kiddushin* 2b, s.v. *DeAssar*. See Chapter 5, note 6; Chapter 18, note 7. Other sources, however, indicate that *mekudesheth* means "prepared," as in Exodus 19:6, denoting that she will be available to her husband as a wife; *Matteh Moshe* 7.

the 32 "Paths of Wisdom" *(Nethivoth Chokhmah)*.[38] They also parallel the 32 times that God's name Elohim (אֱלֹהִים) occurs in the account of creation (Genesis 1).[39] Every marriage is a re-enactment of the act of creation.

In Hebrew, the number 32 is written out *lamed beth* (לב). This spells out the word *lev* (לֵב), Hebrew for heart.[40] This statement (*harey at*) therefore indicates that the groom is giving his heart to his bride. It also denotes that the two love each other with all their hearts.

Furthermore, the first letter of the Torah is the *beth* (ב) of *Bereshith*, while the last letter is the *lamed* (ל) of *Yisrael*. Thus, the statement, *harey at*, encompasses the entire Torah.[41] In this respect, it alludes to the Torah as the subject of the marriage between God and Israel.[42]

In the same context, ancient sources note that the formula *harey at* begins with the letter *heh* (ה), which has a numerical value of five. It thus alludes to the five books of the Torah, which were the subject of the marriage between God and Israel.[43] As we have noted earlier, the Torah was, in a sense, the "wedding ring" in this divine marriage.[44]

Before the wedding, the groom should be sure to have the formula, *harey at,* memorized. The rabbi should also make sure that the groom knows it.

Nevertheless, it is the custom in most circles for the rabbi to

38. Rabbi Yaakov Kopel, *Siddur Kol Yaakov*, p. 122a. See *Sefer Yetzirah* 1:1.

39. Raavad on *Sefer Yetzirah* 1:1; *Tikkuney Zohar Chadash* 112c; *Sefer HaPeliyah* (Koretz, 1784), p. 213a; *Pardes Rimonim* 12:1; *Mavo Shaarim* 5:2:6; *Etz Chaim, Shaar HaTzelem* 2.

40. *Bahir* 106; Rabbi Yehudah ben Barzilai of Barcelona, Commentary on *Sefer Yetzirah* (Berlin, 1885), p. 106; *Tikkuney Zohar* 30, 75a.

41. Rabbi Yehudah ben Barzilai of Barcelona, Commentary on *Sefer Yetzirah,* p. 107; Rabbi Yitzchak of Acco, *Otzar Chaim* (Moscow, Guenzberg Collection, Ms. 775), p. 111b. See *Bahir* 147.

42. Original.

43. *Tashbatz* 466.

44. See Chapter 6, note 16.

recite the formula word by word with the groom.[45] This is so as not to embarrass a groom who does not know it.[46]

It is important that both the bride and groom understand the meaning of the formula that is said when the ring is placed on the bride's finger. If there is any chance that they do not understand it, the formula should be repeated in English, or any other language that the couple understands.[47]

The bride need not respond.[48]

As soon as the ring is placed on the bride's finger, the couple is considered legally married according to Jewish law.

It is customary for the people to respond *mekudesheth* (מְקוּדֶשֶׁת) after the ring is placed on the bride's finger. The word *mekudesheth* means "consecrated" and "married," and signifies that the bride is now considered married.[49] In some circles, it is also customary for the people to say *Mazal Tov* (מַזָל טוֹב, "Good Fortune") at this point.[50]

It is the custom to read the kethubah after the kiddushin is completed.[51]

45. *Kether Shem Tov* 16. The rabbi should not say the word *li* ("to me") with the groom, since it would appear as if the bride were being married to the rabbi; *Nachalath Shiva* 12:3; *Shulchan HaEzer* 8:2:12; *Kether Shem Tov*, note 712.

46. Original.

47. See *Ba'er Hetiv* 27:5; *Kether Shem Tov*, note 712.

48. *Metzudoth David* 125, p. 25d.

49. *Chupath Chathanim* 6, p. 34; *Teshuvah MeAhavah* 117; *Shulchan HaEzer* 8:2:13.

50. *Teshuvoth Maharam Mintz* 109; *Siddur Derekh HaChaim; Eduth LeYisrael*, p. 73. The expression, "*Mazal Tov*," is associated with weddings; Rashi, *Pesachim*, 49a, s.v. *Ain Zivugam*. Also see *Sefer HaTishbi*, s.v. *Mazal; Tzemach David*, s.v. Mazal.

51. *Evven HaEzer* 62:9 in *Hagah*; *Shulchan HaEzer* 8:3:1. However, it appears that it was not a universal custom; see Rabbenu Yerocham 23:2, 186a; Maharil 64b.

It was also a custom among Sephardim; *Kether Shem Tov* 1. It was also a custom in Cochin, India; *Evven Sappir* 2; *Kether Shem Tov*, note 697. In Egypt, it was customary not to read the kethubah at all at the ceremony;

This is to separate the two parts of the marriage ceremony, the erusin (or kiddushin) and the nesuin. Also, a separate blessing over wine is said for the kiddushin and the nesuin, as we shall discuss. The reading of the kethubah provides an interruption in the proceedings so that there should be no question that the blessing on the second cup might be unnecessary.[52]

It appears that the custom of reading the kethubah as part of the ceremony was instituted by Rashi (Rabbi Shlomo Yitzchaki).[53]

The interruption is provided by the reading of the kethubah in particular, and not by anything else, so that the groom is made aware of the obligations that he has undertaken in his marriage.[54]

The custom of reading the kethubah may also be related to the great wedding between God and Israel, which was the receiving of the Torah. There, it is written that "Moses took the Book of the Covenant and read it to the people" (Exodus 24:7). After that, the Israelites "stood under the mountain" (Exodus 19:17), which was being held above them like a chupah.[55]

In some circles, the kethubah is read by the officiating rabbi.

Nahar Mitzraim, p. 184. In the Sephardic community of London, the custom was to read it in English; *Kether Shem Tov* 1.

In some communities, it was customary to read the kethubah before the beginning of the ceremony; *Kether Shem Tov* 1; *Yad Aaron* 62:13.

52. *Tosafoth, Pesachim* 102b, s.v. *SheAin*; Rosh, *Pesachim* 10:8 end; *Teshuvoth Maharam Mintz* 109; *Hagahoth Maimonioth, Ishuth* 3:60; *Ba'er Hetiv* 62:3; *Nachalath Shiva* 12:4:1; *Otzar Kol Minhagey Yeshurun* 16:10.

53. *Sefer HaYashar, Teshuvoth* 620, 621; Mordechai, *Kethuboth* 132; *Hagahoth Asheri, Kethuboth* 1:12; *Arukh HaShulchan* 62:8. For discussion, see *Eduth LeYisrael* 3:6.

54. *Mataamim* 143.

55. Original. See *Metzudoth David* 125, 26c. The reading of the Book of the Covenant occurred before the Israelites stood under the mountain; see Rashi on Exodus 24:1.

Also, after Adam and Eve were married, the Torah says; "This is the book (kethubah) of the chronicles of Adam" (Genesis 5:1); *Sefer Chassidim* 1139; *Mataamim HaChadash* 21.

In others, it is read by a learned guest or dignitary.[56]

After the kethubah is read, it is customary for the rabbi to give it to the groom, who then gives it to the bride.[57] The groom can also give it to a representative of the bride.[58] It is very important that the kethubah be given to the bride or her designee, since according to many authorities, if the bride is not in possession of the kethubah, she is forbidden to live with her husband.[59] Since the second part of the ceremony, the chupah, symbolizes the bride and groom living together, she should have the kethubah in her possession at this time.[60]

56. *Shulchan HaEzer* 8:3:2; *Eduth LeYisrael* 3:6. See *Teshuvoth Maharam Mintz* 109. In Sephardic communities, the kethubah is read by the cantor, often in a special chant; *Kether Shem Tov* 1.

57. It is an ancient custom, from the time of the Geonim, for the groom to give the kethubah to the bride after the kiddushin; see *Halakhoth Gedoloth* 36, p. 66d. Also see *Midrash Sekhel Tov*, p. 91; *Eduth LeYisrael* 3:7. Other ancient sources have the groom giving her the kethubah and saying, "Take this kethubah in your hand, through which you come into my domain according to the law of Moses and Israel;" *Siddur Rav Saadia Gaon*, p. 97; see Rabbi Yachia Yosef Tzalach, *Takhliel (Siddur Minhag Teiman*, Jerusalem, 1894).

This may indicate that giving the kethubah also denotes kiddushin by document (*sh'tar*); see *Orachoth Chaim*, quoted in *Eduth LeYisrael*, p. 19.

There is an allusion to this in the Torah. First it says, "Then they began to call in God's name" (Genesis 4:26), which alludes to the wedding prenuptial blessing. The Torah then says, "This is the book (kethubah) of the chronicles of Adam" (Genesis 5:1), which denotes giving the kethubah; *Sefer Chassidim* 1134; *Yalkut Chadash, Likutim, Dinim* 74 (end); *Mataamim HaChadash* 21.

The groom gives the kethubah to the bride, just as God gave the Tablets to Israel; *Shmoth Rabbah* 46:1; *Tashbatz* 467; note on *Taamey Minhagim* 964. See *Shulchan HaEzer* 8:3:4.

58. In Talmudic times, the kethubah was given to the bride's attendant; *Shmoth Rabbah* 46:1. It can also be given to her father; *Shulchan HaEzer* 8:3.

59. Maharil 65b; *Darkey Moshe* 66:6. Also see *Teshuvoth Rashbash* 320; *Teshuvoth Levushey Mordechai, Evven HaEzer* 49; *Ba'er Hetiv* 66:3; *Kenesseth HaGedolah, Hagahoth Tur* 66:8. Other authorities, however, maintain that as long as the kethubah has been written, the couple can live together, even if it is not in her possession; Rabbi Aaron Sasoon, *Teshuvoth Maharash* 119.

60. Original. See *Teshuvoth HaGeonim* (Assaf) 1:34 end; *Otzar HaGeonim, Kethuboth* 66, p. 21.

During the wedding and afterward, the bride must be very careful not to lose her kethubah. If there is any danger of it being lost, she should give it to her maid of honor, or another trustworthy person, to hold in safekeeping for her.[61]

61. See *Nethivoth HaShalom, Nethiv* 20; *Shulchan HaEzer* 8:3:5. See above, Chapter 9, note 12.

Chapter 22

THE SEVEN BLESSINGS

With the first part of the ceremony completed, the second part begins. Essentially, the second part of the ceremony consists of the reading of the Seven Blessings (*Sheva Berakhoth,* שֶׁבַע בְּרָכוֹת). The Seven Blessings are recited over the nesuin, the part of the ceremony where the bride and groom actually become permitted to each other.[1]

It is the custom to recite the Seven Blessings over a second cup of wine. In many circles, two filled cups of wine are prepared beforehand.[2] In other circles, the first cup is merely refilled; since it is refilled, it is considered a second cup.[3]

Two cups are required because erusin and nesuin were originally two separate rituals, which could be held even months apart. The first cup, for the Prenuptial Blessing, is for the erusin, while the second cup, for the Seven Blessings, is for the nesuin. Each cup therefore has an entirely different connotation.[4] Although the present custom is to have erusin

1. *Kethuboth* 7b.

2. Two cups are mentioned explicitly in a number of sources; see *Machzor Vitri* 469, p. 587; Maharil 64b; *Teshuvoth Maharam Mintz* 109; *Sefer HaManhig*, p. 541; Abudarham, p. 360; *Chupath Chathanim* 6. From *Evven HaEzer* 65:3 in *Hagah*, it is also obvious that two cups were actually used.

3. See *Shulchan HaEzer* 8:3:6. Some say that, in earlier times, two cups were used because the first one was broken; *Likutey Maharich* 3:133b. Earlier sources indicate that a second cup was used for nesuin because the first cup was given to the bride as the article of value for the kiddushin; *Machzor Vitri* 476, p. 592; *Sefer HaOrah* 2:14; *Evven Sappir* p. 81b. Since these reasons no longer apply, a single cup can be used, as long as it is refilled.

4. *Tosafoth, Pesachim* 102b, s.v. *SheAin*; *Machzor Vitri* 469, p. 587, 588; *Sefer HaYashar, Teshuvoth* 622, s.v. *VeAl; Evven HaEzer* 62:9. Also see *Sefer HaManhig*, p. 541; Abudarham, p. 360; *Maaseh HaGeonim*, p. 53; Yisrael Alphabein ed., *Teshuvoth Rashi* (New York, 1943), p. 218; Avraham Chaim Freiman ed., *Teshuvoth HaRambam* 6 (Jerusalem-Tel Aviv, 1934); Shalom Alback, ed., *Sefer HaEshkol* (Jerusalem, 1935), Volume 2, p. 195; *Orachoth Chaim,* Volume 2, p. 66; *Kol Bo* 75, 44c; *Rokeach* 351, p. 239, 354, p. 239; *Sefer HaOrah* 2:14; *Sefer HaPardes,* p. 100; Rabbenu Yerocham 23:2, p. 186a.

and nesuin together, two cups are still used to recall the original custom, where the two ceremonies were done separately, in different places.[5]

There is also a rule that, "two sanctifications are not made over a single cup."[6] This indicates that the same cup of wine cannot be used for two distinct rituals. Since kiddushin (erusin) and nesuin are two rituals, the same cup is not used for both.[7]

The Seven Blessings are:[8]

בָּרוּךְ אַתָּה יְיָ, אֱלֹהֵינוּ מֶלֶךְ הָעוֹלָם, בּוֹרֵא פְּרִי הַגָּפֶן.

1. Blessed are You, O God our Lord, King of the Universe, Creator of the fruit of the grapevine.

בָּרוּךְ אַתָּה יְיָ, אֱלֹהֵינוּ מֶלֶךְ הָעוֹלָם, שֶׁהַכֹּל בָּרָא לִכְבוֹדוֹ.

2. Blessed are You, O God our Lord, King of the Universe, who created all things for His glory.

בָּרוּךְ אַתָּה יְיָ, אֱלֹהֵינוּ מֶלֶךְ הָעוֹלָם, יוֹצֵר הָאָדָם.

3. Blessed are You, O God our Lord, King of the Universe, Creator of man.

בָּרוּךְ אַתָּה יְיָ, אֱלֹהֵינוּ מֶלֶךְ הָעוֹלָם, אֲשֶׁר יָצַר אֶת הָאָדָם בְּצַלְמוֹ, בְּצֶלֶם דְּמוּת תַּבְנִיתוֹ, וְהִתְקִין לוֹ מִמֶּנּוּ בִּנְיַן עֲדֵי עַד. בָּרוּךְ אַתָּה יְיָ, יוֹצֵר הָאָדָם.

4. Blessed are You, O God our Lord, King of the Universe, who created man in His image[9] — in the image set forth by

A second cup is mentioned as early as Netrunai Gaon (719 c.e.); *Otzar HaGeonim, Kethuboth* 82, 83, p. 26; *Kol Bo* 75, 44c; *Halakhoth Pesukoth* 94; Nachman Nathan Koroniel, *Teshuvoth HaGeonim* 55 (Vienna, 1871). Rabbi Menachem Meiri also writes that it is a custom from the time of the Geonim; *Magen Avoth*, pp. 30-32 (London, 1905). See below, note 30.

5. *Mataamim* 26.

6. *Pesachim* 102b.

7. See note 4.

8. *Kethuboth* 7b, 8a; *Mesekhta Kallah* 1:1; *Yad, Ishuth* 10:3, *Berakhoth* 2:11.

9. As it is written, "Let us make man in our image" (Genesis 1:26). The "image" here is the blueprint devised by God for man; Rashi on Genesis 1:27. Alternatively, this is speaking of God's conceptual "image," since man has free will just like God; *Yad, Teshuvah* 5:1. Man also shares the attributes that God uses to interact with His creation; *Nefesh HaChaim* 1:1.

His plan[10] — and who prepared from him a structure[11] to last for all time.[12] Blessed are You, O God, Creator of mankind.[13]

שׂוֹשׂ תָּשִׂישׂ וְתָגֵל הָעֲקָרָה, בְּקִבּוּץ בָּנֶיהָ לְתוֹכָהּ בְּשִׂמְחָה. בָּרוּךְ אַתָּה יְיָ, מְשַׂמֵּחַ צִיּוֹן בְּבָנֶיהָ.

5. May the barren [land][14] rejoice[15] and be glad, when its children are gathered back to it in joy.[16] Blessed are You, O

10. See Rashi on Genesis 1:27, Mizrachi, *Levush HaOrah ad loc.* This phrase would be translated literally, "in the image of the resemblance of His structure." This is the spiritual structure (*tavnith*); *Sefer Hafla'ah*, p. 8; see *Perush HaTefilloth* of Rabbi Yehudah ben Yakar, p. 38; *Sefer HaKaneh* 99a. The word *tavnith* relates to the Merkava; see I Chronicles 28:18. Also see Ezekiel 8:3, 10:8.

Other sources indicate that the word *tavnith* should not be applied to the Divine, from Deuteronomy 4:16-18. They therefore translate this phrase, "in the image of the resemblance of [man's] structure," or, "[man's] structure in the image of a resemblance"; Ritva, *Kethuboth* 8a; *Shitah Mekubetzeth Ibid.* quoting Radbaz; Rabbi Yosef Caro, *Teshuvoth Avkath Rokhel* 27 (Jerusalem, 1960), p. 31c; Abudarham, p. 362. Some sources omit this phrase completely; *Halikhoth Kedem* (Amsterdam, 1847), from *Moreh Nevukhim* 1:3; *Kether Shem Tov*, note 708; see *Otzar HaTefillah*.

However, the word *tavnith* may relate to the woman, just as the word *binyan* (from the same root) does; see below, note 11.

11. *Binyan* (בִּנְיָן) in Hebrew, literally something that is built. This denotes Eve, the first woman, as it is written, "God *built* the rib (or side) that He took from the man into a woman" (Genesis 2:22); Rashi, *Kethuboth* 8a, see *Perishah* 62:3.

12. Rashi, *Kethuboth* 8a. Or, "a most perfect structure," from Ezekiel 16:7 (see Radak, *Metzudoth ad loc); Sefer Hafla'ah, Kethuboth.*

13. The word *adam* here is used in a generic sense, denoting the entire human race, especially woman; Meiri, *Kethuboth* 8a, from Numbers 31:35, Isaiah 45:18; *Shitah Mekubetzeth* 40a.

14. Or Jerusalem; Rashi, *Kethuboth* 8a. Or the nation Israel; Maharsha *Ibid.*

15. As it is written, "Rejoice, barren woman, who does not have children..." (Isaiah 54:1); Abudarham; Maharsha.

16. The entire verse says, "Rejoice, barren woman, who does not have children... for more are the children of the desolate one than the children of the married wife..." (Isaiah 54:1). Hence, the "children" are the Israelites; *Perush HaTefilloth* of Rabbi Yehudah ben Yakar, p. 39.

God, who makes Zion rejoice in her children.[17]

שַׂמֵּחַ תְּשַׂמַּח רֵעִים הָאֲהוּבִים, כְּשַׂמֵּחֲךָ יְצִירְךָ בְּגַן עֵדֶן מִקֶּדֶם. בָּרוּךְ אַתָּה יְיָ, מְשַׂמֵּחַ חָתָן וְכַלָּה.

6. May You grant great joy to these dearly beloved,[18] just as You granted happiness to the work of Your hands long ago[19] in the Garden of Eden.[20] Blessed are You, O God, who grants joy to bridegroom and bride.

בָּרוּךְ אַתָּה יְיָ, אֱלֹהֵינוּ מֶלֶךְ הָעוֹלָם, אֲשֶׁר בָּרָא שָׂשׂוֹן וְשִׂמְחָה, חָתָן וְכַלָּה, גִּילָה רִנָּה, דִּיצָה וְחֶדְוָה, אַהֲבָה וְאַחֲוָה שָׁלוֹם וְרֵעוּת. מְהֵרָה יְיָ אֱלֹהֵינוּ יִשָּׁמַע בְּעָרֵי יְהוּדָה וּבְחוּצוֹת יְרוּשָׁלָיִם קוֹל שָׂשׂוֹן וְקוֹל שִׂמְחָה, קוֹל חָתָן וְקוֹל כַּלָּה, קוֹל מִצְהֲלוֹת חֲתָנִים מֵחֻפָּתָם וּנְעָרִים מִמִּשְׁתֵּה נְגִינָתָם. בָּרוּךְ אַתָּה יְיָ, מְשַׂמֵּחַ חָתָן עִם הַכַּלָּה.

7. Blessed are You,[21] O God our Lord, King of the Universe, who created happiness and joy,[22] bridegroom and bride,

17. In general, the Israelites are the "sons of Zion"; see Abudarham, p. 362, from Isaiah 62:5.

18. The bride and groom; Rashi, *Kethuboth* 8a; see *Mishnath Chassidim* 1:7, p. 64b. Others translate *reyim ahuvim* as "good friends," denoting the members of the wedding party; Maharsha; *Perush HaTefilloth* of Rabbi Yehudah ben Yakar, p. 40. One source has "friends and beloved," denoting the wedding guests and the bridal couple; *Sheiltoth* 16 (*Chayay Sarah*), p. 102.

19. *MiKedem* (מִקֶּדֶם) in Hebrew; see Ritva. See *Yad, Ishuth* 10:3. Or, "In the Garden of Eden to the east," as it is written, "God planted a garden to the east of Eden" (Genesis 2:8); Rashi, *Kethuboth* 8a. However, some sources actually translate this verse, "God planted a garden in Eden from ancient times"; see *Targum Yonathan ad loc; Pesachim* 54a; *Nedarim* 39b.

20. Where God made ten canopies for Adam and Eve; *Bava Bathra* 75a; *Siddur of Rabbi Shlomo of Garmiza,* p. 249. The marriage between Adam and Eve was the most compatible marriage possible, since they were both created from the same flesh; *Sefer Hafla'ah.*

21. This is a blessing for all Israel; Rashi, *Kethuboth* 8a; Ran, *Kethuboth,* Rif 2a. It is for all brides and grooms; *Siddur of Rabbi Shlomo of Garmiza,* p. 248. It speaks of the joy of intimacy between bride and groom; *Tosafoth HaRid, Kethuboth* 8a. It also speaks of the complete joy that will exist in the Messianic Age; Maharsha; Cf. *Mishnath Chassidim* 1:7, p. 64b.

22. Happiness and joy precede the bride and groom (Adam and Eve), since happiness is the way of knowing God, and is the first ingredient of

rejoicing and song, delight and cheer, love and harmony, peace and fellowship. Soon, O Lord our God, may there be heard in the cities of Judah and in the streets of Jerusalem, a sound of gladness, a sound of joy, the sound of the bridegroom, and sound of the bride,[23] the sound of rejoicing from bridegrooms at their weddings, and young people at their feasts[24] of song.[25] Blessed are You, O God, who grants joy to the bridegroom with the bride.[26]

Like the Prenuptial Blessing (*Birkath Erusin*), the Seven Blessings begin with a blessing over wine, for very much the same reason.[27] However, another reason for the blessing over wine is to make the total number of blessings equal to seven.[28] Six of the blessings are mentioned in the Talmud, and the blessing over wine makes seven.

creation; *Matteh Moshe* 12. Some say that the blessing is speaking of the spiritual "rivers of joy" mentioned in *Hekhaloth Rabathai* 9:3; *Perush HaTefilloth* of Rabbi Yehudah ben Yakar, p. 40.

23. This is based on Jeremiah 7:9; Maharsha, *Kethuboth* 8a; *Perush HaTefilloth* of Rabbi Yehudah ben Yakar, p. 40. The five "sounds" in this verse parallel those in Jeremiah 7:34; see *Berakhoth* 6b.

34. Since there cannot be a wedding without a feast; Abudarham, p. 362. See above, Chapter 5, note 32; *Otzar HaGeonim, Kethuboth*, p. 24.

25. This is based on the verse, "*bachurim* from their song" (Lamentations 5:14), but it is changed to "young people" (*naarim*) because the verse denotes a curse, since the *bachurim* spoke profanity and were therefore punished; *Eikhah Rabbah ad loc*; Meiri, *Kethuboth* 8a; Abudarham, p. 362.
    Some sources say that the *naarim* here denote the righteous, who sing to rejoice the bridal couple; *Perush HaTefilloth* of Rabbi Yehudah ben Yakar, p. 40; from *Ruth Rabbah* 3, on Ruth 2:8.
    Music is an integral part of the wedding, see above, Chapter 5, note 32.

26. See below, note 45.

27. Also to "give a portion to Levi"; *Sefer HaKaneh* 99a; *Metzudoth David* 125; *Shnei Luchoth HaBrith, Shaar HaOthioth* 1:162b. Wine is Judgment (*din*); *Zohar* 1:238a. Similarly, the Levites are associated with Judgment; *Zohar* 3:179b; *Tikkuney Zohar* 70, 124a. Hence wine is the portion of Levi.

28. See *Kallah Rabathai* 1:1. Also see *Yad, Ishuth* 10:4; *Machzor Vitri* 469, p. 587.

It appears that beginning with a blessing over wine was originally a custom only among the Jewish mystics.[29] However, in the year 756 c.e., Rav Yehuda Gaon legislated that the blessing over wine be said by all.[30] It has been the universal practice ever since.[31]

The second blessing is, "who created all things for His glory." This is said because people assemble for the wedding,[32] and it is written, "In a multitude of people is the King's *glory*" (Proverbs 14:28).[33]

The blessing also alludes to a "multitude of people" in another way. One of the purposes of marriage is to increase the world's population. Since a "multitude of people is the King's glory," marriage tends to increase God's glory. Hence, the order

29. *Zohar* 2:169a, 3:44b. This is why it is mentioned in the *Zohar* but not in the Talmud.

30. Rabbenu Tam, *Sefer HaYashar* 622. Also see *Halakhoth Pesukoth* 13; Rav Yaakov HaGozer, *Zikhron Brith LeRishonim* (Cracow, 1892), quoted in *Eduth LeYisrael,* p. 28.

31. See *Otzar HaGeonim,* p. 25; *Siddur Rav Amram Gaon,* p. 181; *Siddur Rav Saadia Gaon,* p. 108; *Midrash Sekhel Tov,* p. 91; Rosh, *Kethuboth* 1:16; *Evven HaEzer* 62:1. See *Gilyoney HaShas* on *Kethuboth* 87a.

32. Rashi, *Kethuboth* 8a. Some say that this blessing relates to the gathering of elders at a wedding, since Boaz took ten elders to bless Ruth (Ruth 4:2), and it is written, "toward elders there is glory" (Isaiah 24:23); Raavan on *Kethuboth* 8a, p. 128.

Some say that this blessing pertains to the Shekhinah, which is called "all"; *Perush HaTefilloth* of Rabbi Yehuḍah ben Yakar, p. 38.

Some sources maintain that the second and third blessings here ("who created all things for His glory," and "who created man") do not pertain to the wedding, but are general blessings; Rashi, *Kethuboth* 7b; Ran, *Kethuboth,* Rif 2b; *Sefer Mitzvoth Gadol,* Positive Commandment 48, p. 126a.

For a general discussion of the blessings, see *Machzor Vitri* 572, p. 590; *Sefer HaManhig,* p. 542; *Midrash HaItamri* 2, p. 11c.

For Kabbalistic discussions, see *Zohar* 2:169a; *Shnei Luchoth HaBrith, Shaar HaOthioth* 1:162b (which translates the *Zohar* into Hebrew); *Siddur HaAri* of Rav Asher, p. 149b; *Siddur HaAri* of Rav Shabbathai, 2:102b; *Siddur Rav Shneur Zalman of Liadi,* pp. 132c, 136c; *Mishnath Chassidim, Mesekhta Chatunah U'Millah* (Livorno, 1722), p. 64b; *Sefer HaKaneh* 99a.

33. *Tosafoth Rid, Kethuboth* 8a, s.v. *SheHaKol.*

begins with a blessing for God's glory.[34]

Furthermore, God created the entire universe for His glory, as He said, "Everything is for My glory; I have created it, I have formed it, and I have made it" (Isaiah 43:7).[35] However, man was the goal of creation, so God's glory was not fulfilled until man was made. Furthermore, man was not complete until woman was created and Adam and Eve were married. Therefore, creation was not complete until the first marriage. Every marriage is similarly a completion of creation, and hence, of God's glory.[36]

The Seven Blessings pertain primarily to the chupah, and the chupah is uniquely related to glory in scripture, as it is written, "over all glory shall be a chupah" (Isaiah 4:5). Hence, the blessings begin with God's glory.[37]

The above quoted verse, "Everything is for My glory; I have created it, I have formed it, and I have made it" (Isaiah 43:7), speaks of three stages of creation: creation, formation, and making.

"Creation" denotes creation *ex nihilo* — something from nothing. This is represented by this blessing: "who *created* all things for His glory."

"Formation" denotes "something from something." This is represented by the next blessing, which is literally translated, "who *forms* man."

"Making" denotes completion of a project. This is alluded to by the blessing, "who created man in His image," which speaks of the making of mankind into an ongoing species through the creation of woman. The creation of Eve was the culmination of all creation.[38]

34. Abudarham. Cf. Meiri; *Shitah Mekubetzeth*, s.v. *Mai,* quoting Ramah.

35. Maharsha, *Kethuboth* 8a. See below, note 38.

36. *Sefer Hafla'ah, Kethuboth* 8a.

37. Original.

38. *Perush HaTefilloth* of Rabbi Yehudah ben Yakar, p. 38; *Sefer HaIttur* 2:4, 64c; *Tanya Rabathai* 91, 98d; Abudarham, p. 362; *Shitah Mekubetzeth* 40a; *Matteh Moshe* 12; Maharsha, *Kethuboth* 8a.

The fourth blessing, *asher yatzar*, speaks of Eve; Rashi, *Kethuboth* 8a. See above, notes 11, 13.

After the initial blessings, which speak of creation, a blessing is recited for Zion. This is Jerusalem, which, according to tradition, was where Adam was created.[39] Since Adam was subsequently brought to the Garden of Eden, this blessing is followed by a blessing recalling the joy of Adam and Eve in Eden.[40]

The blessing for Zion's joy is recited before a blessing is said for the joy of the bridal couple. This is to fulfill the verse, "Let my tongue stick to my palate if I do not place Jerusalem at the head of my joy" (Psalms 137:6). The joy of Jerusalem must take precedence over the joy of the bride and groom.[41]

Furthermore, this blessing is a prayer for the restoration of Zion, which is also likened to a wedding. It is thus written, "God will rejoice over you, as a bridegroom rejoices over a bride" (Isaiah 62:5).[42]

The sixth blessing is a prayer that the bride and groom have the same joy that Adam and Eve had in the Garden of Eden. This is a blessing for the bride and groom separately, rather than as a couple. It therefore ends, "who makes groom and bride rejoice."[43]

The last blessing speaks of the joy of the couple together. It contains ten synonyms for joy, paralleling the ten sayings with which the world was created.[44] It concludes with the words,

39. *Targum Yonathan* on Genesis 2:7; *Yerushalmi, Nazir* 7:2; *Bereshith Rabbah* 14.

40. Original.

41. Rashi, *Kethuboth* 8a; Meiri; *Shitah Mekubetzeth* 40a; *Sefer HaKaneh* 99a. See above, Chapter 17, note 49.

42. Abudarham, p. 362.

43. Rashi, *Kethuboth* 8a.

44. *Zohar* 1:265a, 2:169a; Bachya, *Kad HaKemach* (in *Kithevey Rabbenu Bachya*) p. 184; *Sefer HaKaneh* 99a; *Sefer HaPeliyah* (Koretz, 1784), p. 65a. These are the Ten Sefiroth.

The ten expressions also represent the ten things that God will bring about in the World to Come: the ten times in scripture that Israel is called a bride (*Pesikta* 147b); and the ten synonyms for joy found in the Midrash; *Pesikta* 141b; *Perush HaTefilloth* of Rabbi Yehudah ben Yakar, p. 41.

"who makes the bridegroom rejoice *with* the bride," thanking God for the particular joy that a couple can experience together.[45]

The Seven Blessings are alluded to in the sevenfold blessing that God gave Adam and Eve: "[1] be fruitful [2] and multiply, [3] fill the world, [4] and conquer it, [5] dominate the fish, [6] the birds, [7] and all the animals" (Genesis 1:28).[46]

The main reason that the blessings are seven in number is because every marriage is a re-enactment of the creation of the world, which took place in seven days.[47] The six blessings mentioned in the Talmud represent the six days of creation. The blessing over wine represents the Sabbath; just as the Sabbath is sanctified with the Kiddush over a cup of wine, so the Sabbath here is represented by the blessing over wine.[48]

The six days of creation actually represent the masculine forces of creation. The six weekdays are therefore the time when men go out to work to support their families. The Sabbath, on the other hand, represents the bride and queen; hence, it is the feminine element of creation. In the seven days of the week, the six masculine days are united with the Sabbath, which is the feminine day. Similarly, in the Seven Blessings, the masculine and feminine elements are united. Since the bride and groom are being united, it is appropriate that a similar unification occur in their blessings.[49]

45. Rashi, *Kethuboth* 8a.

46. Radal on *Pirkey Rabbi Eliezer* 12:60. See *Midrash Tadshei* 5.

47. *Matteh Moshe* 12; *Yalkut Yitzchak* 552:51; *Sefer HaKaneh* 95a. These are the seven Sefiroth; *Tikkuney Zohar* 47, 84a. These are likened to the "seven doubled letters," which in *Sefer Yetzirah* 4:1 represent the seven days of the week; Ramban, *D'rush LeChathunah* (in *Kithevey Ramban*) 1:138. Also see *Zohar* 2:102b, 2:169a, 2:255b, 3:44b, 3:124a; *Zohar Chadash* 24a; *Tikkuney Zohar* 10, 26a.

48. Bachya, *Kad HaKemach*, s.v. *Chathan BeVeth HaKenesseth*, p. 184. See *Zohar* 2:169a.

49. *Maaver Yaavak* 2:9, from *Bahir* 172; *Yalkut Yitzchak* 552:53. See *Tolaath Yaakov*; Recanti, *Taamey HaMitzvoth*, p. 26.

It is taught that when Adam and Eve were married, God covered them with seven chupah canopies.[50] These seven canopies represented all seven forces of creation. Thus, when God created Adam and Eve, He said, "Let *us* make man in our image" (Genesis 1:26). God said, "let *us*" in the plural because He was speaking to all the forces of creation.[51] These forces of creation were basically seven in number, one for each of the days of creation. The seven forces of creation are seen as the seven chupah canopies.[52] The Seven Blessings represent these seven canopies used for the first wedding, the one between Adam and Eve.[53]

Furthermore, at the great wedding between God and Israel, it is written, "all the people saw the voices" (Exodus 20:15). It is taught that the Israelites saw seven Voices, representing the seven forces of creation.[54] The giving of the Torah was the fulfillment of creation, and therefore, all the forces of creation were present there. The Seven Blessings at every wedding represent the seven Voices at the giving of the Torah.[55]

Significantly, God's name appears fourteen times in the Seven Blessings. In the Ten Commandments, God's name also appears fourteen times.[56]

Every day, we also say seven blessings, for the "marriage" between God and Israel. It is taught that "in the morning two blessings are said before the Sh'ma, and one afterward. In the evening, two blessings are said before the Sh'ma, and two afterward."[57] Thus, a total of seven blessings are said every day

50. *Zohar* 2:245a. The Talmud says that Adam had ten chupoth, but in the future world, the righteous will have seven chupoth; *Bava Bathra* 75a. See Chapter 18, note 53.

51. See *Targum Yonathan,* Ramban, *ad loc*; *Bereshith Rabbah* 8.

52. See *Avodath HaKodesh, Chelek HaAvodah* 43 (end).

53. *Kol Bo* 44c; *Nachalath Shiva* 12:5:3; *Taamey HaMinhagim* 971. These are the seven Sefiroth, see *Shoshan Sodoth* 70b.

54. *Bahir* 45: *Zohar* 2:270b.

55. *Tashbatz* 466; *Metzudoth David* 125, 26b.

56. *Tashbatz* 466.

57. *Berakhoth* 11a.

over the Sh'ma. Regarding these blessings, King David said, "Seven each day I praise You" (Psalms 119:164)[58] These seven daily blessings parallel the Seven Blessings said for the bride and groom.[59]

It is significant to note that, in the daily service, the last words before the Sh'ma praise God, "who has chosen His people Israel in *love*." Just before saying the Sh'ma, the word "love" is said — speaking of God's love for Israel. The first expression after the Sh'ma is, "You shall *love* God your Lord, with all your heart...." (Deuteronomy 6:5). This speaks of Israel's love for God.

The Sh'ma itself consists of the words, "Listen Israel, God is our Lord, God is One" (Deuteronomy 6:4). This is an expression of unity. The Sh'ma is therefore an expression of unity and love.

Even more significantly, the Hebrew word *echad* (אֶחָד), meaning "one," has a numerical value of thirteen. This is the same as the numerical value of *ahavah* (אַהֲבָה), meaning "love." The Seven Blessings are thus a prayer that the love between bride and groom will be as permanent and indestructable as the love between God and Israel.[60]

It is also taught that when a person gets married, he gains seven benefits: [1] full human stature, [2] joy, [3] good, [4] blessing, [5] Torah, [6] protection, and [7] peace.[61] One blessing is said for each of these seven benefits.[62]

In this respect, the wedding blessings are just like any other blessings said over enjoyment.[63] It is taught that it is forbidden to derive any pleasure from the world without reciting a blessing.[64] Enjoying God's world without offering a blessing to

58. *Yerushalmi, Berakhoth* 1:5, 9a; *Tosafoth, Berakhoth* 2a, s.v. *Mebharekh.*

59. *Zohar* 3:230b; *Tikkuney Zohar* 70, 132a.

60. Original.

61. *Yevamoth* 62b; *Tur, Evven HaEzer* 1.

62. *Nachalath Shiva* 12:5:3.

63. *Levush* 61:1; *Shnei Luchoth HaBrith, Shaar HaOthioth* 1:162b.

64. *Berakhoth* 35a.

Him is tantamount to stealing from God.[65] Since a person gains seven benefits in marriage, it is fitting that seven blessings be said. Without these blessings, intimacy between bride and groom is forbidden.[66]

The Seven Blessings complete the wedding ceremony.[67] The ceremony thus consists of three basic elements: the kiddushin, the chupah, and the Seven Blessings.[68] These parallel the three partners in the marriage: the bride, the groom, and God.[69]

Another purpose of the blessings is to sanctify the bride and groom before the wedding is completed. If the blessings are said slowly and deliberately, with full feeling, and the bride and groom meditate on their significance, the blessings will uplift them spiritually before their marriage. This will begin their married life on a good, firm spiritual basis.[70]

Although the Seven Blessings have an element of thanks to God, they are also a blessing that the bride and groom should have a good life, as can be seen from their context.[71]

The earliest hint of these blessings is found in the case of Rebecca. Just before Rebecca left home to marry Isaac, the Torah says that her family blessed her (Genesis 24:60).

65. *Berakhoth* 35b. This is specifically related to the Seven Blessings; *Zohar* 3:44b.

66. *Mesekhta Kallah* 1:1. For discussion as to whether it is literal, see above, Chapter 18, note 27. The Talmud says that "eating matzah on the day before Pesach is like being intimate with one's betrothed bride in her father's house"; *Yerushalmi, Pesachim* 10:1, 68b; see above, Chapter 18, note 12. Just as matzah cannot be eaten before the seven blessings in the Haggadah, so the betrothed cannot be taken without Seven Blessings; *Metzudoth David* 107, p. 20b.

67. Abudarham, p. 357.

68. See Ramban, *D'rush LeChathunah* 1:62b.

69. Original. These are the three partners in making a child; *Niddah* 31b; *Kiddushin* 30b; *Koheleth Rabbah* 5:13. See *Zohar* 2:93a, 3:83a. Also see *Sotah* 17a.

70. *Shnei Luchoth HaBrith, Shaar HaOthioth* 1:162b.

71. *Arukh HaShulchan* 62:9.

Rebecca, the first Jewish bride, was thus blessed for her wedding. This remained the tradition for all generations to come; all Jewish brides are blessed, just as Rebecca was.[72]

It appears that in Biblical times it was the custom to bless the bride publicly.[73] Thus, when Boaz wanted to marry Ruth, it is written that Boaz "took ten men from the elders of the city" (Ruth 4:2).[74] Later, along with the other people present, these elders blessed Ruth and said to her, "May God make the woman who came to your house like Rachel and Leah, the two [women] from whom the house of Israel was built" (Ruth 4:11).[75]

From this, we also see that ten men must be present when the Seven Blessings are recited.[76] One reason for this is so that the marriage will be publicized, and so that it will be generally known that the couple is married.[77] Although marriage may be a private affair, the community has an interest in every marriage, and therefore, must participate in it.

On a mystical level, the ten men present at the wedding

72. *Mesekhta Kallah* 1:2. From this, some say that the blessings are a Torah law; see *Machzor Vitri*, p. 718. From context, it is speaking of the Seven Blessings; *Kissey Rachamim* on *Mesekhta Kallah*, p. 3b, s.v. *U'LePhum*. This also seems to be the opinion of *Sefer HaIttur* 2:4, 65b; *Tanya Rabathai* 91, 99a. There was a minyan (ten men) present; see *Hadar Zekenim; Chizzkuni;* on Genesis 24:6; *Torah Sh'lemah* 24:70. There was also a cup of wine; *Torah Sh'lemah* 24:244.

Others, however, maintain that the blessing to Rebecca was the Erusin Blessing; see *Tosafoth, Kethuboth* 7b, s.v. *SheNe'emar;* also see *Birkey Yosef, Evven HaEzer* 34:4.

73. It was also a custom in early post-Biblical times; see Tobias 8:5-7.

74. *Kethuboth* 7a, 7b; *Mesekhta Kallah* 1:2. Also see *Levush* 61:1.

75. This is considered a blessing; see *Kissey Rachamim* on *Mesekhta Kallah*, 3b s.v. *SheNe'emar*.

76. *Kethuboth* 7a, 7b. It is also derived from the verse, "In congregations bless God, the Lord, from the source of Israel" (Psalms 68:27); *Ibid.* Some say that the word "congregations" is in the plural, since two congregations are needed, one for the Erusin Blessing, and one for the Seven Blessings; *Peney Yehoshua, Kethuboth* 7b. See Chapter 20, note 12. Also see *Megillah* 23b; *Yad, Berakhoth* 2:10, *Ishuth* 10:5; *Evven HaEzer* 62:4.

77. See *Perush HaTefilloth* of Rabbi Yehudah ben Yakar, p. 38. Also see *Torah Temimah* on Ruth 4:2.

represent the sayings of creation. It is taught that the world was created with Ten Sayings.[78] If one looks at the first chapter of Genesis, the expression, "and God said," occurs nine times. In addition, the first verse, "In the beginning God created the heaven and the earth" (Genesis 1:1), is considered a "saying," making the total ten.[79] The ten men required for the wedding blessings parallel these Ten Sayings of creation.[80]

A quorum (*minyan*) of ten adult Jewish males (over thirteen years of age) must therefore be present at the wedding ceremony. Even if it is a small, private ceremony, ten men must be present.

If there is no minyan present, a wedding may be held in an emergency, but the Seven Blessings cannot be recited.[81] If it is possible to assemble a minyan during the week after the marriage, the Seven Blessings may be said then.[82] If the Seven Blessings are not said during the first week of marriage, the couple should attend another wedding and ask to be included in the blessings that are recited.[83]

78. *Avoth* 5:1.

79. *Rosh HaShanah* 32a; *Megillah* 21a.

80. Bachya, *Kad HaKemach, Chathan BeVeth HaKenesseth,* p. 184; *Metzudoth David* 125, p. 26b; *Yalkut Yitzchak* 552:55.

81. *Terumath HaDeshen, Pesakim U'Kethavim* 140; *Chelkath Mechokaa* 62:3; *Beth Shmuel* 62:4; *Arukh HaShulchan* 62:12; *Shulchan HaEzer* 8:6:8. Also see *Chelkath Mechokak* 55:12; *Beth Shmuel* 55:7. This follows the opinion that "a bride without a blessing is forbidden..." is not literal; see above, Chapter 18, note 27.

82. They can be said later; *Yad, Ishuth* 10:6; *Evven HaEzer* 55:3. This is because the blessings are not strictly associated with the wedding; *Perishah* 62:9; *Beth Shmuel* 55:8.

    The blessings can be said up to seven days after the wedding; see Ritva, *Kethuboth* 7b; *Yam Shel Shlomo, Kethuboth* 1:19. Other authorities, however, maintain that they can be said up to a year after the wedding; *Sefer HaMakneh, Kuntres Acharon* 55:3; *Arukh HaShulchan* 62:12; *Shulchan HaEzer* 8:6:9.

83. The couple should tell the person or persons reciting the blessings to have them in mind. See *Teshuvoth Nodah BeYehudah, Evven HaEzer* 56; *Pith'chey Teshuvah* 62:7.

In many communities, it is the custom for the cantor or rabbi to recite all seven of the blessings.[84]

In many circles, however, it is customary to honor as many as six different men with the blessings. The first man recites the blessing over wine together with the blessing, "who created all things for His glory" (*she-ha-kol bara li-kh'vodo*). The remaining five blessings are then parceled out as honors to other important guests.[85] The determination is made by the bride and groom and their families.[86]

After the Seven Blessings, the second cup is given to the groom to sip, and then to the bride. In this respect, it is like the first cup.[87]

84. This appears to be the most ancient custom; see *Pirkey Rabbi Eliezer* 12; Radal *ad loc.* 12:60; *Zohar* 3:44b; *Tikkuney Zohar* 10, 26a. This is also the Sephardic custom; note #5 on *Tikkuney Zohar loc. cit.*; *Shulchan HaEzer* 8:3:18. It is also the custom in Algiers; *VaYigash Eliahu* 104:8. Some say that the blessings should not be divided; *Shaarey Ephraim*, quoted in *Igroth Moshe, Evven HaEzer* 94.

85. See *Igroth Moshe, Evven HaEzer* 94. The author maintains that there should not be an interruption between blessings, and that all the men saying them should be included as each blessing is recited.

An earlier custom was for one person to say the first six blessings, and for a second person to say the seventh; Rabbi Noach Chaim Tzvi (ben Avraham) Maya, *Atzey Arazim* on *Evven HaEzer* 62:1 (Fürth, 1790); *Shulchan HaEzer* 8:3:18; *Minhagey Belza*, p. 85.

This can be done because any one of the blessings can be said without any of the others; similarly, if the blessings are said out of order, they are still valid; *Tanya Rabathai* 91, 99a; *Sheyarey Kenesseth HaGedolah, Hagahoth HaTur* 62:3 quoting *Igroth HaRambam* 3; *Nethivoth HaShalom* 18:4; *Atzey Arazim* 62:1; *Chokhmath Adam* 129:8. According to this, the requirements stated in *Igroth Moshe*, that there be no interruption, and that each man be included in all the blessings, may not be necessary. In general, the custom is not to abide by these requirements.

The concept of these blessings being recited by friends or attendants (*shoshvinin*) is found in an ancient source; *Sefer HaKaneh*, p. 99a.

In any case, the groom himself should not say these blessings; *Maaseh Rokeach* on *Yad*, p. 1, quoting Rabbi Avraham ben HaRambam; *Chida, Shiurey Berakhah* 62; *Sedey Chemed, Chathan VeKallah* 18; *Teshuvoth China VeChisda*, part 1, p. 110c; Rabbi Chaim Benveneste, *Dina DeChayay* 26c; *Shulchan HaEzer* 8:3:19.

86. *Teshuvoth Maharik* 169, quoted in *Shulchan HaEzer* 8:3:18.

87. *Shulchan HaEzer* 8:3:20. Some say that the person saying the blessing should also take a sip from the cup; *Maaseh Rokeach loc. cit.* See above, Chapter 20, note 36.

It is a custom for the groom[88] to break a glass goblet or cup to conclude the ceremony.[89] This custom has its roots in the Talmud,[90] and it became popular some eight hundred years ago.[91]

The usual practice is for the master of ceremonies to wrap the glass in a napkin, and place it near the groom's foot. The groom then shatters the glass with his right foot.[92]

88. The groom in particular; *Darkey Moshe, Orach Chaim* 560; *Evven HaEzer* 65:3 in *Hagah*; *Rokeach* 353; Maharil 64b; *Teshuvoth Maharam Mintz* 109; *Kerem Shlomo* 65.

Other sources, however, indicate that someone else would break the cup; see *Sedey Chemed, Asifath Dinim, Zayin* 12 (6:462); *Shulchan HaEzer* 8:3:23.

At the engagement (*tenaim*), the mothers-in-law would break the plate; above, Chapter 4, note 32. Here, however, the groom himself breaks it, since at this moment, his joy is greatest; *Mataamim HaChadash* 5.

89. *Orach Chaim* 560:2 in *Hagah*; *Evven HaEzer* 65:3 in *Hagah; Eduth LeYisrael* 5:2; *Ezer LeYitzchak* 17:9; *Sedey Chemed, Chathan VeKallah* 2.

In the Talmud, the custom was to break the glass at the meal; *Berakhoth* 31a; below, note 90. Now, however, the custom is to break the glass under the chupah; Rabbi Yitzchak Atiya, *Rov Dagan* (Livorno, 1823); *Teshuvoth Oth LeTovah* 30; *VaYaged Moshe,* p. 18. In some circles, it was the custom to break the glass after the kiddushin; *Ibid.; Kether Shem Tov* 25. The prevalent custom, however, is to break the glass after the Seven Blessings; *Machzor Vitri* 476, p. 593.

The custom of breaking a glass, however, was not universal, and in Algiers it was not observed; *VaYigash Eliahu* 104; *Zeh HaShulchan,* p. 213, note 14.

In some circles the cup used for the wedding blessings was used, and the wine was poured out before the cup was broken; *Kether Shem Tov* 23. In some places, it was the custom to bury the broken pieces; *Kether Shem Tov* 27. In Baghdad, a porcelain, rather than a glass, cup was shattered; *Ben Ish Chai, Shoftim* 11.

Normally, it is forbidden to destroy anything wantonly, since this comes under the heading of "do not destroy" (Deuteronomy 20:19); *Bava Kama* 91b; *Yad, Melakhim* 6:10. This does not apply to breaking the glass, because it is done for a purpose; Maharatz Chayos, *Berakhoth* 31a; *Pri Megadim, Mishbetzoth Zahav* 560:4; *Sedey Chemed, Asifath Dinim, Zayin* 12 (6:462); *Arukh HaShulchan* 65:5. Some authorities, however, opposed the custom on these grounds; Raavan 171. Some say that an already broken glass should be used; *Kerem Shlomo.*

90. *Berakhoth* 31a; *Tosafoth ad loc.* s.v. *Iisu.*

91. *Machzor Vitri* 470, p. 589; *Sefer HaOrah* 2:14, p. 177.

92. *Shulchan Ha Ezer* 8:3:23,24; *Eduth LeYisrael* 5:2. The older custom was to

The primary reason for shattering the glass is that a person must always temper his joy in this world.[93] Too much joy can lead a person to forget God and neglect his spiritual responsibilities.[94] It is thus written, "In all sadness there is reward" (Proverbs 14:23).[95] Thus, in a time of joy, a person must do something to remind him of his fear of God, as it is said, "Serve God in awe, rejoice with trembling" (Psalms 2:11).[96]

The glass is also broken to recall the destruction of Jerusalem and the Holy Temple. It is to remind people that there is still much sadness and heartbreak in the world.[97]

At the great wedding between God and Israel, the first Tablets were broken. The breaking of the glass recalls this first tragedy.[98]

In a sense, however, the Tablets were destroyed instead of the Israelite nation. After they made the Golden Calf, the

throw the cup against a wall; *Machzor Vitri* 470, p. 589; Maharil 64b; *Teshuvoth Maharam Mintz* 109.

93. *Levush, Orach Chaim* 560:2.

94. See Rashi, *Berakhoth* 30b, s.v. *DeHava*.

95. *Machzor Vitri* 470, p. 589. See *Berakhoth* 30b.

96. *Ibid.; Rokeach* 353, 355, p. 240; *Taamey HaMinhagim* 976; *Yalkut Yitzchak* 552:45. It is also to frighten the people, and quench their joy; *Pri Megadim, Mishbetzoth Zahav* 560:4. This is related to the destruction of the Temple; *Yam Shel Shlomo, Kethuboth* 1:17; *VaYaged Moshe*, p. 49. See next note.

97. *Kol Bo, Tisha B'Av* 62, p. 25d; *Orach Chaim* 560:2 in *Hagah*; *Yalkut Yitzchak* 552:43. Since the Temple was destroyed, joy is no longer complete; *Mataamim* 36.

In some circles, when the glass was broken, it was the custom to say, "If I forget you, Jerusalem, let my right hand forget" (Psalms 137:5); *Turey Zahav, Orach Chaim* 560:4; *Kether Shem Tov* 26.

One reason that glass, in particular, is broken is that, after the destruction of the Temple, glass became very rare; see *Tosafoth, Shabbath* 20b, s.v. *VeAnan; Hagahoth Rabbi Betzalel Regensberg, Berakhoth* 31a (in Vilna Talmud); *Sotah* 48a; *Pith'chey Olam, Orach Chaim* 560:7.

98. Bachya, *Shulchan Shel Arba; Yam Shel Shlomo, Kethuboth* 1:17; *Pri Megadim, Mishbetzoth Zahav* 560:4; *VaYaged Moshe*, p. 49. The Tablets were broken on 17 Tammuz, the same day that Jerusalem was breached; *Taanith* 26b.

Israelites deserved to die, but Moses destroyed the Tablets in their place.[99]

Similarly, the groom breaks a glass to give the Angel of Death its due, so to speak. If anything bad is supposed to happen to the bridal couple, the glass is broken in their place.[100]

The breaking of the glass also alludes to the breach that occurred right after the wedding of Adam and Eve, that is, the eating of the Tree of Knowledge. It was through that sin that death came to the world.[101] The glass is broken to remind us that we are mortal, and will some day be shattered just like the glass.[102] However, humanity became mortal right after the first wedding.

Furthermore, people must marry and reproduce mainly because man is mortal. Since man is mortal, he must reproduce his species. Since our mortality is the main reason for the wedding, we recall it at the close of the ceremony by breaking the glass.[103]

However, the Midrash teaches that man is like glass — if glass is broken, it can be remelted and reblown. Similarly, even when a man dies, his life is not over. We believe in the immortality of the soul and the resurrection of the dead; just as glass can be restored, so can a person after he dies.[104]

99. *Midrash Lekach Tov; Midrash Aggadah,* on Exodus 34:1. See *Yevamoth* 62a; *Bava Bathra* 14b; *Menachoth* 99b; Rashi on Deuteronomy 34:12. It was like when God "poured out His anger on wood and stone," destroying the Temple instead of the Israelite nation; *Eikhah Rabbah* 4:15. See next note.

100. Recanti, *Shoftim,* on Deuteronomy 20:5, p. 50c; *Shnei Luchoth HaBrith, Torah She BiKethav, Shoftim* 3:188a; *VaYigash Eliahu* 104; *Mataamim HaChadash* 34.

The Hebrew word for cup, *kos* (כוס) has a numerical value of 86, the same as that of *Elohim* (אלהים), the name associated with judgment; *Mataamim HaChadash* 8.

The cup is also broken to avoid the evil eye; Rabbi Uri Feivel ben Aaron, *Or HaChokhmah, D'rush al Adar* (Lachov, 1815).

101. Original.

102. Maharsha, *Berakhoth* 31a; *Ezer LeYitzchak* 17:9.

103. Chida, *Pethach Eynayim, Berakhoth* 31a; *Mataamim* 37.

104. *Bereshith Rabbah* 14:7. See *Perashath Derakhim,* end of 25.

This is why we break glass, as opposed to pottery.[105] The breaking of glass recalls our mortality, but it also recalls the divine promise of immortality.[106]

Another allusion to the breaking of the glass is that just as glass can be remelted and restored, so can man, even after his soul has been shattered and blemished by sin. No matter what sins a person may have committed, if he repents, God forgives him. It is thus taught, "Nothing can stand up before repentance."[107] The bridal couple have all their sins forgiven on their wedding day; therefore, this is a particularly appropriate time to break the glass. It indicates that no matter how broken they are spiritually, they can be restored just as the glass can.[108]

Another reason that a glass vessel in particular is broken is because of the tradition that King Solomon built a special gate for bridegrooms.[109] According to one tradition, this gate was made of glass.[110] The glass is broken to recall that with the destruction of the Temple, the glass gate was also shattered.[111]

When the glass is broken, the people respond *Mazal Tov* (מַזָל טוֹב "good fortune").[112] The band then strikes up the recessional.

Some say that the expression Mazal Tov is used at the end of

105. See above, Chapter 4, notes 32, 34.

106. *Tzion LeNefesh Chayah (Tzelach), Berakhoth* 31a; quoted in *Etz Yosef* on *Eyn Yaakov; Mataamim* 40; *Yalkut Yitzchak* 552:44.

107. *Yerushalmi, Peah* 1:1.

108. *Tzion LeNefesh Chayah, Berakhoth* 31a; *Mataamim* 38; *Yalkut Yitzchak* 552:46.

109. *Pirkey Rabbi Eliezer* 17. See above, Chapter 10, note 7.

110. *Shevet Yehudah,* quoted in Radal on *Pirkey Rabbi Eliezer* 17:70. It is stated in name of *Yossipon,* but see *Yossipon* 55. Also see Josephus, Antiquities 8:3:2, 15:11:5.

111. *Mataamim HaChadash* 51; *Shulchan HaEzer* 8:3:24.

112. *Shulchan HaEzer* 8:3:26. The Sephardic custom is to say, "If I forget you, Jerusalem, let my right hand forget" (Psalms 137:5); *Ibid.; Kether Shem Tov* 26; see above, note 97. It is also a custom to say Psalms 124:7.

a wedding because after Eve was made, Adam "named her Woman (*Ishah*) because she was taken from Man (*Ish*)" (Genesis 2:23). In the original Hebrew, the expression "she was taken from man" is *me-ish lukacha zoth* (מֵאִישׁ לֻקְחָה זֹאת). The initial letters of this phrase spell out *mazal* (מַזָּל).

It is furthermore written, "He who finds a wife finds good (*tov*)" (Proverbs 18:22).[113] The two words are therefore combined into Mazal Tov.[114]

According to Torah standards, it is very bad taste for the bride and groom to kiss under the chupah. It may be a gentile custom, but it has no place in a Jewish wedding. Such a sign of intimacy is reserved for when the couple is alone together.[115]

In many circles, immediately after the ceremony, people throng up to the chupah for a few moments to wish the bride and groom mazal tov personally.[116]

One traditional tune for the recessional is *VaYehi BeYeshurun Melekh* — "And there was a king (the groom) in Jeshurun (Israel), when the people were gathered — all the tribes of Israel together" (Deuteronomy 33:5).[117] The bride and groom exit at a lively pace, with men dancing either behind or around them.[118]

113. He finds the good that was missing, when it was said, "It is not good for man to be alone" (Genesis 2:18).

114. *Mataamim HaChadash* 9. Also, *mazal* (מזל) is the initial letters of *mazria zera le-minehu* — "which produces seed of its kind" (Genesis 1:12); *Kehilath Yaakov*, s.v. *Mazal*.

115. See *Evven HaEzer* 21:5 in *Hagah*.

116. *Betrothed Forever*, p. 30.

117. *Ibid.* p. 31.

118. They are accompanied to the Yichud Room with dance; *Mataamim* 83, 84. The people dance around them in a circle, because marriage is part of the cycle of the world; *Mataamim HaChadash* 14. Also see *Ibid.* 55. See *Mishneh Halakhoth* 7:249.

Chapter 23

SECLUSION

Immediately after the guests finish congratulating the bride and groom, the couple exit toward the Yichud (seclusion) Room. In many circles, it is the custom for the groom to take the bride's hand and lead her there.[1] The bride and groom are led to the Yichud Room amid singing and dancing.

The word *yichud* (יחוד) literally means seclusion. After the wedding ceremony is over, it is customary[2] for the bride and groom to be alone in a room for a short period of time.[3] This is an ancient custom,[4] which also has mystical overtones.[5]

The main reason for this seclusion is that, according to many authorities, the marriage is not complete until the couple has had a chance to be alone together.[6] As we discussed in

1. The custom of the groom taking the bride by the hand is discussed in *Sheyarey Kenesseth HaGedolah, Orach Chaim* 339:10; *Pri HaAdamah* 3, p. 14; *Shulchan HaEzer* 8:8:3. Some say his taking her hand to lead her to yichud completes the ceremony; Rabbi Raphael Aaron of Cairo, *Nahar Pakud* on *Shaar HaMafkid* (Cairo, 1908). Of course, he can only do this if the bride has been to the mikvah, and is not a niddah; Rabbi Yitzchak Badhab, *Kobetz Yerushalmi, Kiddushin* 10 (Jerusalem, 1930), p. 63b; *Eduth LeYisrael* 10:1.

2. Sephardim do not have the custom of yichud; *Shulchan HaEzer* 8:8:3; *Teshuvoth Yabhia Omer, Evven HaEzer* 5; *Siddur Imrey Phi*, p. 415. See *Arukh HaShulchan* 55:15.

3. The time required to fry a small egg and eat it; *Evven HaEzer* 178:4, from *Sotah* 4a. This is the time required to attain intromission; *Ibid.*

4. Maharil 65a. See *Evven HaEzer* 55:1 in *Hagah*; *Shulchan HaEzer* 8:8.

5. *Zohar* 3:141b.

6. *Chelkath Mechokak* 55:9; *Beth Shmuel* 57:4; *Siddur Derekh Chaim; Arukh HaShulchan* 55:11; *Pith'chey Teshuvah* 62:1; *Chokhmath Adam* 129:1; *Kitzur Shulchan Arukh* 148:1. Also see *Teshuvath Massah Binyamin* 90; *Teshuvoth Chavath Yair* 50 (end).

   Other authorities, however, maintain that being under the wedding canopy is sufficient, and that yichud is not required by law; *Turey Zahav* 57:4; see *Pith'chey Teshuvah* 55:2; *Eduth LeYisrael* 10:1.

Chapter 18, there are authorities who maintain that chupah itself is seclusion.[7] Thus, only after the couple has been alone together are they considered completely married according to *all* opinions.

The reason for this is self-evident. According to Torah law, until a couple is married, and the Seven Blessings have been recited, they are forbidden to be completely alone, without any chaperone.[8] The fact that they are alone together is therefore an indication of their married state. The yichud is public, to show the world that they are now married.[9]

There are some authorities who maintain that the marriage is complete with the Seven Blessings, and that the main reason for yichud is to give the couple time to be alone together. Rather than spending their first moments as a married couple among throngs of guests, the couple spends these first precious minutes alone with each other. This is a time when their love is at a peak, and they should be able to savor the moment alone together, without outside interference.[10]

In most Jewish wedding halls, there is a special Yichud Room. If the wedding is held where there is no Yichud Room available, any place where the couple can have complete privacy is suitable.[11] In a synagogue, the rabbi's study is

One source holds that the couple should be together alone immediately after the ceremony, so that he will not be required to divorce her if she is not a virgin; HaGra 55:11, from *Yerushalmi, Kethuboth* 1:1, 1b.

7. See above, Chapter 18, note 31.

8. See *Evven HaEzer* 55:1 in *Hagah*. Also see Mordechai, *Kethuboth*, Chapter 1.

9. Just as the giving of the Torah was public; *Avodath Yisrael, Ki Thisa,* s.v. *Shnei*, p. 36b; *Mataamim HaChadash* 1, p. 9b.

10. Maharil 65b; *Nachalath Shiva* 12:9. This is also so that the groom will not be too bashful later to initiate intimacy; *Mataamim* 130. See *Teshuvoth Ramah* 54.

11. *Beth Shmuel* 55:5; *Kitzur Shulchan Arukh* 148:1; *Mishneh Berura* 139:32. However, if the bride is a niddah, and has not been to the mikvah, the seclusion cannot be absolute; *Kitzur Shulchan Arukh* 148:2. If it is the bride's second marriage, however, only absolute yichud completes the marriage; *Kitzur Shulchan Arukh* 148:3; see *Evven HaEzer* 64:4.

sometimes used for this purpose. According to some authorities, the room should be given over to the groom, so that he will actually be taking the bride into his domain.[12]

It is the custom in most circles to designate two men as witnesses for the seclusion.[13] They examine the Yichud Room before the bride and groom enter, to ascertain that no one else is there and that the couple will actually be secluded alone.[14]

It is customary for the bride to enter the Yichud Room first, and to welcome in the groom.[15] It is also an ancient custom for the bridal couple to eat together in the Yichud Room.[16] They have been fasting all day, and they now have their first meal of the day together.[17]

12. *Siddur Derekh Chaim; Mishneh Berurah* 139:32; *Shulchan HaEzer* 8:8:4.

13. See Chapter 18, note 24. Also see *Shulchan HaEzer* 8:8:2; Rabbi Raphael Mordechai Solovey, *Yad Ramah* 52 (Bilgorei, 1923); Rabbi Aryeh Leib Tzinz, *Yaalath Chen, Beth Chatunoth* 12.

14. *Betrothed Forever,* p. 31

15. *Shulchan HaEzer* 7:4:3; *VaYaged Moshe*, p. 17; *Agra DeParka* 67. It is thus taught that the groom does not enter until the bride gives him permission; *VaYikra Rabbah* 9:6. See *Zohar* 1:49a, 2:133b, 3:141b.

    It is a Lubavitcher custom to place a silver spoon on the threshold, and have the groom step over it, entering the room *before* the bride; *Sefer HaMinhagim*, p. 76.

16. *Zohar* 3:141b; *Evven HaEzer* 55:1 in *Hagah*. Some sources mention that honey and cheese were eaten; *Rokeach* 353. Others note that egg and chicken were eaten; Maharil 65a. In some places, chicken soup, known as "golden soup," was served to the couple; *Mataamim* 23, 130.

17. *Betrothed Forever*, p. 31.

Chapter 24

THE MEAL

After the ceremony, the guests seat themselves for the wedding meal. This meal is an integral part of the wedding.[1] It is considered a mitzvah (virtuous act) to participate in this meal.[2]

Since it is a mitzvah meal, the demeanor should be appropriate. There is much room for joy, cheer, and even some frivolity, but coarse entertainment should be avoided. Nor is this a place for popular entertainment. The songs should have a strong Jewish flavor, consisting of verses in praise of God and His Torah.[3] As noted earlier, there is much good, modern, popular Jewish music that is appropriate.

The general practice is to have the meal at night. One reason for this is that Isaac and Rebecca, the first Jewish couple, first met each other in the evening (Genesis 24:63).[4] Similarly, the wedding between Jacob and Leah took place at night.[5] It is therefore common to have the wedding meal at night. This is not by any means a strict rule, and afternoon or morning weddings are permitted and often held.[6]

1. The kiddushin must be accompanied by a meal; see *Otzar HaGeonim, Kethuboth* 60, p. 18; *Teshuvoth HaGeonim* (Assaf) 1:113. See above, Chapter 22, note 24.

2. See *Yad, Deyoth* 5:2, *Eruvin* 6:6, *Chametz U'Matzah* 3:9; *Tosafoth, Pesachim* 114a, s.v. *VeAin; Chok Yaakov* 444:10; *Charedim, Mitzvoth of the Mouth and Gullet* 4:3; *Teshuvoth Chavath Yair* 70; *Shulchan HaEzer* 9:1:3; *Eduth LeYisrael* 7:1.

3. Mordechai, *Pesachim* 605; *Magen Avraham* 670:4; *Likutey Maharich* 3:134a; *Yalkut Yitzchak* 552:59.

4. *Mataamim* 134; *Shulchan HaEzer* 9:1:2; *Yalkut Yitzchak* 552:58, quoting Rabbi Naftali Tzvi Yehudah Berlin (Netziv), *Harchev Davar* (published with *HaAmek Davar*, Vilna, 1879) on Genesis 24:63; *Otzar Kol Minhagey Yeshurun* 16:15, p. 49.

5. *Mataamim* 133.

6. See Chaim Palaggi, *Ruach Chaim* 61:10, quoting *Yalkut Shimoni,*

The tables should be set nicely for the wedding, with tablecloths and settings.[7] The usual rule for a mitzvah meal requires that bread, meat, and wine be served.[8] The traditional meal also usually includes fish; just as man was blessed to "be fruitful and multiply" (Genesis 1:28), so were the fish (Genesis 1:22). The traditional menu therefore is fish, soup, a meat or chicken dish, and dessert. It goes without saying that the meal must be absolutely kosher. Care must be taken that all wine served is also kosher.

It is a very beautiful custom in many circles to set aside a special table for the poor, where any poor person can come in and partake of the wedding meal.[9] When the poor are invited to a meal, the table becomes like an altar, atoning for all the host's sins.[10] It is considered very auspicious for the newlywed couple that their wedding is open to the poor.

It is also a custom to allow the poor to collect charity at a wedding.[11] It is written, "Charity saves from death" (Proverbs 10:2, 11:4). Generosity to the poor can help guarantee that the couple will have a long, happy life together.

The meal usually begins while the bride and groom are alone together in the Yichud Room. All the guests wash in the traditional manner, by pouring water from a cup, first over the right hand, and then over the left. After washing and drying the hands, the usual blessing is recited:

בָּרוּךְ אַתָּה יְיָ, אֱלֹהֵינוּ מֶלֶךְ הָעוֹלָם, אֲשֶׁר קִדְּשָׁנוּ בְּמִצְוֹתָיו וְצִוָּנוּ עַל נְטִילַת יָדָיִם:

Blessed are You, O God our Lord, King of the Universe, who

Bereshith 16; *Nishmath Kol Chai* 2:2; *Kenesseth HaGedolah, Hagahoth HaTur* 26:1, 27:1.

7. See *Chidushey HaRan, Sanhedrin* 32b, s.v. *Ohr.*

8. *Shulchan HaEzer* 9:1:4. This is the usual standard for a mitzvah meal; see *Orach Chaim* 551:10; *Magen Avraham* 249:6. It was a custom to drink wine at a wedding from Talmudic times; *Berakhoth* 9a.

9. *Chupath Chathanim; Shulchan HaEzer* 9:1:12; *Eduth LeYisrael* 7:1.

10. *Chagigah* 27a; Rashi *ad loc.* s.v. *Shulchano.*

11. See *VaYigash Eliahu* 104: 40; *Shulchan HaEzer* 7:5:3.

sanctified us with His commandments, and commanded us to wash the hands.

The guests take their seats. No one should talk between washing the hands and reciting the blessing over bread. Each guest takes the bread in both hands, and recites the usual blessing over the bread:

בָּרוּךְ אַתָּה יְיָ, אֱלֹהֵינוּ מֶלֶךְ הָעוֹלָם, הַמּוֹצִיא לֶחֶם מִן הָאָרֶץ.

Blessed are You, O God our Lord, King of the Universe, who brings forth bread from the earth.

The meal is then begun. The bride and groom eventually make a grand entrance, usually before the main course. The band strikes up a spirited tune, and the guests surround the bride and groom, dancing around them in circles. At one point, the bride and groom are often lifted up in chairs, and carried around with the dancers. Then, toward the end, the bride and groom are seated together, and various guests dance before them, often performing all sorts of antics.[12]

The groom then washes his hands, sits at his place, and the guests become quiet so that he can recite the blessing over bread.[13] It is customary to have a special large challah loaf for the bridegroom.[14] After he takes a piece for himself and the bride, the rest of the loaf is distributed to the guests.

The practice of a cake cutting "ceremony" has no place in Jewish tradition.

12. See *Kethuboth* 17a. People dance before the groom as they would before a king; *Midrash Talpioth*, s.v. *Chathan VeKallah*. It is a custom to jump and spring in the dancing; *Yerushalmi, Chagigah* 2:1, 9a. In some circles, it was customary to make somersaults before the bride and groom; *Sichoth HaRan* 86.

13. Rashi, *Berakhoth* 47a, s.v. *Kadim; Or Zarua* 192; *Magen Avraham* 167:29; *Machatzith HaShekel ad loc; Ba'er Hetiv* 167:17; *Kenesseth HaGedolah, Hagaoth Beth Yosef, Evven HaEzer* 62:10; *Teshuvoth Be'er Sheva* 50; *Shulchan HaEzer* 9:1:7; *Eduth LeYisrael* 7:4. Other authorities, however, maintain that the honor should be given to the rabbi or another prominent person; *Chupath Chathanim.*

14. See *Teshuvoth Massah Binyamin* 1; *Shulchan HaEzer, Hashmatoth* 9:1, p. 128a.

A dais is usually set up, where the bride and groom, along with their parents and the rabbi, sit at the head table.[15] The groom sits at the head, since on this day, he is like a king.[16]

In many circles, at the end of the meal, it is customary for the cantor to recite a *Mi SheBerakh* ("May He who Blessed") prayer:[17]

מִי שֶׁבֵּרַךְ אֲבוֹתֵינוּ, אַבְרָהָם, יִצְחָק וְיַעֲקֹב, הוּא יְבָרֵךְ אֶת הֶחָתָן וְאֶת הַכַּלָּה וְיַצְלִיחַ אֶת דַּרְכָּם אֲשֶׁר יֵלְכוּ מֵהַיּוֹם וָהָלְאָה. יַחְדָּו יִמְצְאוּ תָּמִיד חֵן וָחֶסֶד בְּעֵינֵי כָּל רוֹאֵיהֶם, וְיִזְכּוּ לִבְנוֹת בַּיִת בְּיִשְׂרָאֵל לְשֵׁם וְלִתְהִלָּה, וִיהִי שָׁלוֹם בְּבֵיתָם וְשַׁלְוָה וְהַשְׁקֵט בִּלְבּוֹתָם כָּל הַיָּמִים אֲשֶׁר הֵם חַיִּים עַל הָאֲדָמָה. וְאֶת הַשּׁוֹשְׁבִינִים וְאֶת כָּל הַיּוֹשְׁבִים פֹּה יְבָרֵךְ בְּכָל הַטּוֹב, וְיַאֲרִיךְ יְמֵי כֻלָּם בַּנְּעִימִים. וְיִשְׁלַח בְּרָכָה וְהַצְלָחָה בְּכָל מַעֲשֵׂה יְדֵיהֶם, עִם כָּל יִשְׂרָאֵל אֲחֵיהֶם, וְנֹאמַר אָמֵן.

May [God] who blessed our fathers, Abraham, Isaac, and Jacob, bless the bridegroom and bride, and make their path successful wherever they may go from this day forth. Together may they always find grace and favor in the eyes of all they encounter. May they be worthy to build a house in Israel with good name and praise. May there be peace in their home, and contentment and happiness in their hearts as long as they live. May the members of the wedding party and all the guests be blessed with all good, and may their lives be prolonged in happiness. May [God] send blessing and success in all the work of their hands, along with all their fellow Israelites; and let us say Amen.

15. *Moed Katan* 28b; *Taamey Minhagim* 979; *Eduth LeYisrael* 7:3.

16. *Midrash Talpioth,* s.v. *Chathan VeKallah; Mataamim HaChadash* 46, from Psalms 89:20. See *Pirkey Rabbi Eliezer* 16 (end).

17. This is taken from *HaMadrikh.* See *Eduth LeYisrael* 7:8; Cf. *Or Zarua* 113.

Chapter 25

THE GRACE

After the meal is finished, preparations are made for the Grace after Meals (*Birkath HaMazon*). In many circles, it is customary to have special "benchers" (Grace booklets), imprinted with the name of the bride and groom, for the wedding.

Two cups are set out before the Grace begins, one for the Grace itself, and one for the Seven Blessings, which are recited a second time after the Grace.[1] As in the ceremony itself, two cups are used, because two rituals cannot be performed over a single cup.[2] The first cup is for the Grace, since whenever three or more men say the Grace together (especially at a special occasion), it is customary to recite the Grace over a cup of wine.[3] Similarly, the Seven Blessings are said over a cup of wine.[4]

Both cups should be carefully rinsed inside and out before

1. *Evven HaEzer* 62:9 and *Hagah; Tosafoth, Pesachim* 102b, s.v. *SheAin; Mesekhta Sofrim* 19:11; *Beth Shmuel* 62:11; *Chupath Chathanim* 8; *Chokhmath Adam* 129:7; *Arukh HaShulchan* 62:18. See *Machzor Vitri* pp. 53, 602, 715; *Otzar HaGeonim, Kethuboth* 81, p. 25; *Teshuvoth Rabbenu Tam,* p. 100; *Sefer HaYashar* p. 74c; *Taamey HaMinhagim* 985; *Yalkut Yitzchak* 552:60. Also see *Tanya Rabathai* 91, 98d; Rabbenu Yerocham 23:2, p. 186b; *Sefer HaIttur*; Ritva, *Kethuboth* 7b; *Orachoth Chaim* p. 80; *Sefer HaManhig*, p. 541; *Tzedah LaDerekh, Nashim* 3:1:1; *Hagahoth Maimonioth, Berakhoth* 2:10 §5, *Ishuth* 2:23 #60; Mordechai, *Kethuboth, Hagahoth* 283.

   Other authorities, however, maintained that only one cup was necessary; *Evven HaEzer* 62:9. For discussion see *Shulchan HaEzer* 9:3:1; *Pachad Yitzchak*, s.v. *Birkath Chathanim* 60d; *Eduth LeYisrael, Birkath HaMazon*, p. 81.

   Some say that both cups should be identical (Tzanzer custom). Paper cups, preferably, should not be used (Rabbi Moshe Feinstein).

2. *Tosafoth, Pesachim* 102b, s.v. *SheAin*. See above, Chapter 22, notes 6,7.

3. Orach Chaim 182:1. This is a sign of respect for God; *Levush* 182:1; *Mishnah Berurah* 182:1.

4. See Chapter 22, notes 29-31.

being filled.[5] Then, both cups are filled before the Grace is started.[6] Both cups should be filled all the way to the top.[7]

Although dirty dishes and food should be cleared off the table before the Grace, some bread should be left on the table. It is considered a blessing from God if one can eat and have something left over, as Elisha said to his servant: "Thus says God, 'Eat and have some left over' " (2 Kings 4:43). Furthermore, in the Grace, we ask for God's blessing, and a blessing cannot rest on nothingness. Some bread is left on the table, upon which the blessing can rest.[8]

It is customary to remove all knives from the table before the Grace. The table is likened to the altar, regarding which it is written, "If you lift your sword upon it, you will have profaned it" (Exodus 20:22). We are blessing God for food and life, and knives are a source of death.[9]

At a wedding, when the Seven Blessings are recited, it is customary to have the men and women sit separately. This Grace is a time of divine joy, paralleling the joy between bridegroom and bride, and it is a time when there should not be any emotion between any other man and woman present.[10]

5. *Orach Chaim* 183:1

6. *Derishah* 62:4; *Turey Zahav* 62:7; *Machatzith HaShekel* 147:11;*Levush, Minhagim* (at end) 30;*Teshuvoth Tzvi Tifereth* 82; *Teshuvoth Levushey Mordechai, Orach Chaim* 115. Cf. *Machzor Vitri*, p. 53;*Eduth LeYisrael, Birkath HaMazon*, p. 81.

   Many other authorities, however, maintain that the cup for the Seven Blessings is not filled until after the grace; *Beth Sh'muel* 62:11; *Ba'er Hetiv* 62:11; *Korban Nathanel* on *Rosh, Pesachim* 10:7; *Magen Avraham* 147:11; *Chupath Chathanim* 8:13;*Chokhmath Adam* 129:7; *Kitzur Shulchan Arukh* 149:1;*Shulchan HaEzer* 9:3:2. For discussion, see *Likutey Maharich* 3:134b.

7. *Orach Chaim* 183:3 in *Hagah*. However, if the cup is very large, and there is insufficient wine, it is sufficient that a *revi'ith* (3.4 oz.) of wine be placed in it; *Mishnah Berurah* 183:9, 271:42.

8. *Orach Chaim* 180:2;*Levush* 180:5;*Kitzur Shulchan Arukh* 44:3. See *Sanhedrin* 92a; *Zohar* 2:87b. Some say that food should be left on the table in case a beggar comes after the meal; Rashi, *Sanhedrin* 92a.

9. *Orach Chaim* 180:5; *Magen Avraham* 180:4; *Turey Zahav* 180:3; *Kitzur Shulchan Arukh* 44:4. See *Rokeach* 33, p. 230; Abudarham, p. 320.

10. *Sefer Chassidim* 393, 1120; *Bayith Chadash* 62; *Beth Shmuel* 62:11; *Kitzur*

During the Grace, however, the bride and groom sit together.[11] This indicates that among everyone present, their relationship is unique.

Before the Grace, it is customary to recite or sing *Shir HaMaaloth* (Psalm 126). This is to recall the Temple as well as God's promise of its restoration:[12]

שִׁיר הַמַּעֲלוֹת
בְּשׁוּב יְהֹוָה אֶת שִׁיבַת צִיּוֹן
הָיִינוּ כְּחֹלְמִים.
אָז יִמָּלֵא שְׂחוֹק פִּינוּ
וּלְשׁוֹנֵנוּ רִנָּה.
אָז יֹאמְרוּ בַגּוֹיִם:
הִגְדִּיל יְהֹוָה לַעֲשׂוֹת עִם־אֵלֶּה.
הִגְדִּיל יְהֹוָה לַעֲשׂוֹת עִמָּנוּ
הָיִינוּ שְׂמֵחִים.
שׁוּבָה יְהֹוָה אֶת־שְׁבִיתֵנוּ
כַּאֲפִיקִים בַּנֶּגֶב.
הַזֹּרְעִים בְּדִמְעָה
בְּרִנָּה יִקְצֹרוּ.
הָלוֹךְ יֵלֵךְ וּבָכֹה נֹשֵׂא מֶשֶׁךְ הַזָּרַע;
בֹּא יָבֹא בְרִנָּה נֹשֵׂא אֲלֻמֹּתָיו.

A song of steps: When God returns the captives of Zion, we will be like dreamers. Our mouths will then be filled with laughter, and our tongues with singing. It will then be said among nations, "God has done great things with them!" God has indeed done great things with us; we are very happy.

Return our exiles, O God, like the flood streams in the Negev. May those who planted in tears, harvest in joy. May he who went along weeping, carrying his bag of seed, soon come back singing, carrying his bundle of grain.

Shulchan Arukh 149:1; *Shulchan HaEzer* 9:4:6; *Eduth LeYisrael* 3:3, p. 88; *Brith Olam* on *Sefer Chassidim* 393; Chida, *Yosef Ometz* 47; Rabbi Yehudah Assad, *Teshuvoth Yehudah Yaaleh* 2:45; *Nohag KeTzon Yosef, Nesuin* 12.

However, some say that it is permitted, since nowadays men are not so easily aroused by the presence of women; *Levush, Minhagim* 36.

11. *Yam Shel Shlomo, Kethuboth* 1:20; *Urah Shachar* 2:24; *Shulchan HaEzer* 9:4:8, 9:6:3; *Darkey Chaim* (customs of Rabbi Chaim Halberstam of Tzana) 126. See *Eduth LeYisrael* p. 94. Among some Chassidic circles, however, the custom is that the bride stands at the door; *Ibid.* See *Chelek LeShiva* on *Nachalath Shiva,* p. 18.

12. *Shnei Luchoth HaBrith; Magen Avraham* 1:5; *Mishneh Berurah* 1:11. This is said before the final washing of the hands; *Arukh HaShulchan* 181:9.

After this, a small cup of water is passed around, from which the people wash their fingers after the meal. This is referred to as *mayim acharonim*, literally, "final water." It is a custom in most circles to wash in this manner after every meal.[13] There should be no interruption between this washing and the Grace.[14]

One of the guests is then given the honor of leading the Grace. In some circles, it is customary for this honor to be given to one of the rabbis present.[15]

A person sitting next to the man honored to lead the Grace lifts the first cup and gives it to the leader. The leader takes it in both hands, and then transfers it to his right hand.[16] In some circles, he holds the cup from the bottom, so that it rests on the palm of his hand.[17] The cup should be held at least one handbreadth (around 4 inches) above the table.[18]

The leader begins the Grace by saying:

רַבּוֹתַי נְבָרֵךְ

Gentlemen, let us say Grace.

In some circles, it is the custom to say this introduction in Yiddish rather than Hebrew:[19]

רַבּוֹתַי, מִיר וֶועלֶן בֶּענְטְשִׁין.

Everyone present responds:[20]

יְהִי שֵׁם יְיָ מְבוֹרָךְ מֵעַתָּה וְעַד עוֹלָם

13. *Orach Chaim* 181:1; *Kitzur Shulchan Arukh* 44:1.

14. *Magen Avraham* 181:5; *Shulchan HaEzer* 9:3:4.

15. *Shulchan HaEzer* 9:3:5—9,

16. *Orach Chaim* 183:4; *Berakhoth* 51a.

17. *Ba'er Hetiv* 182:5; *Mishneh Berurah* 183:15; *Arukh HaShulchan* 183:5; *Shulchan HaEzer* 9:4:2. See *Zohar* 1:1a.

18. *Orach Chaim* 183:4; *Berakhoth* 51a.

19. *Magen Avraham* 192:0; *Mishneh Berurah* 192:2; from *Pesachim* 103a; *Aruch HaShulchan* 192:2; *Zohar* 3:186b.

20. *Magen Avraham; Mishneh Berurah; loc. cit.*

May God's name be blessed now and forever (Psalms 113:2). The leader repeats this verse:

יְהִי שֵׁם יְיָ מְבוֹרָךְ מֵעַתָּה וְעַד עוֹלָם

May God's name be blessed now and forever.

If there are ten adult Jewish men present, he continues with the poem *Davay Haser:*

דְּוַי הָסֵר וְגַם חָרוֹן וְאָז אִלֵּם בְּשִׁיר יָרוֹן. נְחֵנוּ בְּמַעְגְּלֵי צֶדֶק, שְׁעֵה בִּרְכַּת בְּנֵי יְשׁוּרוּן (בְּנֵי אַהֲרוֹן).

בִּרְשׁוּת (הַכֹּהֵן) מָרָנָן וְרַבָּנָן וְרַבּוֹתַי, נְבָרֵךְ אֱלֹהֵינוּ שֶׁהַשִּׂמְחָה בִּמְעוֹנוֹ שֶׁאָכַלְנוּ מִשֶּׁלוֹ

Remove distress, and also wrath,[21]
Then the dumb will burst forth in song;
He shall lead us in straight paths,[22]
Accepting the blessing of the children of Jeshurun
(the children of Aaron).[23]

With the permission of the masters, rabbis, and others present, let us bless our God, in whose domain is joy,[24] whose food we have eaten.

Everyone responds:

בָּרוּךְ אֱלֹהֵינוּ שֶׁהַשִּׂמְחָה בִּמְעוֹנוֹ שֶׁאָכַלְנוּ מִשֶּׁלוֹ וּבְטוּבוֹ חָיִינוּ.

Blessed be our God, in whose domain is joy, whose food we have eaten, and through whose goodness we live.[25]

21. Divine wrath, as in Lamentations 4:11; see *Eduth LeYisrael*. Or "frustration."

22. See Psalms 23:3.

23. See *Eduth LeYisrael*, p. 92.

24. The word "and" is not included here; see *Machzor Vitri* 492, p. 600; *Evven HaEzer* 62:13; *Yam Shel Shlomo, Kethuboth* 1:19; *Kitzur Shulchan Arukh* 149:1; *Arukh HaShulchan* 62:39. Some authorities, however, maintain that the word "and" should be said here; see *Siddur Avodath Yisrael; Siddur Derekh HaChaim; Otzar HaTefillah; Shulchan HaEzer* 9:4:3; *Eduth LeYisrael*, p. 93.

One source only has *she-ha-simcha be-me'ono*, and omits *she-akhalnu mi-shelo; Siddur Rav Saadia Gaon*, p. 107.

25. The last phrase, "through whose goodness we live," is not in the Talmud; see *Orach Chaim* 192:1; *Magen Avraham* 192:0. However, it is in the *Zohar*; see *Zohar* 2:168b; *Zohar Chadash* 87c; *Bayith Chadash* 192; *Shaarey Zohar, Berakhoth* 49a.

The leader repeats:

בָּרוּךְ אֱלֹהֵינוּ שֶׁהַשִּׂמְחָה בִּמְעוֹנוֹ שֶׁאָכַלְנוּ מִשֶּׁלּוֹ וּבְטוּבוֹ חָיִינוּ.

Blessed be our God, in whose domain is joy, whose food we have eaten, and through whose goodness we live.

Everyone responds:[26]

בָּרוּךְ הוּא וּבָרוּךְ שְׁמוֹ

Blessed be He, and blessed be His name.

Everyone then completes the Grace, on page *221*

The initial letters of the poem *Davay Haser*, spell out the name Dunash (דּוּנָשׁ). The poem is attributed to Rabbi Dunash ben Labrat (circa 950 c.e.), a student of Saadia Gaon (882 — 942 c.e.).[27] This Rabbi Dunash is also known as the author of the Sabbath table song, *Deror Yikra,* which also spells out his name with the first letter of each line.

Davay Haser is said only in the presence of ten men, when the Seven Blessings are said at the end of the Grace.[28] The poem is said because exuberant joy and song have been forbidden since the destruction of the Temple — except at weddings. We pray that the Temple be rebuilt, so that the situation will be normalized, and joy will be permitted at all times.[29]

26. This is not a universal custom.

27. *Shulchan HaEzer* 9:4:5; *Eduth LeYisrael, Birkath HaMazon* 2, p. 85. See *Toledoth Rav Nissim ben Yaakov* (Constantinople, 1519), quoted in Rabbi Matithyahu ben Mordechai Gerji, *Oneg LeShabbath* (Jerusalem, 1913), quoted in *Avney Shoham.*

The earliest mention of this poem is in Maharil 65a. Also see *Beth Shmuel* 62:11; *Turey Zahav* 62:7; *Derishah* 62:4; *Kitzur Shulchan Arukh* 149:1.

28. *Beth Shmuel* 62:11; *Arukh HaShulchan* 62:18. If there is no minyan, then *Davay Haser* is not said, but rather, *Nodeh LeShimkhah,* as at a circumcision ceremony; *Ibid.* However, the custom is not to say *Nodeh LeShimkhah; Shulchan HaEzer* 9:4:7. It is only said in the presence of a "new face" *(panim chadashoth); Eduth LeYisrael, Birkath HaMazon* 2:2. There is some discussion as to over which cup it is said; *Ibid.* 2:4.

29. Rabbi Yehudah Liva ben Shmuel Oppenheim, *Matteh Yehudah* (Offenbach, 1721); quoted in *Taamey HaMinhagim* 986; *Shulchan HaEzer* 9:4:5; *Eduth LeYisrael* 2:3. Also see *Otzar Kol Minhagey Yeshurun* 16:16.

This poem is also said during the week after the wedding, wherever the Seven Blessings are recited. Some circles, however, have a custom of not reciting it on the Sabbath.[30]

Also added to the introduction to the Grace are the words *SheHaSimcha BiMe'ono* (שֶׁהַשִּׂמְחָה בִּמְעוֹנוֹ), meaning, "in whose domain is joy."[31] This is also said only when the Seven Blessings are said.[32]

This phrase is added to the Grace because a wedding is a particular time of joy, both on high and below. It is thus written, "On the day of his wedding, on the day his heart rejoiced" (Song of Songs 3:11).[33]

This phrase is said at a wedding also because it is a duty to make the bride and groom rejoice.[34] However, we must recognize that the joy does not come from us, but from God's domain. We therefore acknowledge that God is the One "in whose domain is joy."[35] The domain of God is seen as a place totally devoid of sadness, as it is written, "Strength and delight are before Him" (1 Chronicles 16:27).[36]

The phrase is also said because creation was not completed until Adam and Eve were married. It is written, "God rejoices in His works" (Psalms 104:31). However, it was only with the marriage of Adam and Eve that the divine joy in creation was

30. *Likutey Maharich* 3:135b. However, the earliest source states that it was said on the Sabbath; Maharil 65b. Other places therefore had the custom to say it on the Sabbath; see *Minhagey Mattersdorf* 115; *Minhagey Belza*, p. 85. See *Eduth LeYisrael, Birkath HaMazon* 2:6.

31. *Kethuboth* 8a; *Yad, Berakhoth* 5:5.

32. *Evven HaEzer* 62:13. The only time it is said is at a wedding feast or the like; *Kethuboth* 8a; *Yam Shel Shlomo, Bava Kama* 7:37; *Kol Bo* 75, 45a; *Arukh HaShulchan* 62:40. It is not said at a Pidyon Ha-Ben; *Yoreh Deah* 305:10 in *Hagah*.

33. *Metzudoth David* 125, 26c.

34. *Berakhoth* 6b.

35. *Perush HaTefilloth* of Rabbi Yehudah ben Yakar, p. 42; Bachya, *Kad HaKemach*, p. 185; Abudarham, p. 364.

36. *Sefer Chassidim* 393; Abudarham, p. 364. See *Chagigah* 5b; *Zohar* 1:163b.

complete. This divine joy is reflected at every wedding.[37]

We recognize that true joy comes only from God. A wedding may represent one of the greatest human joys, but it is not complete. Man must marry because he is mortal; therefore he must propagate the species. The joy of marriage is tinged by the realization of our mortality. Therefore, although a wedding represents our highest joy, we recognize that true joy can only be found in "His domain."[38]

However, whenever there is joy on earth, there is also joy on high, as it is written, "Let the heavens rejoice and let the earth be glad" (1 Chronicles 16:31). When the joy on high combines with the joy below, there is a great realization of the Divine. Therefore, the first letters of this verse, which in Hebrew is *Yismechu ha-shamayim ve-thagel ha-aretz* (יִשְׂמְחוּ הַשָּׁמַיִם וְתָגֵל הָאָרֶץ) spell out the Tetragrammaton of (יהוה, YHVH), God's unpronounceable Name. This is the joy that is recognized at a wedding.[39]

The word used for "domain" here is the Hebrew *Ma'on* (מָעוֹן), which is actually one of the seven heavens mentioned in the Talmud, where it is described as the abode where angels live and sing before God.[40] The song of the angels is seen as a reflection of the joy on high.[41] The heaven ma'on is thus seen as the place of the "rivers of joy."[42] Therefore, ma'on is mentioned in the Grace.

Furthermore, it is taught that the angels who served the "bridal meal" at Adam and Eve's wedding were angels from

37. *Mataamim* 49.

38. *Aruch HaShulchan* 62:40. This is erroneously attributed to *Yam Shel Shlomo; Shulchan HaEzer* 9:4:6.

39. *Sefer Chassidim* 393; *Nohag KeTzon Yosef* 12.

40. *Chagigah* 12b.

41. *Machzor Vitri* 492, p. 600; *Sefer HaIttur* 2:4, 64b; *Sefer HaManhig* p. 539; *Tanya Rabathai* 91, p. 98b; *Yalkut Yitzchak* 552:62. Also see *Tzedah LaDerekh, Kiddushin* 3:1; *Orachoth Chaim*, p. 73. See above, note 29.

42. *Perush HaTefilloth* of Rabbi Yehudah ben Yakar, p. 42; Bachya on Exodus 25:18, p. 277; *Kad HaKemach*, p. 185. These "rivers of joy" are mentioned in *Hekhaloth Rabathai* 9:3.

ma'on. Therefore, at every bridal feast, we speak of the joy that is in God's heaven, ma'on.[43]

Finally, the word ma'on also denotes the Holy Temple. This was the place of true joy for the Jewish people — joy in serving God. The words, "in whose domain (*ma'on*) is joy" are thus, in a sense, a prayer for the restoration of true joy in the Holy Temple.[44]

The Grace is then said just as it is after any meal:

בָּרוּךְ אַתָּה יְהֹוָה, אֱלֹהֵינוּ מֶלֶךְ הָעוֹלָם, הַזָּן אֶת הָעוֹלָם כֻּלּוֹ, בְּטוּבוֹ בְּחֵן וּבְחֶסֶד וּבְרַחֲמִים, הוּא נוֹתֵן לֶחֶם לְכָל בָּשָׂר כִּי לְעוֹלָם חַסְדּוֹ, וּבְטוּבוֹ הַגָּדוֹל, תָּמִיד לֹא חָסַר לָנוּ, וְאַל יֶחְסַר לָנוּ מָזוֹן לְעוֹלָם וָעֶד. בַּעֲבוּר שְׁמוֹ הַגָּדוֹל, כִּי הוּא אֵל זָן וּמְפַרְנֵס לַכֹּל וּמֵטִיב לַכֹּל, וּמֵכִין מָזוֹן לְכָל בְּרִיּוֹתָיו אֲשֶׁר בָּרָא. כָּאָמוּר: פּוֹתֵחַ אֶת יָדֶךָ, וּמַשְׂבִּיעַ לְכָל חַי רָצוֹן: בָּרוּךְ אַתָּה יְהֹוָה, הַזָּן אֶת הַכֹּל.

Blessed are You, O God our Lord, King of the Universe, who feeds all the world with His goodness, kindness, love and mercy. He gives bread to all flesh, for His love is endless.[45] In His great goodness, He has never left us in need, and He will never leave us in need of food, forever and ever, for the sake of His great Name. For He is God who feeds and provides for all; He is good to all, and prepares food for all His creatures that He created. Blessed are You, O God, who feeds all things.

נוֹדֶה לְךָ יְהֹוָה אֱלֹהֵינוּ, עַל שֶׁהִנְחַלְתָּ לַאֲבוֹתֵינוּ, אֶרֶץ חֶמְדָּה טוֹבָה וּרְחָבָה, וְעַל שֶׁהוֹצֵאתָנוּ יְהֹוָה אֱלֹהֵינוּ מֵאֶרֶץ מִצְרַיִם, וּפְדִיתָנוּ מִבֵּית עֲבָדִים, וְעַל בְּרִיתְךָ שֶׁחָתַמְתָּ בִּבְשָׂרֵנוּ, וְעַל תּוֹרָתְךָ שֶׁלִּמַּדְתָּנוּ, וְעַל חֻקֶּיךָ שֶׁהוֹדַעְתָּנוּ, וְעַל חַיִּים חֵן וָחֶסֶד שֶׁחוֹנַנְתָּנוּ, וְעַל אֲכִילַת מָזוֹן שָׁאַתָּה זָן, וּמְפַרְנֵס אוֹתָנוּ תָּמִיד, בְּכָל יוֹם וּבְכָל עֵת וּבְכָל שָׁעָה.

43. Geonim, quoted in *Shitah Mekubtzeth, Kethuboth* 8a; *Yalkut Yitzchak* 552:61 (who erroneously attributes it to *Kol Bo*).

God was, as it were, the "best man" (*shoshvin*) at Adam's wedding, and shared in his joy; *Shulchan HaEzer* 9:4:6.

44. *Sefer HaIttur* 2:4, 64b; *Tanya Rabathai* 91, 98b.

45. Psalms 136:25.

We thank You, O God our Lord, for You granted our fathers a desirable, good, spacious land; for You brought us out, O God our Lord, from the land of Egypt, and rescued us from the place of slavery; for Your covenant that You sealed in our flesh, for Your Torah that You taught us, for Your laws that You revealed to us; and for the food we eat, that You grant and provide for us always, every day, at all times, every hour.

וְעַל הַכֹּל יְהֹוָה אֱלֹהֵינוּ אֲנַחְנוּ מוֹדִים לָךְ, וּמְבָרְכִים אוֹתָךְ, יִתְבָּרֵךְ שִׁמְךָ בְּפִי כָּל חַי, תָּמִיד לְעוֹלָם וָעֶד. כַּכָּתוּב, וְאָכַלְתָּ וְשָׂבָעְתָּ וּבֵרַכְתָּ אֶת יְהֹוָה אֱלֹהֶיךָ, עַל הָאָרֶץ הַטּוֹבָה אֲשֶׁר נָתַן לָךְ: בָּרוּךְ אַתָּה יְהֹוָה, עַל הָאָרֶץ וְעַל הַמָּזוֹן.

And for everything, O God our Lord, we thank You and bless You. May Your name be blessed by all life always and forever. It is thus written, "You shall eat and be satisfied, and bless God your Lord for the good land He gave you" (Deuteronomy 8:10).[46]

Blessed are You, O God, for the land and for the food.

רַחֵם נָא יְהֹוָה אֱלֹהֵינוּ, עַל יִשְׂרָאֵל עַמֶּךָ, וְעַל יְרוּשָׁלַיִם עִירֶךָ, וְעַל צִיּוֹן מִשְׁכַּן כְּבוֹדֶךָ, וְעַל מַלְכוּת בֵּית דָּוִד מְשִׁיחֶךָ, וְעַל הַבַּיִת הַגָּדוֹל וְהַקָּדוֹשׁ, שֶׁנִּקְרָא שִׁמְךָ עָלָיו. אֱלֹהֵינוּ אָבִינוּ רְעֵנוּ זוּנֵנוּ פַּרְנְסֵנוּ וְכַלְכְּלֵינוּ וְהַרְוִיחֵנוּ, וְהַרְוַח לָנוּ יְהֹוָה אֱלֹהֵינוּ מְהֵרָה מִכָּל צָרוֹתֵינוּ. וְנָא אַל תַּצְרִיכֵנוּ יְהֹוָה אֱלֹהֵינוּ, לֹא לִידֵי מַתְּנַת בָּשָׂר וָדָם, וְלֹא לִידֵי הַלְוָאָתָם, כִּי אִם לְיָדְךָ הַמְּלֵאָה הַפְּתוּחָה הַקְּדוֹשָׁה וְהָרְחָבָה, שֶׁלֹּא נֵבוֹשׁ וְלֹא נִכָּלֵם וְלֹא נִכָּשֵׁל לְעוֹלָם וָעֶד:

Have mercy, O God our Lord, on Your people Israel, on Your city Jerusalem, on Zion, home of Your glory, on the royal house of David Your anointed one, and on the great and holy Temple that bears Your name. Our God, our Father, our Shepherd, feed us, support us, nourish us, and sustain us. Quickly grant us relief, O God, from all our troubles. And please, O God our Lord, do not make us rely on gifts from flesh and blood, nor upon their loans, but let [all] come from Your full, open, generous hand, so that we will never be shamed or disgraced.

46. This is seen as a commandment to recite the grace.

וּבְנֵה יְרוּשָׁלַיִם עִיר הַקֹּדֶשׁ בִּמְהֵרָה בְיָמֵינוּ: בָּרוּךְ אַתָּה יְהֹוָה, בּוֹנֵה בְּרַחֲמָיו יְרוּשָׁלָיִם, אָמֵן.

And build Jerusalem, the holy city, soon, in our days. Blessed are You, O God, who in His mercy builds Jerusalem. Amen.

בָּרוּךְ אַתָּה יְהֹוָה אֱלֹהֵינוּ מֶלֶךְ הָעוֹלָם, הָאֵל אָבִינוּ מַלְכֵּנוּ אַדִּירֵנוּ בּוֹרְאֵנוּ גּוֹאֲלֵנוּ יוֹצְרֵנוּ קְדוֹשֵׁנוּ קְדוֹשׁ יַעֲקֹב רוֹעֵנוּ רוֹעֵה יִשְׂרָאֵל הַמֶּלֶךְ הַטּוֹב וְהַמֵּטִיב לַכֹּל שֶׁבְּכָל יוֹם וָיוֹם הוּא הֵטִיב. הוּא מֵטִיב. הוּא יֵיטִיב לָנוּ. הוּא גְמָלָנוּ. הוּא גוֹמְלֵנוּ. הוּא יִגְמְלֵנוּ לָעַד לְחֵן וּלְחֶסֶד וּלְרַחֲמִים וּלְרֶוַח הַצָּלָה וְהַצְלָחָה בְּרָכָה וִישׁוּעָה נֶחָמָה פַּרְנָסָה וְכַלְכָּלָה וְרַחֲמִים וְחַיִּים וְשָׁלוֹם וְכָל טוֹב וּמִכָּל טוּב לְעוֹלָם אַל יְחַסְּרֵנוּ.

Blessed are You, O God our Lord, King of the Universe — the God who is our Father, our King, our Mighty One, our Creator, our Redeemer, our Maker, our Holy One — the Holy One of Jacob — our Shepherd — the Shepherd of Israel. [He is] the good King — good to all — who every day did good, does good, and will do good for us. He has granted us, is granting us, and will grant us our needs, with kindness, love, mercy and abundance. May help, success, blessing, salvation, comfort, livelihood, support, mercy, life, peace, all good, and all that comes from good, never fail us.

The cup is put down at this point.[47]

הָרַחֲמָן הוּא יִמְלוֹךְ עָלֵינוּ לְעוֹלָם וָעֶד.

May the Merciful One rule over us forever and ever.

הָרַחֲמָן הוּא יִתְבָּרַךְ בַּשָּׁמַיִם וּבָאָרֶץ.

May the Merciful One be blessed in heaven and earth.

47. *Arukh HaShulchan, Orach Chaim* 190:7; Rabbi Yaakov Emden, *Siddur Amudey Shamayim*, quoted in *Shaarey Teshuvah* 190:1. Some sources maintain that it is held until the end of the grace; *Teshuvoth Chakham Tzvi* 168.

הָרַחֲמָן הוּא יִשְׁתַּבַּח לְדוֹר דּוֹרִים וְיִתְפָּאַר בָּנוּ לָעַד וּלְנֵצַח נְצָחִים וְיִתְהַדַּר בָּנוּ לָעַד וּלְעוֹלְמֵי עוֹלָמִים.

May the Merciful One be praised for all ages, glorified among us forever and ever, and honored by us until the end of time.

הָרַחֲמָן הוּא יְפַרְנְסֵנוּ בְּכָבוֹד

May the Merciful One sustain us with honor.

הָרַחֲמָן הוּא יִשְׁבּוֹר עֻלֵּנוּ מֵעַל צַוָּארֵנוּ וְהוּא יוֹלִיכֵנוּ קוֹמְמִיּוּת לְאַרְצֵנוּ.

May the Merciful One break the yoke from our necks, and bring us standing tall to our land.

הָרַחֲמָן הוּא יִשְׁלַח לָנוּ בְּרָכָה מְרֻבָּה בַּבַּיִת הַזֶּה וְעַל שֻׁלְחָן זֶה שֶׁאָכַלְנוּ עָלָיו.

May the Merciful One send a great blessing to this house, and to this table upon which we have eaten.

הָרַחֲמָן הוּא יִשְׁלַח לָנוּ אֶת אֵלִיָּהוּ הַנָּבִיא זָכוּר לַטּוֹב וִיבַשֶּׂר לָנוּ בְּשׂוֹרוֹת טוֹבוֹת יְשׁוּעוֹת וְנֶחָמוֹת.

May the Merciful One send us the prophet Elijah (may he be remembered for good), and may He bring us good tidings of salvation and comfort.

הָרַחֲמָן הוּא יְבָרֵךְ אֶת־הֶחָתָן וְאֶת־הַכַּלָּה, וְאֶת־כָּל הַיּוֹשְׁבִים פֹּה, אוֹתָנוּ וְאֶת־כָּל־אֲשֶׁר לָנוּ כְּמוֹ שֶׁנִּתְבָּרְכוּ אֲבוֹתֵינוּ אַבְרָהָם יִצְחָק וְיַעֲקֹב בַּכֹּל מִכֹּל כֹּל כֵּן יְבָרֵךְ אוֹתָנוּ כֻּלָּנוּ יַחַד בִּבְרָכָה שְׁלֵמָה וְנֹאמַר אָמֵן.

May the Merciful One bless the bridegroom and bride, as well as all those present.[48] [May He also bless] us and all that is ours, just as our fathers, Abraham, Isaac, and Jacob were blessed, with all, from all, and in every way.[49] So may He bless us all together, with a full blessing; and let us say Amen.

48. *HaMadrikh*. Similar blessings are found in *Chupath Chathanim* 9:12, p. 42; see *Siddur Rav Saadia Gaon*, p. 107; *Machzor Vitri* 83; p. 53.

49. These blessings are found in Genesis 24:1, 27:33, 33:11.

בַּמָּרוֹם יְלַמְּדוּ עֲלֵיהֶם וְעָלֵינוּ זְכוּת שֶׁתְּהֵא לְמִשְׁמֶרֶת שָׁלוֹם וְנִשָּׂא בְרָכָה מֵאֵת
יְהֹוָה וּצְדָקָה מֵאֱלֹהֵי יִשְׁעֵנוּ וְנִמְצָא חֵן וְשֵׂכֶל טוֹב בְּעֵינֵי אֱלֹהִים וְאָדָם:

May they speak in our favor on high, so that we have the protection of peace. May we have a blessing from God, and charity from the Lord who saves us, and may we find favor and good understanding in the eyes of God and man.

הָרַחֲמָן הוּא יְזַכֵּנוּ לִימוֹת הַמָּשִׁיחַ וּלְחַיֵּי הָעוֹלָם הַבָּא: מַגְדִּיל יְשׁוּעוֹת מַלְכּוֹ
וְעֹשֶׂה חֶסֶד לִמְשִׁיחוֹ לְדָוִד וּלְזַרְעוֹ עַד עוֹלָם.
עֹשֶׂה שָׁלוֹם בִּמְרוֹמָיו הוּא יַעֲשֶׂה שָׁלוֹם עָלֵינוּ וְעַל כָּל יִשְׂרָאֵל וְאִמְרוּ אָמֵן:

May the Merciful One let us be worthy of the days of the Messiah and of life in the World to Come. He is a great salvation to His king, and He shows mercy to His messiah, to David and his children forever.[50] May He who makes peace in His lofty heights, grant peace to us and to all Israel; and say Amen.

יְראוּ אֶת יְהֹוָה קְדֹשָׁיו, כִּי אֵין מַחְסוֹר לִירֵאָיו. כְּפִירִים רָשׁוּ וְרָעֵבוּ, וְדוֹרְשֵׁי
יְהֹוָה לֹא יַחְסְרוּ כָל טוֹב. הוֹדוּ לַיהֹוָה כִּי טוֹב, כִּי לְעוֹלָם חַסְדּוֹ. פּוֹתֵחַ אֶת יָדֶךָ,
וּמַשְׂבִּיעַ לְכָל חַי רָצוֹן. בָּרוּךְ הַגֶּבֶר, אֲשֶׁר יִבְטַח בַּיהֹוָה, וְהָיָה יְהֹוָה מִבְטַחוֹ.
נַעַר הָיִיתִי, גַּם זָקַנְתִּי, וְלֹא רָאִיתִי צַדִּיק נֶעֱזָב, וְזַרְעוֹ מְבַקֶּשׁ לָחֶם. יְהֹוָה עֹז
לְעַמּוֹ יִתֵּן, יְהֹוָה יְבָרֵךְ אֶת עַמּוֹ בַשָּׁלוֹם:

Let [you], His holy ones, fear God, for those who fear Him will not be in need. The rich will grow poor and hungry, but those who seek God will not lack any good.[51] Give thanks to God for He is good, for His love is endless.[52] You open Your hand, and satisfy the desires of all living things.[53] Blessed is the man who trusts in God, and God will be his trust.[54] I was young, and have now grown old, and I

50. Psalms 18:51.

51. Psalms 34:10,11

52. Psalms 118:1.

53. Psalms 145:16.

54. Jeremiah 17:7.

have never seen a good man forsaken, nor his children begging bread.[55] God will give His people strength; God will bless His people with peace.[56]

After the Grace is completed, the first cup is set aside, and the second cup is taken for the Seven Blessings.[57] The Seven Blessings are said, as they are during the wedding ceremony.[58] In many circles, it is customary to honor six different people with the first six blessings.[59]

בָּרוּךְ אַתָּה יְיָ, אֱלֹהֵינוּ מֶלֶךְ הָעוֹלָם, שֶׁהַכֹּל בָּרָא לִכְבוֹדוֹ.

1. Blessed are You, O God our Lord, King of the Universe, who created all things for His glory.

בָּרוּךְ אַתָּה יְיָ, אֱלֹהֵינוּ מֶלֶךְ הָעוֹלָם, יוֹצֵר הָאָדָם.

2. Blessed are You, O God our Lord, King of the Universe, Creator of Man.

בָּרוּךְ אַתָּה יְיָ, אֱלֹהֵינוּ מֶלֶךְ הָעוֹלָם, אֲשֶׁר יָצַר אֶת־הָאָדָם בְּצַלְמוֹ, בְּצֶלֶם דְּמוּת תַּבְנִיתוֹ, וְהִתְקִין לוֹ מִמֶּנּוּ בִּנְיַן עֲדֵי עַד. בָּרוּךְ אַתָּה יְיָ, יוֹצֵר הָאָדָם.

3. Blessed are You, O God our Lord, King of the Universe, who created man in His image—in the image set forth by His plan—and who prepared from him a structure to last for all time. Blessed are You, O God, Creator of mankind.

55. Psalms 27:25.

56. Psalms 29:11.

57. Rabbenu Yerocham 23:2, 186b; *Bayith Chadash* 62; *Beth Shmuel* 62:11; *Magen Avraham* 147:11; *Shulchan HaEzer* 9:5:1; *Eduth LeYisrael* 2:3, p. 83. Some authorities maintain that the second cup is filled at this point; see above, note 6.

58. See *Evven HaEzer* 62:5. Cf. *Siddur Rav Amram Gaon*, quoted in *Otzar HaGeonim, Kethuboth* 79, p. 25. Also see *Sefer HaOrah* 2:7; *Darkey Moshe* 62:10; *Perishah* 62:10. They can only be said after a meal; Rabbenu Yerocham 23:2, 186b. Some say that the blessings can also be said before a meal; see *Sofrim* 19:11; Ran, *Kethuboth,* Rif 3a. See *VaYaged Moshe*, p. 21.

59. See above, Chapter 22, note 85. Also see *Eduth LeYisrael* 1:9, p. 85.

שׂוֹשׂ תָּשִׂישׂ וְתָגֵל הָעֲקָרָה, בְּקִבּוּץ בָּנֶיהָ לְתוֹכָהּ בְּשִׂמְחָה. בָּרוּךְ אַתָּה יְיָ, מְשַׂמֵּחַ צִיּוֹן בְּבָנֶיהָ.

4. May the barren [land] rejoice and be glad, when its children are gathered back to it in joy. Blessed are You, O God, who makes Zion rejoice in her children.

שַׂמֵּחַ תְּשַׂמַּח רֵעִים הָאֲהוּבִים, כְּשַׂמֵּחֲךָ יְצִירְךָ בְּגַן עֵדֶן מִקֶּדֶם בָּרוּךְ אַתָּה יְיָ, מְשַׂמֵּחַ חָתָן וְכַלָּה.

5. May You grant great joy to these dearly beloved, just as You granted joy to the work of Your hands long ago in the Garden of Eden. Blessed are You, O God, who grants joy to the bridegroom and bride.

בָּרוּךְ אַתָּה יְיָ, אֱלֹהֵינוּ מֶלֶךְ הָעוֹלָם, אֲשֶׁר בָּרָא שָׂשׂוֹן וְשִׂמְחָה, חָתָן וְכַלָּה, גִּילָה רִנָּה, דִּיצָה וְחֶדְוָה, אַהֲבָה וְאַחֲוָה, שָׁלוֹם וְרֵעוּת. מְהֵרָה יְיָ אֱלֹהֵינוּ יִשָּׁמַע בְּעָרֵי יְהוּדָה וּבְחוּצוֹת יְרוּשָׁלָיִם קוֹל שָׂשׂוֹן וְקוֹל שִׂמְחָה, קוֹל חָתָן וְקוֹל כַּלָּה, קוֹל מִצְהֲלוֹת חֲתָנִים מֵחֻפָּתָם וּנְעָרִים מִמִּשְׁתֵּה נְגִינָתָם. בָּרוּךְ אַתָּה יְיָ, מְשַׂמֵּחַ חָתָן עִם הַכַּלָּה.

6. Blessed are You, O God our Lord, King of the Universe, who created happiness and joy, bridegroom and bride, rejoicing and song, delight and cheer, love and harmony, peace and fellowhip. Soon, O God our Lord, may there be heard in the cities of Judah and in the streets of Jerusalem, the sound of gladness, the sound of joy, the sound of the bridegroom, the sound of the bride, the sound of bridegrooms rejoicing at their weddings, and young people at their feasts of song. Blessed are You, O God, who grants joy to the bridegroom with the bride.

After the first six blessings are said, the cup for the Seven Blessings is put down. The man who led the Grace lifts the first cup, and recites the blessing over wine, which is now the seventh blessing:[60]

60. *Tosafoth, Pesachim* 102b, s.v. *SheAin; Machzor Vitri* p. 53; Rosh, *Pesachim* 10:8; Rabbenu Yerocham 23:2, 186c. See *Pesachim* 103a, Ritva *ad loc; Darkey Moshe* 62:5; *Shulchan HaEzer* 9:5; *Eduth LeYisrael* 1:5. See below, note 64.

However, some authorities maintain that the blessing over wine is said on the first cup; see *Pachad Yitzchak*, s.v. *Birkath Chathanim*, p. 61a; *Likutey Maharich* 3:134b; *Shulchan HaEzer* 9:5:3; *Eduth LeYisrael*, p. 84.

בָּרוּךְ אַתָּה יְיָ, אֱלֹהֵינוּ מֶלֶךְ הָעוֹלָם, בּוֹרֵא פְּרִי הַגָּפֶן.

7. Blessed are You, O God our Lord, King of the Universe, Creator of the fruit of the grapevine.

During the actual wedding ceremony, the blessing over wine is the first of the Seven Blessings. After the Grace, it is the last blessing. This is so that it will be apparent that the blessing over wine pertains to the Seven Blessings, and not just to the Grace.[61] After the Grace, the blessing over wine is usually said just before the wine is sipped, and now, after the Seven Blessings, the wine blessing is also said just before the wine is sipped.[62]

After reciting the blessing over the first cup, the man who led the Grace takes a sip from it.[63] The custom is not to recite a blessing over the second cup, over which the Wedding Blessings are said.[64]

After the first cup is sipped, the two cups are mixed

61. *Beth Hillel*, quoted in *Beth Shmuel* 62:2; *Machatzith HaShekel* 190:1; *Taamey HaMinhagim* 989.

62. Mordechai, *Pesachim* (in Vilna Talmud), p. 36a; *Magen Avraham* 190:1; *Shulchan HaEzer* 8:3:11. Cf. *Sefer HaMakneh, Kuntres Acharon* 62:1; *Arukh HaShulchan* 62:2.

Some say that this is because the couple can enjoy each other now that they are married, and this takes precedence over the blessing for wine; Rabbi Tzvi Elimelekh Shapiro of Dinov, *Maggid Taalumoth* (Przemysl, 1876), p. 73, quoted in *Taamey HaMinhagim* 990; *Shulchan HaEzer* 9:5:2; *Yalkut Yitzchak* 552:50.

The blessing over wine is also said last because wine is not needed for the Seven Blessings; therefore, the Seven Blessings would be an interruption between the wine blessing and drinking the wine; *Siddur Derekh Chaim; Taamey HaMinhagim* 991.

63. Some say a *revi'ith,* while others say a mouthful; see *Orach Chaim* 190:1; *Shulchan HaEzer* 9:5:6; *Eduth LeYisrael*, p. 84.

64. Since it is exempt with the blessing over the first cup; see *Sefer HaMakneh, Kuntres Acharon* 62:1; *Bayith Chadash* 62; *Pith'chey Teshuvah* 62:178; *Magen Avraham* 147:11; *Pri Megadim, Eshel Avraham* 147:11; *Chokhmath Adam* 129:7; *Kitzur Shulchan Arukh* 149:1; *Siddur Derekh Chaim; HaAmak Sh'elah* 16:9 end; *Eduth LeYisrael, Birkath HaMazon* 1:7; *Shulchan HaEzer* 9:5:5.

together.[65] The two cups are then given to the bride and groom.[66] After they taste from the cups, the remaining wine is divided among those present.[67]

In many circles, it is customary for the closest friends and relatives of the bridal couple to remain after the meal, and have a private "mitzvah dance" with the bride and groom. In some circles, various rabbis, dignitaries, and relatives dance with the bride, with the man holding one end of a handkerchief, and the bride the other.[68] In this regard, customs vary widely.

65. *Machzor Vitri* p. 53; *Chupath Chathanim* 8:21; *Arukh HaShulchan* 62:18; *Shulchan HaEzer* 9:5:7. Some mix the cups before sipping from the first cup; *Chupath Chathanim*. Others sip first; *Arukh HaShulchan*. See *Yam Shel Shlomo, Kethuboth* 1:21, end.

66. *Machzor Vitri* p. 53 (which appears to indicate that only the groom and bride drink it); *Shulchan HaEzer* 9:5:8. Some say that one cup is given to the bride and groom, and the other to everyone else present; *Shulchan HaEzer*. Giving wine to the bride and groom is part of the mitzvah of making them rejoice, since wine induces joy; Rabbi Chaim Eleazar Spiro of Munkatch, *Divrey Torah* (Munkatch, 1929), quoting Rabbi Tzvi Elimelekh of Dinov; in *Shulchan HaEzer* 9:5:8.

67. *Shulchan HaEzer* 9:5:7; *Eduth LeYisrael*, p. 85. Some say that only the bride and groom drink; *Machzor Vitri* p. 53; *Arukh HaShulchan* 62:18.

68. See *Shulchan HaEzer* 9:8:5.

Chapter 26

THE BRIDAL WEEK

It is not the Jewish practice for the bride and groom to "escape" on a honeymoon right after the wedding. Rather, they remain in their home community. They are beginning their married life, not separated from the community, but as an integral part of it.

During the first week, the bride and groom remain together, learning to enjoy each other's company. It is taught that Moses ordained that the bride and groom should rejoice together for the first week after marriage.[1]

Although this was ordained by Moses, it was a custom even much earlier. Thus, after Jacob married Leah and realized that he had been tricked, he demanded that Rachel be given him as a wife. Laban, Rachel's father, told him, "Wait until this week with [Leah] is over, and then we will give you the other girl" (Genesis 29:27). From this, it is evident that even in the time of the Patriarchs, the normal period of wedding celebration was seven days.[2]

We also find that when Samson was married, a seven day

1. *Yerushalmi, Kethuboth* 1:1, 2b; *Sefer HaIttur* 2:4, 65c; *Tanya Rabathai* 91, 99a; *Yad, Avel* 1:1. Some say that this is a Torah law; *Korban HaEdah; Shiurey Korban;* on *Yerushalmi loc. cit*; Cf. *Moed Katan* 7b. Others, however, maintain that it is a rabbinical law; *Turey Zahav, Yoreh Deah* 342:1. Cf. *Tosafoth, Berakhoth* 47b, s.v. *Mitzvah*; also see *Yad, Ishuth* 10:12; Rosh, *Moed Katan* 3:3.

   Some say that only the first day is stipulated by Torah law; based on the verse, "On the *day* of his wedding, on the day his heart rejoiced" (Song of Songs 3:11); Rosh, *Kethuboth* 1:5; Rabbenu Yerocham 23:2, 185d. See *Eduth LeYisrael*, p. 52; *VaYaged Moshe* p. 50. Also see *Evven HaEzer* 64:1, *Kitzur Shulchan Arukh* 149:12; *Likutey Maharich* 3:135a; *Shulchan HaEzer* 12:6:1.

2. Rashi, Ramban, *ad loc*; *Yov'loth* 28:28; *Pirkey Rabbi Eliezer* 16; *Sefer HaIttur* 2:4, 65c; *Tanya Rabathai* 91, 99a; *Perush HaTefilloth* of Rabbi Yehudah ben Yakar, p. 42.

"feast period" was kept.[3] It has been the Jewish practice ever since.

During this seven day period, the groom should not go out to work or to business.[4] He should be completely free to spend time with his new bride. Furthermore, the groom is like a king, and just as a king does not engage in work or business, neither does the groom.[5]

Similarly, just as a king never goes out alone, neither does the groom or bride.[6] Therefore, during the seven days after the wedding, neither the bride nor the groom should go out alone.[7]

During this period, if the groom is present in synagogue, the Tachanun prayer of supplication is not said.[8]

These seven days are observed if it is a first marriage for either the bride or the groom. However, if it is a second marriage for both, only three days are observed.[9]

The seven day period parallels the seven days of creation. As noted earlier, every marriage is a re-enactment of the creation of the universe.[10]

During the bridal week, it is customary for close relatives or friends to make special meals for the bridal pair. Such meals are known as *Sheva Berakhoth* (literally, "Seven Blessings"),

3. See Judges 14:12,17; *Yalkut Shimoni ad loc* 70.

4. *Evven HaEzer* 64:1 in *Hagah*; *Yad, Ishuth* 10:12; see *Maggid Mishneh, ad loc; Pachad Yitzchak*, s.v. *Chathan VeKallah*, p. 60d. Work is forbidden as it is on an intermediate day of a festival (*Chol HaMoed*); *Eduth LeYisrael* (Henkin) 45, p. 141. Getting haircuts is also forbidden; *Pachad Yitzchak*, s.v. *Chathan VeKallah*, p. 61a.

5. Rashba (actually, Ramban, see *Shitah Mekubetzeth*), *Kethuboth* 5b, s.v. *Iy Nami*; Ran, *Kethuboth*, Rif 2a, s.v. *VeDeOmrinin*.

6. *Pirkey Rabbi Eliezer* 16; *Evven HaEzer* 64:1 in *Hagah*.

7. *Sefer HaMinhagim* (Lubavitch), p. 76, includes the bride. Both the bride and groom need safeguarding during this week; *Berakhoth* 64b; *Magen Avraham* 239:7; *Mataamim HaChadash* 56.

8. *Orach Chaim* 131:4; *Shulchan HaEzer* 12:7.

9. *Kitzur Shulchan Arukh* 149:12. See *Evven HaEzer* 64:2.

10. Bachya, *Kad HaKemach*, p. 184.

since the Seven Blessings are said after the Grace, just as at the wedding.

For the Seven Blessings to be said, at least one person must be invited who was not present at the wedding or at any previous Sheva Berakhoth meal. Such a person is known as a *Panim Chadashoth* ("new face").[11]

On the Sabbath, however, it is not required to have a "new face" to recite the Seven Blessings, since the Sabbath itself is considered a "new face."[12] There are various customs as to whether the Seven Blessings are said at the third Sabbath meal (Shalosh Seudoth).[13] There are also varied customs as to whether or not *Davay Haser* is said on the Sabbath.[14]

The Seven Blessings cannot be said unless there is a minyan (ten adult Jewish men) present.[15] They are then said just as they are after the wedding meal.

If there is no minyan present, however, or if there is no "new face," then the Seven Blessings cannot be said. In such a case, as long as there are three adult men present, and others besides the immediate household, the last blessing, *Asher Bara*, is said, as well as *SheHaSimcha BeMe'ono*. In such a case, the custom is to omit *Davay Haser*.[16]

On the Sabbath after the wedding, it is customary for the

11. *Kethuboth* 8a; *Evven HaEzer* 62:7.

12. *Tosafoth, Kethuboth* 7b, s.v. *VeHu; Evven HaEzer* 62:8. The same is true of a festival; *Ibid.*

13. *Evven HaEzer* 62:8 in *Hagah*. See *Teshuvoth of Rabbi Menachem Azarya of Fano* 60; quoted in *Pith'chey Teshuvah* 62:16. Some had a custom of not saying it; see *Darkey HaChaim VeHaShalom* 1055.

After the third meal, the cup cannot be tasted; *Ba'er Hetiv, Orach Chaim* 299:5. Other authorities, however, maintain that it can; *Hagahoth Chokhmath Shlomo, Ibid.; Teshuvoth Zikhron Yehudah, Orach Chaim* 87; *Shaarim Metzuyanim BeHalakhah* 149:4. Some say that only the bride can sip the cup; *Likutey Maharich.*

14. See Chapter 25, note 30.

15. *Kethuboth* 7b.

16. *Evven HaEzer* 62:7 and *Hagah; Kitzur Shulchan Arukh* 149:3.

groom's friends to accompany him to synagogue.[17] Similarly, the bride's friends accompany her to the synagogue.[18] The groom is called up to the reading of the Torah.[19] In many circles, it is a custom for the families of the bridal couple to present a Kiddush in the synagogue on this Sabbath.[20]

17. Some say he wears his wedding clothes; *Minhagey Mattersdorf* 113.

18. *Mataamim HaChadash* 54; *Shulchan HaEzer* 12:9:3; from *Yevamoth* 118b.

19. *Machzor Vitri* 477, p. 593; *Shulchan HaEzer* 12:9:7; Cf. Maharil 65a. See Chapter 10, note 9.

20. Cf. *Minhagey Belza*, p. 86.

Chapter 27

MAKING MARRIAGE WORK

The wedding is only the beginning. Even the most elaborate wedding will not guarantee a happy marriage.

Making a wedding is like planting a seed in the ground. If the seed is to grow, it must be carefully tended. It must be watered, weeded, and pruned. Only then will it produce good fruit. The same is true of a marriage. What a couple puts into a marriage is what they will get out of it.

MARRIAGE RECORD

MARRIAGE RECORD

Name of Bride ....

Hebrew name ....

Name of Groom ....

Hebrew name ....

Bride's Father ....

Hebrew name ....

Bride's Mother ....

Hebrew name ....

Groom's Father ....

Hebrew name ....

Groom's Mother ....

Hebrew name ....

Wedding Date ....

Hebrew Date ....

Place Held ....

Rabbi Performing wedding ....

of Congregation ....

Witnesses to wedding:

1. ....

2. ....

Witnesses to Kethubah:

1. ....

2. ....

Reading Kethubah

Seven Blessings:

1. ....

2. ....

3. ....

4. ....

5. ....

6. ....

7. ....

Grace led by ....

Seven Blessings at Grace ....

1. ....

2. ....

3. ....

4. ....

5. ....

6. ....

7. ....

Sheva Berakhoth during Bridal Week given by ....

1. ....
2. ....
3. ....
4. ....
5. ....
6. ....
7. ....

Date ....

ADDITIONAL NOTES ....